PINTER

AT SIXTY

DRAMA AND PERFORMANCE STUDIES
Timothy Wiles, general editor

PINTER

edited by
Katherine H. Burkman
and
John L. Kundert-Gibbs

Indiana University Press
Bloomington & Indianapolis

AT SIXTY

Title page credit: Pinter photo by Snowdon. Others by Brad Feinknopf.
Collage design by Ellen Hoover.

The paper used in this publication meets the minimum requirements of American
National Standard for Information Sciences—Permanence of Paper for Printed
Library Materials, ANSI Z39.48-1984.

♾™

Manufactured in the United States of America

Library of Congress Cataloging-in-Publication Data

Pinter at sixty / edited by Katherine H. Burkman and John L. Kundert-Gibbs.
    p. cm. — (Drama and performance studies)
    Includes bibliographical references (p.   ) and index.
    ISBN 0-253-34499-9 (cloth). — ISBN 0-253-20811-4 (paper)
    1. Pinter, Harold, date. —Criticism and interpretation.
I. Burkman, Katherine H. II. Kundert-Gibbs, John L. III. Title:
Pinter at 60. IV. Series.
PR6066.I53Z737 1993
822'.914—dc20   92-35160
1 2 3 4 5 97 96 95 94 93

For Allan, Deborah, David, Joan, Lee, and Kristin

Contents

Preface

To celebrate the distinguished playwright Harold Pinter's sixtieth birthday, over 250 scholars and artists from around the world came together at The Ohio State University for *A Pinter Festival: An International Meeting*. The idea for the gathering emerged at the annual Harold Pinter Society meeting at the Modern Language Association Convention in 1987. The Ohio State University had hosted the 1981 symposium honoring Samuel Beckett in 1981, and its mix of scholarly papers and artistic performances became the model for this meeting, which was held somewhat after Pinter's October birthday, April 19–21, 1991.

The festival's poster (see title page) may reveal something of our attitude toward the meeting: trying not to take ourselves too seriously in this endeavor, we wished to celebrate as well as cerebrate. Hence, Pinter hovering over the proceedings, but Stuart Pimsler of Stuart Pimsler Dance & Theater (at the podium) and his company, at the table, suggesting a parody of the usual panel, with less than full attention on the speaker. Susan Costello, the figure at the far right at the table, is also the figure behind the mountain, and from reactions to the poster, we can only conclude that she is properly ambiguous, either in agony, in ecstasy, or both.

Although Pinter's birthday was celebrated by many productions in England, this American-hosted meeting was the first international gathering solely devoted to a study of his work, making it, as one participant suggested, something of a historic occasion. Some three hundred people registered for the meeting, coming from The Netherlands, England, Greece, Canada, Germany, Korea, Italy, and Newfoundland, as well as many areas of the United States. It was not surprising, perhaps, that the writer of *The Birthday Party* chose not to attend his own, but in a sense his absence freed us to focus on the work, not on the man. Far from being disinterested in the meeting, however, Pinter very generously sent us his script for a new play, *Party Time*, scheduled for a world premiere in London at the Almeida Theatre the following November, and permitted us to give it a staged reading at the meeting. He also sent a remarkable recording of himself reading both parts in *The New World Order: A Sketch* (printed in the September/October, 1991 issue of *Granta*), which we listened to twice at the meeting, an event which brought everyone together into the heat of Pinter's urgency as actor, writer, and political humanist.

The three keynote speakers, Martin Esslin, Carey Perloff, and Louis Marks, all of whose essays appear in this book, touched on some of the major concerns of the meeting: Pinter as a political writer (Esslin), Pinter as a man of the theatre (Perloff), and Pinter's work in film and television (Marks). The excitement they conveyed about working with him set the tone for a meeting at which there was a healthy controversy about how to approach Pinter at the same time that everyone seemed to come together in an effort to understand the importance of his voice as artist and person in our world today, to get a renewed sense of that importance, and to celebrate his work.

Productions presented at *A Pinter Festival* were *The Hothouse,* an Ohio State University Theatre Department Studio production, directed by Stephen Gray; *Betrayal,* performed by NXT (New Cross Theatre), a professional company based at the University of London; a reading of Pinter's poetry by CATCO (Contemporary American Theater Company), a group from Columbus, Ohio, at the Riley Hawk Glass Gallery in Columbus's Short North; *Monologue,* performed by Robert Gordon in conjunction with the staged reading of *Party Time;* and *Pimsler Honors Pinter,* an evening commissioned especially for the meeting, performed by the Columbus-based group Stuart Pimsler Dance & Theater.

The reading of *Party Time* was directed by John Clum, and the actors were from NXT, Duke University, and The Ohio State University—an English/American mix. Performance, moreover, was incorporated into many workshop/scholarly presentations by the Illinois Repertory Theatre, members of the Department of Theatre at Western Illinois University and Miami University in Ohio, Maggie Rose of the University of Milan, who showed us an Italian production of *A Kind of Alaska* on video, and Grandparents' Living Theatre, a Columbus-based group who performed a part of *A Slight Ache. My Terrible Cap,* a song cycle based on Pinter's poetry and composed by Theodore Wiprud, was presented on audio tape along with Pinter's audio tape of himself performing both parts in *The New World Order.* Video tapes of several of Pinter's works were also available for viewing at the Wexner Center for the Arts, courtesy of Pinter's BBC television producer, Louis Marks, so that the richness of Pinter's work on screen was realized both in papers and in production. Indeed, with over 40 panels of speakers and three keynote speakers, some of the performances had to take place at 11:00 p.m.—there were simply not enough hours in the three days! We were all so busy at the meeting that we hardly noticed that it rained most of the weekend.

Members of NXT not only performed *Betrayal,* but also participated in the meeting by giving papers; led by Nesta Jones, their director, several members of the group also gave an exciting lecture/demonstration on "Pinter and Englishness," conceived by their dramaturg, William Naismith. The subjects of other panels were "Pinter and Judaism," "Critical Perspectives," "Pinter and Politics," "Minimalism and Metatheatre," "Myth and Ritual," "Voice in Pinter," "Acts in the Present Tense: Knowing, Violence, and the Force of Utterance," "Psychological Perspectives," "Sexual Isolation, Madness, and the Tragicomic in Pinter," "Pinter's Characterization of Women," "Memory and Desire," "Pinter's Film Spies," "Audience and Pedagogy," "Pinter on Television," "Place and Playing Space in Pinter," "Pinter's Films," "Pinter and the Postmodern," "Pinter: America and the Postmodern," and "Changed Names/Hidden Identities; Reading for Jewish Subtext in Pinter, Mamet, and Ionesco."

Panels also contained papers focused on *The Birthday Party,* the film of *The Handmaid's Tale, Betrayal, Old Times, The Collection, The Dwarfs, The Home-*

coming, The Caretaker, Family Voices, A Kind of Alaska, and *Victoria Station.* Others contained papers comparing Pinter to such writers as Storey, Duras, Pedtrushevskaya, Eliot, Havel, Ganbaro, Miller, Shepard, Sartre, Stoppard, Kafka, Beckett, Mamet, and Shakespeare. The papers were of such a consistently fine quality that we had an extremely difficult time selecting a sampling of them for this publication. Some others appear in *The Pinter Review* (1992), and yet others are available through the Pinter archive that Professor Steven Gale has been building for The Pinter Society at Kentucky State University.

Stuart Pimsler Dance & Theater was invited to create a new work in Pinter's honor because of the uncanny affinity between the playwright and the group, whose production of Beckett's *Catastrophe* brought them to our attention. Pimsler shares Pinter's urgent sense of humanistic values, his irony, and his dark humor. He has always been interested in political and social issues as an underpinning for his aesthetic (a point about Pinter's work that is at the forefront of Pinter criticism today), and he shares Pinter's fascination with silence and understatement, going beyond the political to the metaphysical. Other affinities include the use of ritual (although Pinter's Jewishness comes out less directly than Pimsler's) and the lyrical quality of Pimsler's dance, which is akin to the poetry of Pinter's work, in which rhythm is so important.

Pimsler Honors Pinter, which was performed twice, consisted of three parts: a production of *A Kind of Alaska;* a work in the company's repertory of their own, *The Men from the Boys* (which some thought was an unknown Pinter work because of its affinities with Pinter's power struggles); and a new work to honor the playwright that grew out of the company's work on *A Kind of Alaska,* called *Pausing in the Avalanche.* In this dance/drama piece, the setting for *A Kind of Alaska* was reconfigured in a more surreal fashion, some of it flown. As dancers, the company had become fascinated with the movement problems of the patients suffering from the sleeping sickness *encephalitis lethargica,* detailed in Oliver Sacks's *Awakenings,* which had inspired Pinter to write *A Kind of Alaska.* Using some lines from the text of *Alaska,* Pimsler and his entire company, Suzanne Costello, Loraine Jeffery, Romy Noltimier, Janet Parrott, Janet Slifka, and Tim Talty, enacted the moments, so Pimsler explained, just before the awakening of Deborah from her many years of sleep that constitute the action of *A Kind of Alaska.*

The essays gathered in this collection suggest the major concerns of the meeting, which we have placed under headings for the convenience of the reader: production, politics, poetics, influence, film, and, because it resonates with gender issues and was foregrounded in the production commissioned for the festival, *A Kind of Alaska.* The essays, however, overlap their categories. For example, Judith Roof's piece included under "Pinter's Poetics," in which she discusses the question of adaptation from one medium to another, could just as easily be included under the section on film, while Steven Gale's discussion of art objects as metaphor, included under film, could as easily be included under poetics. Jeanne Colleran's article, in which she holds that absurdism always has held the seeds of a political critique, placed under

"Political Pinter," might as easily, with its comparison of Pinter to Gambaro, have been placed under influences or, because of its concern with the absurd, under poetics. As the various discussions of Pinter tend to take up one question about his work, they invariably enter into a dialogue with the other essays.

Pinter has always struck a nerve with his depiction of dispossession from home and self, but what emerges in the essays is something of the way his political passion has always informed his work, as Esslin's piece makes clear, so that the more explicit forms this has taken in his recent work are not only of a piece with his entire oeuvre, but are far more complex than they might first appear to be. Rosette C. Lamont is the first to suggest that *The Hothouse* is a Holocaust play, Susan Hollis Merritt discusses ways in which Havel's outsiders may inform and be informed by Pinter's work, and Phyllis R. Randall shows us how Pinter was drawn to Elizabeth Bowen's mix of the personal and political in his adaptation of her novel *The Heat of the Day* for television.

Although Pinter's debt to Kafka has been long established, his adaptation of *The Trial* for film served as a catalyst for full discussions at the meeting of the Kafka-Pinter connection. When they take up this link between Pinter and Kafka, Louis Marks, Francis Gillen, and John L. Kundert-Gibbs are still, of course, on political as well as aesthetic ground, and their contributions became one of the innovative threads of the meeting.

Another unique contribution of the conference which we wish to capture in the book is the attention received by two other Pinter plays: *Mountain Language* and *A Kind of Alaska*. Carey Perloff, in her discussion of her direction of the early *Birthday Party* and the more recent *Mountain Language,* speaks about how the rehearsal process (with Pinter involved) also reveals much about the political content of Pinter's work and how that is best realized on stage. Moonyoung C. Ham and Katherine H. Burkman take up gender issues in their discussion of *A Kind of Alaska,* issues that clearly resonate throughout Pinter's work, appearing more explicitly in his film adaptations of *A Handmaid's Tale* and the powerful film released in this country just after the meeting, *The Comfort of Strangers.*

The placement of Pinter in the tradition of modern drama from Ibsen, Strindberg, Chekhov, and Pirandello to the more recent Beckett influence that Alice Benston discusses shows Pinter working within a tradition, despite his unique contributions, a tradition that goes back further, as Hersh Zeifman points out in his playfully suggestive look at the Shakespeare-Pinter connection. Working back to Dante via Beckett, Martha Fehsenfeld also explores influences, early and late, offering a provocative interpretation of *Betrayal* in terms of her findings. Not stopping at the modern, both Jon Erickson and Alice Rayner take Pinter up into issues of postmodernism, Erickson with his discussion of minimalism in *Old Times,* Rayner with her concern with indeterminacy in *No Man's Land* and other works.

In some sense, our celebration of Pinter's birthday ties us into the ritual which underlies Pinter's work; yet, as with any "real life" reenactment of ritual, the deep structure of the myth is well hidden behind the trials and triumphs of the living moment. On stage (or on screen), we see in Pinter's work an attempt to come to terms with the reality of life, its good and bad, an attempt to go beyond the mitigating effect of realistic stage and screen conventions, which are commonly accepted as representing life in art. Pinter's writing is, if anything, hyper-real as it focuses with terrible honesty on personal and societal problems, forcing a primal, living, or immediate response as much as an aesthetic one. He confronts the audience with problems outside the bounds of art, breaking the so-called normal boundaries of film and stage in an attempt to find a reality so immediate that one cannot separate oneself from it. If, for example, we watch *The Comfort of Strangers,* is there a way *not* to take the movie personally? And can we ignore its political ramifications?

At the conclusion of *Pausing in the Avalanche,* Stuart Pimsler joined his company on stage with a birthday cake and they all approached the audience singing "Happy birthday to you." Somehow the celebration of Deborah's upcoming birthday in *Alaska* merged with our celebration of Pinter's in a wonderfully comic moment that echoed our feeling about Pinter's work. Not only is Pinter, in our opinion, the world's most important living playwright, but he is also one who looks without flinching at what our world is like and still celebrates it in his own work. Cause for celebration.

Katherine H. Burkman
John L. Kundert-Gibbs

Acknowledgments

We are grateful to those who helped us with *A Pinter Festival,* out of which this book has evolved: Dean G. Michael Riley and Associate Dean Marvin R. Zahniser of the Ohio State University College of the Humanities; Professors Morris Beja and Arnold Shapiro and Messrs. Michael Rupright and Eric Walborn of the Department of English; and Professors Firman H. Brown, Jr., and Mark Shanda and Messrs. Stephen Gray and Joseph F. Scharrer of the Department of Theatre. We are also grateful to Mr. and Mrs. Charles Krown, Mr. and Mrs. David Blumberg, Mr. and Mrs. Ralph Hazelbaker, Mrs. Merilynn S. Kaplin, and Mrs. Melvin Schottenstein for their support, to Stuart Pimsler, Suzanne Costello, Loraine Jeffery, Romy Noltimier, Janet Parrott, Janet Slifka, Tim Talty, and Brad Feinknopf for their creative contributions, and to Professors Steven H. Gale and Francis Gillen of the Pinter Society for all of their help. Our thanks as well to Harold Pinter for his interest in and contributions to the meeting and to our efforts with the book.

We would also like to thank Professor Timothy J. Wiles for his many excellent suggestions. Ms. Judy Daish, Ms. Samantha Ford, Mr. Peter Lyster-Todd, and Mr. John Hofmeister have also been most helpful.

Quotations from the writings of Harold Pinter, *Harold Pinter, Complete Works: One,* copyright 1976; *Complete Works: Two,* copyright 1977; *Complete Works: Three,* copyright 1978; *Complete Works: Four,* copyright 1981; *The Dwarfs: A Novel,* copyright 1990; *Five Screenplays,* copyright 1973; *The Hothouse,* copyright 1980; *Mountain Language,* copyright 1988; *One for the Road,* copyright 1986; and *Other Places,* copyright 1983, are by permission of Grove Press, Inc. and Harold Pinter. Quotations from *The Comfort of Strangers and Other Screenplays,* copyright 1990, and from *The Heat of the Day,* copyright 1989, are by permission of Faber and Faber Ltd. and Harold Pinter.

I. Pinter in Production

ONE

Pinter in Rehearsal:
From *The Birthday Party* to *Mountain Language*

Carey Perloff

It is a truism that a playwright is the last to know what his or her script truly means, and it has often been said of Harold Pinter that he resists analysis of his work. But there is no one who has a cannier sense of the sheer nuts and bolts of making theatre than Pinter, and one can learn a great deal about Pinter's work from observing him and collaborating with him in rehearsal. In particular, when one watches Pinter at work on one of his plays, the "abstraction" for which they are famous drops away, and a frighteningly specific realism takes its place. This essay explores the ways in which Pinter's presence in rehearsal informed and changed the direction of our work on two of his plays.

In the fall of 1989, I directed a double bill of Harold Pinter's work at CSC (the Classic Stage Company) Repertory in New York (of which I was artistic director) with Pinter in attendance at rehearsal. The double bill, starring Jean Stapleton and Peter Riegert, was comprised of Pinter's first full-length play, *The Birthday Party,* and a new work, the American premiere of the one-act play *Mountain Language.* This unusual collaboration came about a year after CSC had produced an acclaimed revival of *The Birthday Party,* about which Pinter became intrigued after an enthusiastic report from his friend Lauren Bacall.

At the time I was surprised at Pinter's interest, since he had been so disenchanted by recent American productions of his work that it had taken six months to wrest the rights to *The Birthday Party* from him in the first place. (Evidently what bothered him about the American productions he had seen was their psychological indulgence. Among American theatre-goers his work often does have the reputation for being dreary and incomprehensible, precisely because it is often performed with a reverence and intense psychological fervor that destroys both its mystery and its comedy.) After having seen our production and meeting with the cast and me, Pinter offered CSC the exclusive

From her address at *A Pinter Festival,* given on 20 April 1991.

American rights to *Mountain Language,* which had premiered a few months before at the National Theatre in London under Pinter's own direction.

Thus, a year after our first rehearsals of *The Birthday Party,* we went through a second rehearsal process in which we paired *The Birthday Party* with *Mountain Language* and worked with Pinter directly in rehearsal. We discovered things about Pinter's work the second time around that we had not even considered during our first encounter with his work.

The first time around, we had worked hard to avoid the traps of psychology and method acting when rehearsing *The Birthday Party.* It had quickly become clear to us that in a Pinter play, language is used to veil or disguise emotion, not to reveal it. For American actors trained in direct emotional expression and unaccustomed to the concealing powers of subtle language, a Pinter text poses formidable challenges. It is critical, when rehearsing Pinter's work, to allow the language to be active rather than to give emotions free play; one has always to construct a complex mask which can only be allowed to slip on very rare and explosive occasions. Most American actors have great resistance to what they consider to be "technical" solutions to character problems: the goal is emotional truth at all costs. Such an attitude is fine if you exist in a culture that believes fundamentally in therapy. The faith that we Americans seem to have in therapeutic confession comes from our belief that honesty is the best policy and that if you tell a stranger the truth (about your emotions, your past, your love affairs, your underwear), you will somehow be absolved and rewarded with tranquility and peace of mind. Thus it is difficult for Americans to conceive of a world in which confession is fatal, in which the revelation of emotional truth leads to potential annihilation. But such is the world of Pinter. On the surface everything is civil, courteous, almost banal. People talk about cornflakes and deck chairs and childhood holidays. But beneath the surface, everyone, or nearly everyone, is out to destroy everyone else. Pinter's world is a predator's world. Survival depends upon not showing what you feel. Tip your hand once and you leave yourself open to emotional blackmail forever.

This kind of work is very difficult for psychologically trained actors because it requires the construction of a mask that must be maintained at all costs. There were moments in rehearsal when this sense of play became particularly difficult because of the enormous temptation (and indeed need) of the actors to tell the truth rather than to play the game. An example of this problem occurred during the work on the Goldberg-Lulu scene in act III. Lulu comes down the stairs after a long and horrifying night in which she has been violated first by Stanley and then by Goldberg. The truth is that she is devastated. But what does she say?

GOLDBERG: Come over here.
LULU: What's going to happen?
GOLDBERG: Come over here.
LULU: No, thank you.

GOLDBERG: What's the matter? You got the needle to Uncle Natey?
LULU: I'm going. (89)

If this were an American naturalistic play, Lulu would come downstairs weeping and a confession of grief would ensue. But it is not and she does not. She knows by now that she is dealing with a consummate operator; thus the more upset she is, the less she dares let it show. She says "I'm going." But she doesn't go.

That's part of the game. If the actress insists upon playing it for obvious "truth," then she has to make the move to go. But then the scene becomes about Goldberg trying to keep Lulu in the room. And it isn't about that at all. The more you listen to Lulu's language, the more you realize that this is about Lulu wanting to have a scene with Goldberg. She has rehearsed all the lines and she's going to say them or bust. "You used me for a night, a passing fancy," she howls. "You made use of me by cunning when my defenses were down." We had a terrible time with these lines in rehearsal because the actress playing Lulu felt caught: if she played it straight, the scene was merely hysterical and her outburst looked like crude melodrama. But if she played these lines as something premeditated, the actress felt that Lulu's pain wouldn't show and the scene would feel formulaic.

What became clear as we worked is that the more desperately Lulu tried to keep up the mask, tried to spout her Harlequin romance dialogue, the more horribly evident and yet hilariously funny her pain was. In fact, her effort to keep up the mask became the true action of the scene. We must have spent five days just on those two pages of dialogue. Masking one's emotional response is a very hard thing to trust. But it's crucial, because if the emotional torture becomes literal in any sense, the subtle evolution of the play's terror is destroyed.

The task of our first work on *The Birthday Party* had thus been the creation of "masks" which would protect and conceal the emotional truths hidden below the surface. We explored the tension that comes from silence and reveled in the musical qualities of Pinter's writing. The second rehearsal process, in which Pinter participated, had a very different focus. Perhaps because we had learned to sing the music, we could now uncover what had prompted the music to begin with.

By placing the two plays next to each other, we found it immediately evident that at least thematically, Pinter's work has been remarkably consistent over time. Much has been made of the fact that Pinter's work has suddenly become political, but the fundamental theme of *Mountain Language,* that of the desperate assertion of individual freedom in the face of public coercion, can already be clearly seen in *The Birthday Party.* Structurally, the two works also display odd similarities; indeed, in a sense *Mountain Language* is a sort of distillation of *The Birthday Party.*

Certainly the casting requirements for both plays are identical, with the exception of the older man playing Petey: each play calls for an older woman, a younger woman, and three men in their forties. I used exactly the same cast for both plays, but I took the cast of *The Birthday Party* and reversed the types for *Mountain Language,* so that the actor playing Stanley, the victim of torture in *The Birthday Party,* became the brutal Officer in scene 1 of *Mountain Language;* the villainous Goldberg became the tormented Prisoner in *Mountain Language;* zany and ever-cheerful Meg became the Old Woman; and Lulu in her magnificent party dress became the sober Young Woman. This role reversal was extremely difficult for the actors, who were playing much more "to type" in *The Birthday Party* than in *Mountain Language;* indeed, two weeks into rehearsal, Peter Riegert told me I was making a grave mistake and that he would never succeed in playing the brutalized Prisoner. But in the totality of the evening, it was the reverse casting after *Mountain Language* that made *The Birthday Party* so chilling. It was almost as if we could play the torture of *The Birthday Party* more subtly because it had been seen so nakedly in *Mountain Language.* At the same time, we were able to find some of *The Birthday Party*'s chilling humor in *Mountain Language.* And the juxtaposition of the two plays meant that the line between prisoner and oppressor, victim and victimizer, became frighteningly blurred.

The Birthday Party* and *Mountain Language* formed a coherent evening that was clearly the product of the same fertile mind. The similarities between the two plays also highlighted their differences. *The Birthday Party,* Pinter's first play, is a full-length domestic comedy with fleshed out characters and seem- ingly recognizable situations. *Mountain Language* is a brutal twenty-minute work set in an abstract, unspecified political prison among characters who remain nameless. During rehearsals for *Mountain Language,* I had to keep reminding myself that this was the same writer as the one who had written in his famous essay "Writing for the Theatre": "Beware of the writer who puts forward his concern for you to embrace, who leaves you in no doubt of his worthiness, his usefulness, his altruism, who declares that his heart is in the right place, and ensures that it can be seen in full view, a pulsating mass where his characters ought to be" (13), and "I've never started a play from any kind of abstract idea or theory and never envisioned my characters as messengers of death, doom, heaven or the milky way, or, in other words, as allegorical representations of any particular force, whatever that may mean" (10-11). We consistently, if silently, wondered how this could be the same writer as the author of *Mountain Language,* a play in which the author's "concern" and "heart" are startlingly clear, and in which a message is urgently being communicated. But Pinter told us during rehearsals that he could never conceive of writing a play like *The Birthday Party* again, a play with characters named Meg and Petey, a play in which the theme of gratuitous torture is subliminal and unspoken, hidden beneath black comedy. He seems to feel that the world has come to such a point that what was implied in *The Birthday Party* now needs to be made explicit. Pinter frequently plucks out Petey's final line to Stanley ("Don't let them tell you what to do") as a line by which he himself has always chosen to live his life "now more than ever." And indeed he says that he always viewed *The Birthday Party* as being a deeply political play on some level, although audiences watching *The Birthday Party,* particularly those first bewildered audiences in London, were often mystified or unaware of the political implications of this black comedy. One of the beauties of the play is the subtle way in which menace reveals itself from beneath a mask of smiling civility.

Audiences watching *Mountain Language* cannot help but be aware of the political message of the play. The charming Goldberg and comic McCann who slowly reveal themselves as villains in *The Birthday Party* become, in *Mountain Language,* brutal prison guards whose villainy is never in question. "I simply cannot see the joke anymore," Pinter said in rehearsal. "I cannot write about torture and make it funny." Having become heavily involved in Ortega's fight against the American-backed contra rebels in Nicaragua in the eighties, Pinter has become a born-again political activist himself, denouncing the United States as a war-mongering imperialist bully that has wreaked havoc on the Third World.

It is disconcerting to hear these kinds of views expressed by a writer who has until recently so assiduously concealed his personal beliefs beneath a complex web of language. And I am not convinced that *Mountain Language* is a better play for expressing his sentiments so boldly. But as a prelude to *The Birthday Party,* it was a startling piece of theatre.

We tried to schedule rehearsals so that the two plays coincided as much as possible; thus what we discovered in one play shed light on the other. It was an exhilarating and grueling five weeks, made more so for me by the birth of my first child three weeks prior to our first rehearsal. Ironically, the presence of Alexandra in the rehearsal room added an eerie reality to these two seemingly abstract plays. She seemed to highlight a major difference between our first rehearsal process of *The Birthday Party* and the second. What changed was that *The Birthday Party* became real to us the second time in a way it had not been before. Because in Pinter's eyes, everything in his plays is utterly real. The reality is viewed through a lens that may seem extraordinary to us but is quite natural to Pinter. Pinter listens to conversations around him with an intensely acute ear and then distills those conversations into a word or phrase or piece of dialogue that interests him. He is first and foremost a playwright of observation, who seems to write best about people he knows. And he writes for actors, the theatre artists with whom he feels most akin.

Perhaps this is why the first thing one encounters in a rehearsal with Pinter is not Pinter the writer but Pinter the actor. When Pinter demonstrates a scene, it is never to intellectualize or abstract it; in fact, he hates having to explain what something means. He trusts the characters so completely that he feels their behavior should be taken as a given and explored, not analyzed. So when asked a question, he often bolts up onto the stage and performs the scene himself, demonstrating why, for example, it is potent to act with one's back to the audience. He seems to know his work almost by heart, which is why he was so deeply offended when photographer Martha Swope asked him during a photo session to hold his script as if he were working on a scene in rehearsal. "I wrote the damn thing" he snarled. "I don't need to carry the bloody script around."

Sometimes Pinter would just offer a word or two of advice in rehearsal, always entirely practical. One day we were having trouble with a small section of the party scene in act II of *The Birthday Party;* the scene seemed too comfortable, too convivial. Why? Pinter thought for a moment and then replied "Irishmen always drink alone." He was right. McCann was being too convivial (a la Goldberg), and therefore the tension of the scene was missing. So we moved him to the staircase where he sat alone, and the scene instantly became more interesting. Pinter's acting instincts are intensely sharp—he is interested not in what one feels but in what works on stage.

Pinter's relationship with the cast of *The Birthday Party* evolved very quickly. He reveled in the "actor talk" that occurred every night over drinks after the show and regaled us with stories about his own nightmares acting in *The Birthday Party.* One story in particular has remained with me: Pinter's description of performing the interrogation scene in act I with Patrick McGee, Pinter playing Stanley and McGee playing McCann. This sequence is particularly difficult to memorize. It goes by at lightning speed and has to build with a series of insane moves that get more and more extreme until Stanley explodes.

McCANN: We'll provide the skipping rope.
GOLDBERG: The vest and pants.
McCANN: The ointment.
GOLDBERG: The hot poultice.
McCANN: The fingerstall.
GOLDBERG: The abdomen belt.
McCANN: The ear plugs. . . . (93)

Naturally, one night when performing the role, Pinter went completely blank and couldn't for the life of him remember the next word. He looked desperately at McGee. McGee sat there smugly, a diabolical grin on his face, as it to say: "You wrote this, you think of the next line." To this day, this actor's nightmare has remained with Pinter.

At first glance, *Mountain Language* seems far less realistic than *The Birthday Party.* The names are generic and the settings abstract. But the interactions are intensely real and specific. In this regard, we found the presence of Alexandra in rehearsal extremely valuable. When the Elderly Woman in *Mountain Language* says to her imprisoned and tortured son, "The baby is waiting for you," she means his own child, a very real infant whom he has never seen because of a political crime that is never identified. Although the characters are nameless and the location left unstated, the situation in *Mountain Language* is brutally real and must be played as such. It was much easier for Peter Riegert to feel the emotional weight of Jean Stapleton's lines when he looked at the real

Carey Perloff and Pinter in rehearsal. Photo by Tom Chargin.

infant in the room and imagined that it was his own and that he had never been allowed to see or touch her.

The first time that we rehearsed *The Birthday Party*, I had been careful not to overanalyze the characters or the situation, being scrupulous about the active powers of the language itself and allowing the script's rhythms to sustain the tension. In the same way, I made sure that the set was not so burdened with naturalistic details that the language would sink into the bric-a-brac. It seems to me that Pinter's sets must be as evocative, spare, and slightly surreal as Pinter's language. Yet his plays are usually produced on literally drawn living rooms. Pinter's scenic requirements are like Brecht's in the extreme selectivity required on the part of the designer: it is not that the real world is absent from the plays, merely that only very particular elements of the real world are allowed in. Less is more in Pinter—the language must float upon a stripped-away world or it will get mired in irrelevant details. The more mysterious the world outside the play is, the better.

Therefore, we placed *The Birthday Party* on a small raised platform with absolutely minimal furnishings, the requisite kitchen hatch, and a frighteningly steep staircase leading to a hidden upper balcony. Performing the play on a thrust stage freed us immediately from the walls and structure of a proscenium arch. Pinter was initially taken aback when he saw the design, because he claims never to have worked in anything but a proscenium house himself. But he became delighted with the set as we began to work on it, because its spareness and minimal suggestions allowed for a world of ambiguity to exist in the darkness that surrounded the central room. The set was in no way abstract; it was just distilled. And the world beyond was a mysterious void, out of which the actors emerged to perform their roles.

One element of our set particularly interested Pinter: the staircase. In a proscenium production, the staircase would never show; it would merely be indicated by a platform leading offstage. But on a thrust stage, it becomes the central element. In Loy Arcenas's design for *The Birthday Party*, the staircase was the most prominent aspect of the design, leading from the small platform to a mysterious and often dangerous world upstairs. It was also the ramp down which Meg paraded grandly with her party dress and drum. It was just a simple staircase, but it took on marvelous overtones, comic or horrific, depending on the way it was used. And because a real staircase was present, all the jokes about "Is Stanley up yet?"; "I haven't seen him down"; "Then he can't be up" could really play. In fact, they played so well that one day in rehearsals Pinter called Peter Riegert (Goldberg) aside as we were rehearsing his exit in act I, and gave him a new line on the spur of the moment. Thus, as Goldberg was following Meg up the stairs into the hidden rooms, he now exclaimed "What a lovely flight of stairs!" The stair game was in full swing.

We found that creating a character in a Pinter play was akin to the process of designing the set: one had constantly to discover the few details, the few tiny suggestions that made the thing real, the suggestions without which the place or character would not be. We are always told just enough and no more about a character, so that mystery is ever present. Pinter never assumes that one can ever be sure about a person's feelings or motivations, so he doesn't manipulate his characters as a playwright. Besides, he loves a good secret. Secrets are buried deep in Pinter, and conspiracy is everywhere. (We asked him why, having assumed the stage name David Baron for a time, he reverted back to his real name in later years. "They always found out in the end" he replied.) Yet this can never imply that Pinter's characters must be regarded as abstract or symbolic; only a small segment of each person may be revealed, but what is offered is always real. Take Petey, for example. Much has been made of Petey's complicity in Stanley's torture; it has been said that he is a kind of Holocaust figure, a symbol of the collaborators who allow individuals to be tortured. This may be so, but Petey is also an extremely specific man, an elderly deck chair attendant who plays bridge once a week and is married to a woman named Meg. "Approach him as you would a man you really know," Pinter told Bill Moor.

It is impossible to play a symbol, yet one is constantly tempted in Pinter's work to intellectualize the situations. Pinter repeatedly warned us against assuming that the characters in his or any play might think the way we think. When we asked him, for example, whether Petey was at all frightened about the two men he'd met on the beach, two men who are supposed to be symbols of disaster, Pinter replied, "Not at all. Petey is a poor working-class man. The well-dressed gentlemen on the beach reminded him that he ran a boarding house, and that the few quid they offered would come in very handy, particularly since he hasn't made any money off Stanley for a year. Thus, Petey should be pleased when telling the story of the two men, and not sniff danger until it is forced upon him at the end of the play." Pinter seemed to feel particular empathy for Petey. After watching actor Bill Moor rehearse the role for a few days, he said to him, "I see two Peteys in what you're playing. One is defeated and weary of life and of his wife. The other is resilient and loves his work. I am more interested in the second Petey. He's a chess player, remember. He's always on to the next move."

Pinter's practical, prosaic way of reading his characters surprised us initially; so much is written about his metaphoric landscape that it is startling to hear the characters discussed as if they were realer than real. Yet this is what makes Pinter's work great theatre as well as great literature. His insistence on that specificity and on the primacy of the present moment was the most useful guideline Pinter offered us during rehearsals. He insisted that if each character remained firmly rooted in the present moment of the play, the menace would creep in surreptitiously, without having to be referred to or made obvious early on. This means of operating, to Pinter's way of thinking, is far more "realistic" (if one can use such a word) than a confessional drama in which characters divulge their past history and present problems in one fell swoop. Pinter insisted, along these lines, that Goldberg and McCann not be portrayed as villains when they first appear. Imagine they are selling dictionaries, he said. The menace will reveal itself. He requested that we get rid of the bowler hats (which are specified in the script) as being too obvious.

One image that was useful to us while rehearsing Pinter's plays was that of a chess game. Games allow for extreme behavior to be cloaked in civility. They also provide a structure for encounters to occur without a single emotional thrust. It helped us avoid the tendency to carry over the emotional weight of one scene to the next, a naturalistic emotional device that Pinter loathes. In life, one thing happens and then something utterly different happens in the next instant, and the two are not necessarily related. It takes calculation to link scenes up emotionally, and Pinter is not calculating. He arranges scenes like moves in a very dangerous game; each time, the move is clean. The actors must accept and relish this. So, for example, at the top of scene 1 of *The Birthday Party*, when Stanley refuses to eat his cornflakes, Meg explodes with the hurt reaction of a lover. Then Stanley and Petey discuss the weather. Petey's terse replies to Stanley's questions might lead one to believe that Meg's outburst and her obvious passion for Stanley have depressed Petey and made him feel hostile to Stanley. Is Petey jealous of Stanley? the actors asked. Not at all. Once Meg has finished flirting with Stanley, it is over in Petey's mind. He never holds this against Stanley. One thing happens, then the next. Petey's a practical man; he's on to the next thing. "In fact," Pinter said, "Petey and Stanley have as much of a friendship as two people can have under these circumstances, and Meg's crises over the cornflakes do not color that."

Pinter's comments about Meg followed the same logic. We asked whether Meg asked Petey to read the newspaper to her in order to establish an emotional bond with him, to keep the conversation going, to connect. "I don't know," Pinter replied. "I think she has forgotten how to read."

Words in Pinter mean what they say. When Stanley says "There's nowhere to go. So we could just go. It wouldn't matter," he means it in a very literal sense. "This must not be a sentimental or defeated moment for Stanley," Pinter warned. "It's a statement of fact." In fact, the man in a seaside boarding house upon whom Pinter based Stanley said exactly that in answer to the question: "Why don't you ever leave?" He stated a fact. "There is nowhere to go."

Rehearsing *The Birthday Party* with Pinter gave us a clear glimpse into the writing process of the play. Pinter had clearly known these characters in his past; in *The Birthday Party*, he put them into a new and yet recognizable setting and then listened to what they had to say. The comedy of the play is crucial to Pinter, who roared appreciatively at all the funny bits and even let us restore a section he'd cut from the second published version because Wendy Makkena's innocent Lulu made it so ridiculously funny:

LULU: Don't you ever go out?
STANLEY: I was out, this morning.
LULU: I didn't see you out.

STANLEY: Perhaps you weren't out when I was out.
LULU: I'm always out.

One had the sense that Pinter was at home with these characters; he never patronized them, he understood them intimately and sympathized with each one. Even, in a sense, with Goldberg, who reveals the best of Pinter's Jewish humor.

Rehearsals for *Mountain Language* had a very different tone, partly because these characters are very different kinds of characters. They are not people Pinter has known in the same way; they are people who have been placed in a certain theatrical landscape to make a political and aesthetic point. The location of the prison is never specified, which is why the design for the play is particularly important: how does one achieve the kind of universality Pinter wants without being merely abstract? Our production of *Mountain Language* differed radically from Pinter's production of the play at the National. Pinter's production was monumental and detailed, with four separate sets for each of the four scenes and a stately time progression. At CSC, we decided to use the environment of our large warehouse-like theatre to create a world in which the entire play could take place without changing sets between scenes. The 40′ by 40′ playing space was covered with a huge grayish-white tarpaulin that was bunched up where the cloth hit the upstage wall, in a sort of abstract shape reminiscent of banks of snow. A single bare bulb hung over the central area, where the tarpaulin covered *The Birthday Party* platform. The effect of the cloth over the platform created a sense of a shroud. On the platform was a simple square metal table and two chairs. The design suggested a military prison without making the uniforms or architecture identifiable with any particular regime.

The play opened with a line of women against the back wall of the theatre. The line existed as the audience entered the theatre; every few moments, another woman would join the line, very slowly and incrementally, as a score by Wayne Horvitz played over the speakers. Slowly the house lights went down, and there was a long pause before the play began. The impression was that the women had been standing there forever. The first scene happened along the back wall. The second scene occurred on the platform under the bare bulb. For the third scene, the Elderly Woman and the Prisoner remained slumped in their chairs, and the hallway scene was played behind them in a strip of light, so that one saw the Prisoner in silhouette as the Young Woman in the hall looked for her husband. Finally, we returned to the platform for the fourth scene to see the tortured Prisoner. The effect of this staging was to allow the scenes to accrue so that the horror became more present and more unbearable as the play progressed. With very little time between scenes, the audience was never offered a moment of relief until long after the final blackout.

Pinter was fascinated by how different the play felt at CSC. CSC seems to have reminded him of the theatres he worked in as a young actor: gritty, sparse, and with a palpable atmosphere. Good design at CSC means using the architecture of the theatre with as few additions as possible, and *Mountain Language* was relentless in its spareness. The design also supported the nonspecific realism of the play. This nonspecificity is particularly difficult to achieve and took a great deal of discussion and work. Where should the play be set? Pinter has revealed in interviews that he wrote *Mountain Language* after a visit to Turkey, in which he met Kurdish dissidents and came to understand the horror of this group of people who were forbidden to speak their own language (the "mountain language" of this play) in public or in the capital. Indeed, following the first preview of *Mountain Language* at CSC, a discussion was held, during which Pinter's "abstraction" was mentioned, whereupon a man stood up and said, "This play is in no way abstract. I am a Kurd, and this play is about my people."

Yet the play is not set in Turkey and no obvious reference to the Kurdish people is made. The situation could equally well be Northern Ireland, or many parts of Latin America, or places much closer to our own backyard. When Harold and I first discussed producing *Mountain Language* in America, I told him I felt it was important that the play not feel "foreign"; the only way it could possibly have an impact on American audiences was if it felt visceral, immediate, recognizable, and not if it felt merely British. Harold thoroughly agreed; he hates the smugness of Americans who blindly assume that they are living in a democracy and feels that it is important that we recognize the totalitarian aspects of our own government, despite its seeming removal from the brutal excesses of Iraq or Uruguay. Thus, our original intention was to remove the obvious Britishisms from the play—"Babycham" would be replaced by an American equivalent, we'd change "bloke" to "guy" and Joseph Dokes to John Doe. Pinter enjoyed sitting around the table trading ideas with the actors about how to make it work American-style, and for a time this seemed to be the only way to universalize the play for Americans. But it quickly became obvious that this transposition was not going to work. Not only were certain phrases in *Mountain Language* British, the entire rhythm of the play was British English and could only be spoken as such. Had Pinter wanted the play to be American, he would have had to rewrite the entire script, or indeed write a new play, which was not his intention. As always with Pinter's work, it is the quality of the language that makes *Mountain Language* interesting. Take that away, and there is no play.

Interestingly enough, this is where Pinter, who has been said by Martin Esslin and others to be approaching a Brechtian style of writing in his recent work, differs so radically from Brecht. Brecht's characters do not necessarily reflect people he had known or even a language he had heard spoken. In his quest for an epic theatre that would bring certain political realities to light, Brecht transcended his regional German beginnings and found a kind of theatrical poetry that is not dependent on the specific cadences of a particular dialect of German speech. With Pinter, as one discovers quickly in rehearsal, the opposite is the case. Even when setting work in nonspecific locations and exploring generically named characters, what always interests Pinter is the English language and how that language, his own language, can be manipulated and distorted to inflict violence on another person. In trying to Americanize the play, we were in effect trying to literalize the events and characters Pinter had created, but this literal framework was not useful to *Mountain Language.* What makes the play frightening is its depiction of how people can destroy each other through language. And oddly enough, when that language is not literally recognizable, it takes on a greater universality. By maintaining the "Britishisms" of Pinter's language, our audiences were never tempted to ask what southern army base this was set in or what part of America the Young Woman came from. The scenes sprang into relief like brutal snapshots that the audience could absorb and examine one at a time.

Although *Mountain Language's* characters have generic names, the interactions in the play are highly personal and emotionally direct. It is considered a "political play," but *Mountain Language's* focus is in fact on personal torture and individual heroism, rather than on the larger political issues that surround that behavior. A work like *Mountain Language* makes no political or ideological statement other than that torture is despicable and ever present and must be guarded against. It does not hold a political or economic system up to scrutiny, as Brecht attempted to do in *In the Jungle of the Cities* and *St. Joan of the Stockyards.* Viewed in this light, *Mountain Language* is not in fact that remote from the earlier *The Birthday Party* in its depiction of the personal effects of gratuitous torture.

Thus, interestingly enough, the task when producing *Mountain Language* was to focus on the personal, the specific and insidious violence that one individual does to another merely because he/she happens to be in power. This is very different from the technique required to rehearse a play like Brecht's *Arturo Ui,* which demands that its actors engage in discussion of the larger political and social forces informing the play and that the actors and director understand the economic and political reasons that certain characters achieve dominance over other characters. The individual is of far less interest to Brecht than the larger social order in which those individuals play a role, whereas to Pinter, the personal is everything. This is what makes rehearsing his plays much more difficult emotionally than rehearsing Brecht's work.

In a culture of total repression such as that depicted in *Mountain Language,* real communication never happens except through silence. In that silence, thoughts are shared. Pinter reveals this in the play through the use of carefully chosen voice-overs that occur at moments of brutality when spoken communication is impossible. In rehearsal, we found that we couldn't record the voice-overs after having rehearsed a scene because the actors' devastation quickly came through in their voices. To Pinter, the tone of the voice-overs should stand in contrast to that of the scenes, so that the voice-overs could offer a moment of transcendence, as if a small bud were pushing through the rest of the muck. They serve as a reminder of the indomitability of the human spirit in the face of destruction. When the Young Woman's voice is light and cheerful during her voice-overs, the contrast between that affect and her current misery is extremely poignant. The voice-overs thus served to echo another happier world long before this horror, just as Krapp's memories of youthful romance serve as a painful contrast to his current dejection in Beckett's *Krapp's Last Tape*. Indeed, the voice-overs in *Mountain Language* are strongly reminiscent of Krapp. In *Mountain Language,* the scene 3 voice-over says: "We are out on a lake." "It is spring." "I hold you. I warm you." Similarly, Krapp sighs,

> —upper lake, with the punt, bathed off the bank, then pushed out into the stream and drifted. . . . I asked her to look at me and after a few moments—(*pause*)— after a few moments she did, but the eyes just slits, because of the glare. . . . I lay down across her with my face in her breasts and my hand on her. We lay there without moving. But under us all moved, and moved us, gently, up and down, and from side to side. (61)

The voice-over technique in *Mountain Language* allowed Pinter to create some of his most lyrical moments on stage, and it is fitting that they come out of the enforced silence of the prison. In "Writing for the Theatre," Pinter had said: "We have heard many times that tired, grimy phrase 'failure of communication' . . . and this phrase has been fixed to my work quite consistently. I believe the contrary. I think that we communicate only too well, in our silence, in what is unsaid, and that what takes place is a continual evasion, desperate rearguard attempts to keep ourselves to ourselves. Communication is too alarming. To enter into someone else's life too frightening" (15).

In *Mountain Language* Pinter has taken this idea to its extreme. Communication is forbidden. Language has become the tool of the oppressor, whose torrent of words infect the atmosphere. The only true connection comes through silence. The power the victims in *Mountain Language* have is the power of their silence, the power of their imaginations. Only in the interstices, in the spaces between, is real communication possible in the world of *Mountain Language*. "There are two silences. One where no word is spoken. The other when perhaps a torrent of language is being employed. . . . When true silence falls, we are still left with echo but are nearer nakedness" ("Writing for the Theatre" 14–15). In *Mountain Language* Pinter has finally found the power of true silence, the silence in which everything is communicated. The voice-overs hang in the air as the characters stand frozen, staring at each other. The guards hear nothing; they feel in the silence that they have conquered. But a torrent of communication is happening, eye to eye, in the minds of those who have been silenced. It is this leap of imagination that still seems to give Pinter hope, despite his melancholy about the world today.

And perhaps this is why in his later life Pinter has returned to Beckett more than to Brecht. Beckett was Pinter's first mentor and the only person to whom he consistently sent his precious new scripts for comment, and it was Beckett who taught him to find humor in the bizarre spectacle of humanity caught in the muck of life. One day during a rehearsal break, the actors performing *Mountain Language* seemed particularly depressed by the material. Whereupon Pinter told us a story, appropriately enough, about Beckett. It seems that during one of his last visits to Beckett, Pinter had commented upon how deeply depressed he was about the state of the world. At that, Beckett had smiled mischievously and replied, "Not as depressed as I am, Harold." And they both laughed.

TWO

Producing Pinter

Louis Marks

What I wish to present is not theory or analysis. I do not feel myself qualified for that. It is simply raw material, culled from my observations and experiences of working with Pinter on a number of productions of his work.

I begin with the letter he sent me with his first draft of the screenplay of *The Trial* in August 1989. He wrote:

> I feel that this draft confirms the conclusions we came to in our talks. What I found absolutely natural was to tell the story straight, as it were, as a hard, taut, objective series of events. The narrative is itself remorseless and inevitable. I have a sense of a constant and implacable force behind it, a constant and implacable presence.
>
> The film does not go from dream to reality, as it were. It is *all* reality or *all* dream. But one must remember that the knife which is plunged into K.'s heart is real.

Although this takes me, so to speak, to the end of the story—my current production—it casts a light on so much of the other work that it deserves to be introduced at the outset. But I will return to it later.

I am a television and film producer, mostly for the drama department of BBC Television, and "producing Pinter" for me has been confined to this medium. Our first professional meeting—we had met informally before on a few occasions—was in the early summer of 1980 at the National Theatre, London, where Harold was directing Simon Gray's *Close of Play,* continuing a collaboration that had already staged *Butley* and was to continue for many other productions. It was one of these earlier productions, *The Rear Column,* we now met to discuss. The proposal was to mount it for BBC TV's "Play of the Month," with Harold directing.

Let me set the context. Although primarily a man of the theatre, Pinter was no stranger to television. Up to the time of *The Caretaker* almost all his early plays had been presented on TV, including *A Night Out* and *The Birthday Party.* Three had indeed been specially written for TV—*Night School, The*

From his address at *A Pinter Festival,* given on 21 April 1991.

Collection, and *The Lover*—and showed a rare aptitude for exploiting to the full the unique potential of the then still new medium.

Pinter was in fact one of that new generation of British writers who emerged in the late fifties and early sixties, which included Mercer, Owen, Hopkins, and Exton, among many others now forgotten, who enthusiastically grasped the opportunities to reach the new, wider audiences offered by the recently established Independent Television Companies, as against the traditionally middle-class, more paternalistic climate of the old monopolistic BBC. The new writers as well as the new audiences tended to come from the broader working class and warmed to the works of writers who were now emerging from this same background and who faced their problems and spoke in their language. A new television play was a national event, talked about the next day in shops, offices and factories. Pinter—though in crucial ways uniquely different from his contemporaries—was part of that revolution which many of us still look back to as a "golden age."

While the ITV companies set the pace, it was not long before the old BBC felt the winds of change and indeed rapidly took the lead. Throughout the sixties and seventies the explosion of drama continued. The vast new Television Centre was built with its eight studios. Technique flourished, especially with the coming of color, and professional skills set a world standard. Also the enormous body of production brought with it more complex organization with formalized "strands," rigid schedules, and tighter budgeting control. "Play of the Month" was one of these strands with the brief to mount eight studio productions a year of major classic plays.

As a new producer of this strand I chose to interpret "classic" as widely as possible. I was free to roam from Sophocles to Athol Fugard, but, since the strand was transmitted on Sunday night prime time on BBC 1, I felt a two-fold obligation: to serve an audience, most of whom would rarely if ever have an opportunity to see great plays in the theatre, and to select works which could be made to "live" for that audience in contemporary terms.

The Rear Column seemed to fit the bill perfectly. The play had run with modest success in the West End of London but had closed after three months. It deserved a much wider audience. The subject matter—a bizarre tale of sadism and cannibalism among a group of British army officers left behind by the explorer Stanley at a base camp to protect his rear—provided vivid insights into the character of the English "officer and gentleman" under stress, which Gray had handled with deep sympathy and irony. Gray understands "Englishness" like no other living playwright and has expressed it nowhere better than in *The Rear Column*.

Harold had never directed a TV play in his life. The initial discussions deciding the broad approach and the cast went smoothly enough. Simon and he agreed that the production should not fall for the temptation to "open up" the play from the hut where the stage play had confined it, to show incidents in the camp outside which were described but not seen. They felt, correctly, that this would not intensify but dilute the dramatic tension which worked essentially through the actors and the language. But inside the hut everything should be totally realistic. So the preparatory work was done and the production dates set.

Three days before the start of the production proper, Harold called me to say he couldn't go through with it. He felt he simply could not handle the complexities of shooting a two-hour play using five cameras and cutting between them during a virtually live performance. He was experiencing a quite understandable panic. But what could we do? Cancel the production? Hire another director? Twenty-four hours later Harold called again. We'd go ahead.

On the first day of "dry" rehearsal the read-through went excellently. Then Harold started to block the action. I should explain. The rehearsal room has an acting area marked out with tape which matches the dimensions of the eventual studio set, but there is no set, just rudimentary props. Harold placed the actors for the opening scene and began the rehearsal. The first assistant interrupted. "Excuse me Harold, but if you place Barry here for that speech Camera One will be in Camera Two's shot." Harold reconsidered. He repositioned the actor and started again. This time the designer, Eileen Diss, spoke up. "If you shoot Barry like that there isn't any scenery behind him."

Harold stopped the rehearsal. He dismissed the actors, sat down with the designer and assistant, opened up the floor plan, and began plotting the shots again from first principles. His concentration was total and over the following weeks he got completely on top of the technicalities and was free to concentrate on the real job of making a show.

By the time of the recording he was enjoying every moment and was thrilled at the immediacy of television which gives the director instant pictures on the monitor in front of him. During intervals and meal breaks he was in rare good humor. As a man of the theatre he shines in the company of actors and relishes theatrical anecdotes. This was the fun part of the whole experience. But it was matched by the work in which he displayed a single-minded logic and clarity reinforced by a total commitment to pursue a point to its conclusion. He will not be side-tracked or relax his grasp on the problem until it is solved. He hates fudge.

Another quality I recognized in him during this first production was his courage in overcoming his initial fears, to which is linked his loyalty—to the play, to the actors, and not least, to Simon Gray, who had entrusted the work to him.

Shortly after completing *The Rear Column*, I went with my wife to see *The Hothouse* at the Hampstead Playhouse. The utter absurdity of the opening dialogue between Gibbs and Roote about the mysterious fate of 6457 made us both laugh out loud. This was not the thing to do at a Pinter play, which surely demands reverent silence. But we laughed again and the audience shushed us. When the play ended we went round to see Harold and told him our experience. He was appalled. He'd just put on what he considered, and still considers, the funniest play he had ever written before an audience that for a bizarre set of reasons felt it was an offense to laugh.

When I met Harold to talk about this lecture and what I should say to you, I brought this experience up and his response was immediate. He calls it "the curse of Pinter." I asked him when he first became aware of it, and he dates it to the 1965 Peter Hall production of *The Homecoming.* Something about that production—maybe the over-long pauses, the underlining of "significances"—*intimidated* the audience, so that they felt they had to calculate their reaction rather than simply respond to the play. And this disturbs him greatly because it gets in the way of the direct communication between the play and the audience.

Anyway, I had no doubts about the serious quality, as well as the brilliant humor of *The Hothouse* (which I believe does for all dehumanizing institutions what *The Great Dictator* did for all tyrannies), and I invited Harold to bring it to the BBC. This time Pinter would be directing Pinter and the result would be immortalized on videotape.

And this time, too, Pinter himself was more confident, the production more ambitious. In visualizing the transition from stage to screen he wanted a simple means to convey the vast institutional coldness of the asylum while also accommodating the intimacy of the various encounters between the members of the staff. He hit on the idea of a huge staircase. This would play no part in the main action. Occasionally a character would walk up or down it. In the final sequence we would see the shadows of the escaping inmates flitting up it. But for many shots it would just be seen as a staircase with perhaps some far-off sound. But it conveyed the sense of place perfectly and was a clear, powerful image that by itself transformed the play for the box.

Other memories of that production? I spent much time watching rehearsals and saw for myself what others had told me of his working methods. His concentration is totally on the practical, never the theoretical. Meanings of lines, subtexts, interest him not at all. "Play the line . . . it will work" is his constant theme. Everything he wants to say is in the line. If he had wanted a different meaning or nuance he would have written the line differently. For this reason it is impossible ever to paraphrase or reorder or, worse, "wing" a Pinter line. His insistence on this is not arrogance. It is quite simply the case that it destroys the work. He writes for actors as an actor. He plays the lines himself. As in every other aspect of his craft, he is precise in what he wants to achieve. In Pinter precision is paramount.

Incidentally, although we never discussed with Pinter the "meaning" of the play—the subject never arose—we did learn how he came to write it. In answer to a question from one of the tape editors Harold volunteered the story of how in the late fifties when he was still a struggling, unknown writer, he saw an advertisement for guinea pigs to take part in experiments at the Maudsley Mental Hospital in South London for which the pay was ten shillings and sixpence (about $1) a session. Harold was taken to a white-walled room where he was given earphones. Suddenly a piercing high-pitched tone assailed his eardrums. The idea for the play was born.

Some weeks after finishing the production of *The Hothouse,* Harold invited me for lunch. This was partly to have our usual postmortem on the production. But the real reason soon emerged. He told me that he had a long-held wish to write and direct a film version of Kafka's *The Trial*. He'd read it first when he was seventeen and then spent three weeks in Hackney Public Library devouring everything he could find by its author. That experience had determined him to be a writer. Now, forty years on, he wanted to return to it and, in a sense, pay his tribute.

He wanted to present it not as some nightmare fantasy, but as taking place in a "normal" world where people went about their work, where everyday commerce took place, and where there were no long dark sinister shadows or even more sinister low-angle camera shots. The nightmare, in other words, was not something *imposed*. It was *in* the reality.

We did not discuss details. But I remember Harold talked about his most vivid memory from the book. It was the moment when, K., walking along the corridor at the bank, hears a noise. He opens a door and finds two men about to be flogged. It is a shatteringly disturbing image, revealed by opening a door. Close the door and it is gone. But it is not a dream or a fantasy. It happens. Harold's eyes shone at the recollection. This was what it was about. We said we would both read the book again and meet further.

I remember walking away from that lunch thinking "Pinteresque . . . Kafka-esque." Two writers—almost the only two this century—whose names have been adjectivalized. It was an exciting but wholly misleading thought.

That was in, I think, 1982. Over the following few years neither of us was able to pursue the idea. We were also both busy in other directions. These were the years when Pinter, in addition to his own writing, was becoming more actively involved politically, especially in traveling widely on behalf of the International PEN. But these experiences bore fruit in his two intensely powerful short plays, *One for the Road* (1985) and *Mountain Language* (1988)—images of oppression.

Both plays have been performed widely and have gained in power. The moustached Alan Bates in *One for the Road* now seems to bear an uncanny resemblance to the similarly moustached Saddam Hussein. The Kurds, the suppression of whose language by Turkey inspired *Mountain Language,* are with us now more than ever. Both plays needed to reach the largest possible audience, and I proposed TV productions with which Harold again was closely involved, directing the latter play himself.

Of these productions there is not a lot to say except to underline yet again Harold's passionate concern with enhancing the reality of the dramatic experience. Both plays could lend themselves so easily to stylized or overly symbolic approaches, but this is not Harold's way. I recall in particular a heated discussion aimed at clarifying the internal geography of the prison in *Mountain Language* so that the relationship between the corridor and the visiting room made sense. Such details always matter deeply to him.

It was shortly after this—early in 1989—that I invited him to lunch and spoke about our earlier conversations on *The Trial*. It seemed to me that the time was right to try to move this ahead. Harold's eyes blazed and we ordered a bottle of champagne. By curious coincidence it was the day the death threat was issued against Salman Rushdie, and that afternoon Harold was leading a delegation of protesting writers to Downing Street.

When Harold sat down to write the screenplay that summer in Corfu, it took him two weeks to produce his first draft, handwritten on a large pad of yellow lined paper. But, as he told me on his return, it had really taken forty years. During the spring and early summer we had met for a number of talks about the film, but I believe from the outset Harold had a clear idea of what he was out to achieve.

He had stated this in our very first discussion. The starting point was normality. Looking back now over the talks, what happened was a gradual clearing away of debris. By this I mean the huge agglomeration of interpretations, associations, and accretions which have been piled on the original text over seventy years since Kafka's death. It seemed to me that all this needed to be discussed in order for us to be clear on our own approach. So we talked about the political, psychological, and existentialist meanings. At one point we had a fascinating discussion on a particular Jewish interpretation which sees the book as symbolizing the situation of the emancipated European Jew of Kafka's day, free from the age-old legal constraints but yet constantly on trial on charges from unseen accusers.

Harold found all the theories interesting, up to a point, but ultimately irrelevant. All that really mattered was Kafka's text. Everything else gets in the way and obscures the view. It was so blindingly simple. Just read the text and let its richness and drama speak directly to you. What I had come to understand about Pinter's own work over the years of working with him he already knew about Kafka. Let the story, the characters speak directly to you. That is the only communication that matters.

In the end, what was there for Harold to do but start at the beginning and tell the story? So it became obvious that we should place the film precisely in the period in which Kafka himself conceived it—the Austro-Hungarian Empire on the eve of World War I. Having taken that decision, we soon saw it as the only possible one. It was a real world, one that could be recreated authentically on film. But also it was a secure, orderly world, a civilized world, little knowing the earthquake that was about to shatter it. This was the "normality" that Pinter needed. The rest would follow.

What Harold himself discovered, as he described in the letter I quoted at the beginning, was that after the debris was cleared away, what emerged was not only a story, a narrative, but one that had a powerful, irresistible dynamic, "remorseless and inevitable." His script remains true to this at every point. I hope we will be able to say this in the end of the film.

Finally, having delivered the screenplay, Harold decided not to direct it himself.

II. Political Pinter

THREE

Harold Pinter's Theatre of Cruelty

Martin Esslin

What has happened to Harold Pinter the playwright—as distinct from the screenwriter who is as busy as ever?

Since 1982, when *A Kind of Alaska* opened as part of a triple bill, he has published only two short plays, *One for the Road* and *Mountain Language*, and a tiny sketch, *Precisely*. And, while all his previous work dealt with problems such as identity, verification, the nature of reality, existential angst, the concerns of Beckett and Kafka rather than those of the committed political playwrights of his and a later generation, since 1982 his work has become entirely political, devoted to attacks on dictators who torture their subjects and civil servants who are unperturbed by the menace of a nuclear holocaust.

Whereas all his previous work was enigmatic, multilayered, relying on pauses, silences, and a subtext of far greater importance than what was actually being said, these later pieces operate unambiguously on the surface, even relying on voice-overs to make the characters' thoughts crystal clear and proclaiming a message of blinding simplicity, a message which is a call to political action.

And at the same time Pinter has assumed a very visible political role as one of the sponsors of Charter 88, a group of British left-wing intellectuals clamoring for a bill of rights and a written consitution for the United Kingdom.

So, how has a previously confessedly unpolitical playwright become a political pamphleteer?

Of course, while his plays were free from an openly political slant, Pinter himself has never been a politically undefined personality. A good deal has recently been written on this question: from Pinter's own utterances in interviews, speeches, and other incidental autobiographical material, it is fairly clear that he has always been politically conscious and committed to a variety of libertarian causes—his registering as a conscientious objector in his youth, because he was disgusted with the cold war, is a case in point; so are his repeated interventions on behalf of political prisoners in various parts of the

From his address at *A Pinter Festival,* given on 19 April 1991.

world, East and West. At the same time he has repeatedly proclaimed his distrust of establishment politics of all kinds, left or right, and his contempt for politicians. That he is now involved in a movement of intellectuals that stands outside the traditional structure of politics further consolidates that impression. In the light of his recent, more openly political output he has also, himself, pointed out that much of his earlier work was, if not on the surface, at least subtextually political: were not the two killers in *The Dumb Waiter* clearly manipulated by a higher authority upstairs, and did not *The Caretaker* and *The Homecoming* describe social conditions in a debased post-war London?

All this is clearly true and relevant. Yet, it seems to me that it poses the question the wrong way round: the question is not whether Pinter's politics engendered certain aspects of his work, but on the contrary, how and in what forms Pinter's basic existential experience, his manner of perceiving the world, his individuality as a human being and an artist activate his imagination and creativity and in turn determine his politics—both his former seeming absten-tion from direct political involvement in his early work and his open com-mitment to politics in his latest work.

For what so many of the early, ostensibly unpolitical, and the later, openly propagandist, works have in common is the image of the torturer, the terrorist: Nick in *One for the Road* and the brutal torturers in *Mountain Language* are directly related to, say, Ben and Gus in *The Dumb Waiter*, who are discussing the mess created by the girl they killed: "They don't seem to hold together like men, women. A looser texture, like. Didn't she spread, eh? She didn't half spread . . ." (146–47). Or the genteelly middle-class Edward in *A Slight Ache*, who revels in the agony of the wasp he is killing in a jar of marmalade. "What a horrible death," exclaims his wife. "On the contrary," he replies (172).

A preoccupation with cruelty in all its varieties and possible manifestations, physical as well as verbal, with the recurring figures of terrorists, torturers, and executioners pervades Pinter's oeuvre and constitutes one of the main thematic strands of its total texture—indeed, it might be argued that it stands at its very center. In this Pinter is a true representative of his century, the century of the Holocaust, genocide, the nuclear bomb.

In his early novel *The Dwarfs* (1990), written between 1952 and 1956 but unpublished for more than a quarter century, Pinter has one of the characters, Pete, a young East London intellectual from the very circles Pinter comes from, express his despair of the world as it exists and his desperate desire to put distance between himself and "them":

> I am of a mind to abdicate. When my sense of distance has been proved wrong. And no one but me can eliminate it. When I have proved distance malleable I shall lay down this sword. Got to prove they exist, then lay down the sword. Because I am the axiom I will not escape. In the act of proof, after all, is the proof. The gas chamber, I won't deny it, is a ripe and purposive unit. I look into my garden and see walking blasphemies. A blasphemy is a terrible thing. They cut the throat of a child over the body of a naked woman. The blood runs down

her back, the blood runs between the cheeks of her arse. In my sight the world commits sacrilege . . . (111–12)

Here the images of heaped corpses at Belsen and other concentration camps that peopled the imagination of the generation growing up in the late forties are brutally present. How were the young people of that generation to deal with these images?

Another of the three main male characters in the book, young intellectuals in postwar East London, Mark, the actor who claims descent from a Portuguese Sephardic background and thus outwardly is the one most like Pinter himself, cultivates a sovereign attitude of indifference to these horrors:

—The world's got nothing on me, Mark said. Where's the bother?
—You're a marked man, said Len.
—Possibly. Marked, but indifferent.
—Would you be indifferent to the torturing wheel? Pete asked.
—Oh no.
—So you're not indifferent to everything? asked Virginia.
—All I'm trying to say is that everything's a calamity, Mark said. There are items within the fact of that fact that I am unable to accept. But I accept that I can't accept them. I accept that which I can't accept. I accept the fact within which I act. In other words I carry on merrily. (116)

Pete's despair and Mark's show of indifference can thus be seen as two sides of the same coin—and these attitudes reappear in many of the characters of later plays, who like, for instance, Mick in *The Caretaker* or Lenny in *The Homecoming* nonchalantly accept the horrible facts of life in this world and try to stand aloof from and above them.

The label of "comedies of menace" that has been applied to Pinter's plays is correct as far as it goes, yet behind the menace there stands the consciousness of an anxiety about the cruelty of the post-Holocaust, postnuclear world itself. In the same way the frantic search for a territory of one's own, a safe haven from which that world can be excluded—the territorial element of Pinter's work—also emerges as merely an aspect of that basic realization of the ruthless brutality of the times, a panic-stricken desire to shelter from a world pervaded by terror and torture.

Pinter's earliest play, *The Room*, can thus be seen as a post-Holocaust nightmare: is Rose, whose real name seems to be Sal—the Nazis forced all Jewish women to carry the second name Sarah—a Jewish woman sheltering in a marriage with a non-Jew? The emissary who has come to remind her of her family is a black man with an Irish name, Riley, thus representing two other despised minority races. In the end he is brutally beaten down by Rose/Sal's racialist husband, who screams "lice!" (inferior races, in his mind, being no more than vermin). "You verminate the sheet of your birth" is one of the taunts hurled at Stanley, another shelterer from the world, in *The Birthday Party*. In *The Room*, moreover, the anxieties of Jewishness are also introduced in Mr. Kidd's musings about whether his mother might have been a "Jewess."

The professional torturers and terrorists make their first appearance in *The Dumb Waiter*; unlike the impulsive racialist Bert Hudd in *The Room*, they are part of an organization—the twentieth century world is one of organized cruelty on a large scale; and terrorist organizations are so intricately and cunningly structured that the executive organs at the bottom, the members of terrorist cells, have only a vague knowledge of the forces above them, the deeper connections and policies that govern their orders. Pinter's period of acting in a touring Shakespearean company in Ireland at the very beginning of his career as an actor has also obviously furnished many echoes of the IRA and its brand of terrorism and terrorist organization to him.

In *The Birthday Party* the outcast hiding from the brutal world and the torturers who are part of a large and mysterious organization are brought together in the same play—and here another aspect of the cruel totalitarian twentieth-century world comes to the fore: the ruthless interrogation that accompanies the application of the instruments of torture. "The third degree" was familiar to boys from Pinter's generation from American gangster pictures of the period, which represent another aspect of the cruelty of the epoch, the corrupt policemen, as well as the Mafia, organizations closely akin to the Kafkaesque secret-police organizations of the totalitarian world that use torture to extract confessions from possible traitors.

Goldberg and McCann, the Jew and the Irishman (here Pinter used stock comic characters from the repertoire of popular drama as he did with Ben and Gus, the stock cockneys of the London East end music hall), are masters of the third degree, verbal torturers, who bombard their victim with an endless stream of verbiage until he is utterly confused and befuddled. "You betrayed the organization . . . we can sterilise you . . . you betray our breed . . . you are a plague gone bad . . . you're nothing but an odour"—these apostrophes, that I have picked out at random from the stream, emphasize the racialist flavor of the assault in the second act (58–62), while in the third act the already brainwashed and blinded victim (his glasses have been broken) is pressed into the new mold of the cowed subject, a preprogrammed cog in the wheel of the organization, the society of whatever kind it might be (rather like Winston Smith in Orwell's *1984*): "From now on we'll be the hub of your wheel"—"We'll watch over you"—"Advise you"—"Give you proper care and treatment"—"Let you use the club bar"—"Keep a table reserved"—"Help you acknowledge the fast days"—"We'll make a man of you"—"And a woman"—"You'll be re-orientated"—"You'll be rich"—"You'll be adjusted"—"You'll be our pride and joy"—"You'll be a mensch" (92–93). These are but a few of the verbal punches under which the victim is made to reel.

Here the horror is precisely that this type of totalitarian third degree is designed to produce the preprogrammed, zombie-like ideal subject of any conformist society, whether totalitarian or bourgeois, conditioned like one of Pavlov's dogs to follow the strictly preordained pattern. There is also here a striking analogy drawn between the terrorism of the secret police, the Gestapo, or the Mafia on the one hand, and the terrorism of bourgeois conformism on the other: the brilliance of the image in *The Birthday Party* is precisely the indeterminacy of the terrorist characters: they may be the emissaries of an underground terrorist organization, or they may merely be the agents of a society that forces Stanley, the potential artist, into the straightjacket of a bowler-hatted, nine-to-five job that effectively castrates his creative impulses.

This image is even more drastically present in *The Hothouse*, a play Pinter wrote shortly after *The Birthday Party*, in 1958–1959, but then decided to withhold until 1980. Here Pinter went further in showing a world in which human beings—the inmates of a bureaucratic institution that might be a mental hospital—are reduced to numbers and subjected to a third degree. Wired to an electrical apparatus that can give them an electrical shock when they answer wrongly, the patients are in a clinical environment devoted to the systematic torture and degrading of its members. It is significant that in explaining why he had decided to put this play—so long withdrawn—before a public more than twenty years after it had been written, Pinter pointed out that reality had caught up with his fantasy: when he had written the play he was unaware of the fact that in Russian mental hospitals actual dissidents were subjected to this kind of torture. (On the other hand it must not be forgotten that in the late fifties there was much talk about the brainwashing techniques used by the Chinese and North Koreans in the Korean war, so the subject of psychological techniques to produce zombie-like conformity was certainly in the air then.) Moreover, that it was not then as topical as it had become twenty years later does not explain why he decided in 1959 to keep this play out of public view. (He lent me a copy of the manuscript when I was writing my book about him: it had a note on the title page that it was not to be performed.) It seems to me much more likely that at the time he felt that this play fell too much into the stereotype of what by then had become know as a "Pinteresque" play, that it merely repeated earlier works, exaggerating some of their characteristics—i.e. a preoccupation with the grotesquely comic aspect of mechanized torture.

The Caretaker, which constituted his breakthrough into worldwide success (it reached Broadway in 1961), can be seen as dealing with the same subject matter in a far more subtle and less "mechanical" manner. Here the grotesquely comical electrified third degree of *The Hothouse* has become the very realistic electro-shock treatment to which Aston has been subjected in the mental hospital, where his mother sent him because he had been too excitable and emotional. In other words, to rid him of the artistic side of his personality and make him conform to the standards of bourgeois existence. In this play, the verbal third degree of *The Birthday Party* as well as *The Hothouse* has become the sadistic teasing to which Mick, Aston's brother, subjects the intruder Davis, by immersing him in endless streams of difficult language that is beyond his comprehension.

Torture through electro-shock within the everyday situation of a National Health Service Hospital allows the preoccupation with such cruelty to be taken into a much more realistic, less grotesquely caricatured framework. With *The*

Caretaker, that is, Pinter abandoned the surrealist, Kafkaesque stage machinery of his earlier plays, to enter an outwardly far more realistic style of representation, while still preserving, under the seemingly traditionally realistic surface, his main thematic preoccupations and the poetic, metaphoric quality that underlay his main concerns as an artist—the evocation of a world awesome in its unfathomable impenetrability, its senseless cruelty and evanescence.

If the grotesque electrical torture chamber of *The Hothouse* has been transformed into the clinical equipment of the mental hospital in *The Caretaker,* the verbal third degree of *The Birthday Party* and *The Hothouse* reemerges in the linguistic teasing and torture Davis is subjected to by Mick. Language as an instrument of torture, language as a medium through which power is exerted between individuals, becomes ever more prominent in Pinter's later work—it was already present in *The Dumb Waiter's* discussions about linguistic minutiae and very much foregrounded in *The Birthday Party* and *The Hothouse.*

In *The Caretaker,* the more articulate can play cat and mouse with the more inarticulate, befuddle him with questions he cannot understand, and terrify him by using words beyond his comprehension, subject him, that is, to a veritable third degree. In the end, it is the interpretation of the word "caretaker" that decides the fate of the unfortunate outcast Davis.

Torture is the most blatantly visible exercise of power by one human being over another. The "third degree" is verbal torture. But all verbal confrontations, all dialogue in fact, contains an element of a power struggle. One of the interlocutors will dominate, the other will have difficulty in getting a word in edgewise; one will have the wider vocabulary, a quicker response reaction than the other. This is the most prominent characteristic of Pinter's use of dialogue. All verbal interchange may not be a "third degree," but it certainly is at least a "second degree," a struggle for momentary, local power—dominance. And as Elias Canetti, the Nobel-Prize writer who has also produced one of the unknown masterpieces of social analysis of our time, *Crowds and Power,* has brilliantly shown, all power, even its most seemingly mild forms, as the power of the parent over the child, the teacher over the pupil, the bus conductor over the traveler, the employer over his worker, is in the last resort reducible to the ultimate sanction: all power is an aspect of the power over life and death. Verbal cruelty, which always lurks in any dialogic situation—all dialogue being a fencing for positions in a pecking order—is thus only different by degrees from physical cruelty as exercised by the torturer and executioner.

The dialogue of Pinter's plays is, more plainly than that of most other dramatists, always a struggle for linguistic dominance, a power struggle, which, in this sense, always ultimately is a life-and-death matter. The terrorist, the torturer thus always lurks behind the verbal exchanges in Pinter's plays.

Harry's diatribe against Bill in *The Collection* is an excellent example:

Bill's a slum boy, you see, he's got a slum sense of humour. That's why I never take him along with me to parties. Because he's got a slum mind. I have nothing against slum minds *per se,* you understand, nothing at all. There's a certain kind of slum mind, which is perfectly all right in a slum, but when its kind of slum mind gets out of the slum it sometimes persists, you see, it rots everything. That's what Bill is. There something slightly putrid about him, don't you find? Like a slug. . . . (154-55)

Because Harry is speaking in the presence of the victim of this outburst, his diatribe is verbal torture—and contains a threat of physical execution, for if Bill is expelled from his cohabitation with Harry, that might be the end of him.

The verbal duels in *The Homecoming* are of an even fiercer and more deadly nature: In this play also the connection between cruelty and sexuality comes very strongly to the surface, more strongly than in earlier plays, where, however, it was always present in the subtext. The prostitution ring Lenny is running is, after all, another version of the Mafia organization, with its torturers and executioners: in Lenny and Joey, the pattern of the pairs of executioners, the slick, intelligent one and the dumb strong man, reappears in a new but very clearly recognizable variation. Lenny's description of his chastising of one of his prostitutes, with which he confronts Ruth at the beginning of the play, is a case in point; so is the story of Lenny's and Joey's rape of two girls on a derelict bombsite. Lenny's verbabl torture of his father is another deadly game of power. And Ruth establishes her dominance over Lenny precisely by taking these descriptions of brutality with the coolness of a professional. There is a life-and-death struggle also going on in the dialogues between Lenny and his father and between Max and Sam. The milieu of *The Homecoming* is the world of terrorist organizations like the IRA or the SS, the world of gas chambers and the nuclear menace projected into a domestic setting: the final tableau, with Sam lying lifeless on the floor and Max vainly begging for recognition of his status as a man, is a graphic illustration of that fact.

What a harsh universe this play presents us with—in its subtle combination of physical cruelty and sexuality. Characters like Lenny clearly derive erotic pleasure from inflicting pain. It is an essentially loveless world. There is sex, but very little tenderness in this and most other plays by Pinter.

It is surely significant that in Pinter's entire oeuvre there is hardly a single genuine love scene: even in *The Lover* the nearest point that the protagonists can reach to love is by playing a game of prostitute and paying client; in *Landscape* the love scene is a wholly one-sided fantasy in the mind of a woman, while the man is an aggressive bully. In *Silence* and *Betrayal* love is shown to have been no more than a fleeting illusion, a cruel self-deception.

And here another of Pinter's main preoccupations enters the picture: the ever recurring problem of verification, the fact that the individual can never be entirely sure that what others tell him is true, that it can be subjected to the test of verification. The most unverifiable statement of all is a profession of love: love, by its very nature, is beyond verification; it can be faked, pretended. And one partner, the one who loves with greater intensity, will always be deceived. There is one exception, as the Marquis de Sade, that archetypal philosopher of torture, has argued: the evidence of suffering, which is always genuine, cannot be faked. The only genuine evidence that an individual can obtain of having true impact on another individual is through the first-hand evidence of suffering, physical suffering inflicted in full view. This Sadian "touch," as Mario Praz has convincingly argued in *The Romantic Agony,* is a topic subtextually present in much of romantic and postromantic literature. It is most openly approached in Brecht's *Jungle of Cities,* where Shlink finally confesses that not even a life and death struggle can establish genuine contact:

> The infinite isolation of human beings makes even enmity an unattainable goal. . . . I have observed the animals. Love, warmth from the proximity of our bodies, is the only grace in our darkness. But the union of organs is the only one possible, it does not bridge the separation created by language. . . . If you stuff a ship full to the point of bursting, with human bodies, there will be such loneliness there, that they will all turn to ice. (307–308)

The sadistic torturers and executioners of Pinter's universe, the characters seeking domination through verbal fencing, are thus engaging in a sado-masochistic quest for human contact; there is a distinctly erotic element in the various forms that cruelty, the striving for dominance and power over the other, is taking in Pinter's plays. This is not to say that he does not show the processes of torture, domination, and struggle for power as reprehensible; he is merely depicting, as a detached and neutral observer, how it is, what he sees. But there can be no doubt also about the fact that he is fascinated by the spectacle.

As the social milieu of Pinter's world is gradually raised in his work of the late sixties and seventies, the power struggles and the cruelty they entail become less overt. Although still powerfully present in the subtext of plays like *Tea Party, Old Times,* or *Betrayal,* these struggles again powerfully rise to the surface in *No Man's Land,* where the two executioners reappear in the guise of Foster and Briggs, who conduct the final ceremony of Hirst's entombment in an eerie parody of a third-degree session, with the executioners pronouncing the sentence:

> BRIGGS: The trees—
> FOSTER: Will never bud
> HIRST: I must ask you—
> BRIGGS: Snow—
> FOSTER: Will fall forever. Because you've changed the subject. For the last time.
> (151)

Uncertainty—the difficulty, or indeed, impossibility of verification, and the anxiety that must accompany such an absence of certainties; the relentless life-and-death struggle for power, linguistic as much as crudely physical; the presence of vast, mysterious organizations threatening torture and execution;

the structure of the world itself experienced as such a vast machine of senseless cruelty—these images form the backdrop to Pinter's universe, however grotesquely comic some of the ludicrous proceedings in the foreground might be. As he himself once said, much in his plays may be funny, but there comes a point where it ceases to be funny—and that, indeed, is the point of it all.

Kafka and Beckett are the patron saints of this vision, with the Marquis de Sade powerfully lurking in the background. The power of a writer like Pinter derives to a large extent from the degree to which his work embodies the *Zeitgeist*, the cultural, ideological, and philosophical undercurrents of his time. The contemporary philosopher who seems to correspond most closely to the existential experience embodied in Pinter's vision seems to me, whether Pinter is aware of his work or not, Heidegger, in whose philosophy the Cartesian definition of being—I think therefore I am—is replaced by "I fear nonbeing— therefore I am."

To point up these connections and to draw these parallels with other writers and philosophers is to situate Pinter's work within a wider context as the expression of a worldview, an *Existenzgefühl*. What this ultimately amounts to saying is that his work, as that of a major poet and artist, embodies its own metaphysics, its own cosmic perspective, which, however far removed from any established or codified body of doctrine, is akin to something like his own "myth," his own metaphor for his experience of the world as a place of awful—in both senses of the word—impenetrable mystery.

What strikes me in Pinter's latest work is, in fact, that this "mythical" element present in his previous works, which all, ultimately, can be seen as metaphors, generalized visions of the world, has now become, as it were, secularized, taken from the general, metaphorical, and ultimately poetic plane to a level of the specific and particular, from the contemplative detached embodiment of general truths to short-term calls for action on a practical, almost immediately topical level. The material is still that of his first vision— the torturers, the executioners, the victims—but now they have lost the metaphorical dimension; they simply are what they are.

Yet even here Pinter still shuns the specific: it has been said that the people deprived of the use of their language in *Mountain Language* are Kurds in Turkish Kurdistan. He has denied this specificity. Nor is the torturer in *One for the Road* identifiable as a member of a particular secret police in a particular totalitarian regime: the setting might be the then still repressive world of Eastern Europe, or Central or South America, or indeed, a country like Iraq. It is the unidimensional nature of the proceedings, however, the clearcut purposiveness of what is depicted that separates these later works from the earlier ones. There is no uncertainty here about what is being shown, nor why it is shown, no multiplicity of levels of possible meanings and interpretations; everything is on the surface, immediately verifiable as what it is and what it intends.

Is this a loss? Or is it a gain? The elegance of the language, the suavity of the style are still there. It is the penumbra, the chiaroscuro, the intriguing opacity of characters and action, that are absent.

On the other hand there is the clear moral and political purpose, the "saeva indignation" about injustice and suffering, the courage to get actively involved in campaigns to combat them, that constitute a breakthrough into the real world. Mark, the character in *The Dwarfs* who is an actor like Pinter, proclaimed himself indifferent even to the threat of the torturing wheel.

—Do you enjoy life? said Virginia.
—Up to the neck, Mark said. But I don't ask questions. (117)

Clearly now Harold Pinter has reached a stage where *he* does feel compelled to ask questions and to abandon the attitude of the suave, elegant, indifferent onlooker. It is a step from *l'art pour l'art* to *engagement,* which, whatever else one may think of it, certainly deserves respect and admiration.

FOUR

Harold Pinter's *The Hothouse:*
A Parable of the Holocaust

Rosette C. Lamont

Written in 1958 but set aside for "further deliberation," Harold Pinter's *The Hothouse* was first presented in April 1980, in a production directed by the author at Hampstead Theatre. In June of the same year it moved to the Ambassador. The shelving of this powerful translation of the Nazi extermination system (under the guise of a British government-run hospital) is much like the decisions of two French Holocaust writers: Charlotte Delbo and Marguerite Duras. In the case of Delbo, who joined the Resistance movement with her husband, George Dudach, and was arrested with him on 2 March 1942, her first Auschwitz memoir, *Aucun de nous ne reviendra* (*None of Us Will Return*), was written shortly after her liberation from Ravensbrück and then placed by her in a drawer to see if it would survive the test of time. Delbo had the infinite patience and courage to wait twenty years before bringing it out. Marguerite Duras doubled the time of waiting (forty years) before she published *La Douleur (War)* in 1985. An active member of the Resistance, Duras survived the years of the German occupation in Paris, but her husband, Robert Antelme, disappeared for many months in what the French call *l'universe concentra-tionnaire*. *La Douleur* is the story of a wife's anguished waiting, of her visionary sharing of the prisoner's near death by starvation. In her preface, Duras tells how she encountered two notebooks (her journal) in the armoire of her house at Neauphlele-Chateau. She had no memory of having written these pages, although she recognized the handwriting. She was also amazed that this text had survived the numerous winter floods. Above all, this "thing" (she hesitates to call it a text) also survived the passage of time; in fact, it is the most important and moving document of her entire life. Both *None of Us* and *War* belong to what Duras calls sacred texts in a short inner foreword to the story "Albert les Capitales." She goes so far as to warn her readers that they must learn to read anew. In his *Survival in Auschwitz,* published in Italian in 1958— the year of the composition of Pinter's play—Primo Levi says much the same thing:

> On the march to work, limping in our large wooden shoes on the icy snow, we
> exchanged a few words, and I found out that Resnyk is Polish; he lived twenty

years in Paris but speaks an incredible French. He is thirty, but like all of us, could be taken for seventeen or fifty. He told me his story, and today I have forgotten it, but it was certainly a sorrowful, cruel and moving story; because so are all our stories, hundreds of thousands of stories, all different and all full of a tragic, disturbing necessity. We tell them to each other in the evening, and they take place in Norway, Italy, Algeria, the Ukraine, and are simple and incomprehensible like the stories in the Bible. But are they not themselves stories of a new Bible? (59)

Neither a camp survivor, nor the child of survivors, Pinter nevertheless responded in a similar way to the strange work which surfaced out of some buried, nightmarish truth. Although he does not say so, claiming only to have judged *The Hothouse* unworthy of stage presentation, it is more than likely that he shrank from a subject that touched him deeply and amazed him with its powerful implications. This mysterious, menacing play is one of the first overtly political comic dramas of Pinter's career; it is also a baring of his Jewish angst.

Although Pinter has repudiated the idea that he might be writing Jewish plays, he is clearly marked by his early years in the ethnically mixed, rough East End of London. The child of Jewish parents, "of remotely Portuguese origin" (Taylor, *Harold Pinter* 3), he could not have failed to register the political events occurring in the 30s on the other side of the Channel. It is more than likely that he overheard his family discuss them, raising the possibility of an invasion of England and the promulgation of similar racial laws. As a Jewish schoolboy he must have been the butt of derision and attack from the roughnecks in the street. As John Russell Taylor so aptly remarks, he was "a Jewish child in the Nazi era, a metaphorical cousin of Anne Frank" ("Pinter's Game" 61).

Much has been written about Pinter's fascination with the scapegoat, its exclusion, expulsion, and extermination, but when *The Hothouse* is read for its subtext, it becomes a parable of the systematic annihilation of "inferior" races by a nation bent on mass death. It is by scrutinizing the vocabulary used by Pinter in this play that one can take hold of the key that opens a secret door, that of his subterranean, oneiric universe.

The Hothouse is not a place for breeding exotic plants. It may be hot, even stifling, but its heat is all consuming, destructive. We are shown the office of the director of a hospital/sanatorium/mental institution, whose inmates have been stripped of their names and identities. They are being designated solely by numbers. As a result of this procedure, instituted by the predecessor of Colonel Roote, the director, though not at the root of this ordinance "which was laid down in the original constitution" (154), the cases of the various patients are getting confused. It is in fact difficult to keep good records of the dying and the dead, of their ages, sexes, and case histories. In fact, two files comically and horrifyingly overlap on account of a mistake in the final digit. Two people are designated merely as 6457 and 6459, the first being a man who died of heart failure—as listed in the official death certificate—an event that happened a week after his conversation with Roote, the second identifying a female patient who has given birth to a male child the previous day, Christmas eve. If death is taken for granted in this hospital, an unexpected birth constitutes a scandal, one that turns the director of this highly controlled, disciplined institution into a wrathful Herod, ready to kill this innocent. He exclaims oxymoronically: "I'm dumbstruck," and launches into a peroration about the fragility of the system, one that "the softest breath" might send "tottering into chaos, into ignominy . . ." (37). Since this is no immaculate conception, the guilty procreator must be identified. For some inexplicable, utterly absurd reason, the finger points to the turnkey and lab guinea pig, Lamb.

The latter will prove to be the sacrificial lamb in this perverse Christmas mystery play. It is strange that a man who has volunteered his body and mind for experimental shock treatment conducted to ascertain the threshold of pain, should have indulged in erotic adventure and sired a child. By his own admission he is still "virgo intacta" (73)—hardly the proper expression for male chastity. However, this state does not seem to clear him of the possibility of paternity, particularly when the other candidate for fatherhood is Roote's mannish mistress/assistant, Miss Cutts. This sadistic Atropos, who implants electrodes into the willing Lamb to study "neural activity" (65), is suspected by the guard, Lush, of being "the father" (92). There is also "a Lorna Lamb in the dispensary department," another one of Lush's weird suppositions. Roote, who will reveal himself kinkier than he sounds at first, shouts: "A man, not a woman, you bloody fool!" (93). Endemic to the Pinter universe, sexual ambiguity is on a rampage in *The Hothouse* (translate as whorehouse). Miss Cutts, who is always wondering out loud whether she is "feminine enough" (49) for Roote (in the brilliant production of the play at *A Pinter Festival,* Roote appears in act 2 wearing a female wig and lacy, satin undies), uses her sexuality to lure victims to their death. Her bizarre seductions (she is also the mistress of Gibbs, and probably the lover of the woman who gave birth) suggest those of Ilse Koch, the ghoulish amateur of beautiful tattoos to be turned into lampshades.

More than anything else, it is the immediate mention of the numbers system at the start of the play that emits the right signal to put the audience on the track. The disappearance of names and personal identities and their replacement by numbers were, of course, practiced at Auschwitz. When the rare survivors returned, we saw the numbers tatooed on their forearms. Primo Levi writes in the "Ka-Be" chapter of *Survival in Auschwitz* that a prisoner, who could only express himself in Yiddish, tried to explain to him the selection process, followed by gassing and the burning of the bodies in the crematorium. The man Schmulek raises some basic questions.

Show me your number: you are 174517. This numbering began eighteen months ago and applies to Auschwitz and the dependent camps. There are now ten

thousand of us here at Buna-Monowitz, perhaps thirty thousand between Auschwitz and Birkenau. *Wo sind die Andere?* Where are the others? (46–47)

The replacement of identity by a number is a leitmotif in *Survival in
Auschwitz.* In the second chapter, "On the Bottom" (the title echoes the title—
in Russian—of Gorky's famous play, *The Lower Depths*), Levi describes the
rite of passage from human being to "phantom," or *"Häftling"* (prisoner): "My
number is 174517; we have been baptized, we will carry the tattoo on our
left arm until we die" (22–23). An inverted rite of baptism! A little earlier in
the same chapter we read: "They will even take away our name" (22). Later,
when the writer is examined in chemistry by Herr Doctor Pannwitz, who will
determine whether he is fit to work in the Chemical Kommando, he thinks,
standing before this tall, blond, thin Aryan, who looks at the prisoner as though
through "the glass window of an aquarium": "I, Häftling 174517, stand in his
office, which is a real office, shining, clean and ordered, and I feel that I
would leave a dirty stain on whatever I touched" (96).

This dehumanization, which penetrates the fibers of the victim's psyche,
is built into the new order. However, it has its drawbacks as Roote points out
to his underling, Gibbs. It is after all a system put in place by his predecessor,
a man who has vanished to leave room for "the next contender." Roote raises
all kinds of issues when he says:

> On this numbers business . . . it would make things so much simpler if we called
> them by their names. Then we'd all know where we were. After all they're not
> criminals. They're only people in need of help, which we try to give, in one way
> or another. They're all people specifically recommended by the Ministry. . . .
> They're not any Tom, Dick, or . . . or . . . er . . . Harry. I often think it must depress
> them . . . somewhat . . . to have a number rapped on them all the time. After some
> of them have been here a few years they're liable to forget what names their
> fathers gave them. Or their mothers. (21)

Who might these people of legitimate or illegitimate birth be since they are
not "criminals" but wards of a repressive, disciplinarian state? Why have they
been "recommended by the Ministry" for confinement? They are not average
Englishmen, not "Tom, Dick, or . . . er (*hesitation*) Harry." Perhaps their real
names, hidden under the numbers, might be Schmuel, Solomon, Aaron, Saul.[1]

Although Pinter is addressing himself to the same horrifying reality Primo
Levi writes so movingly about, he uses a Beckettian mode, the aesthetic that
Margaret Croyden defines as "comic grotesque" (45). *The Hothouse* opens
with a discussion of people as numbers. Roote is standing at the window of
his clean, sterile office, while Gibbs, a man twenty years younger than the
director, is shuffling papers in a filing cabinet.

ROOTE: Gibbs.
GIBBS: Yes, sir?
ROOTE: Tell me . . . How's 6457 getting on?
GIBBS: 6457, sir?

ROOTE: Yes.
GIBBS: He's dead, sir. (13)

Deprived of their individuality, their humanity, these people are elements of statistical facts. Becoming a number is what Lawrence L. Langer calls "humiliated memory" (77). In *Holocaust Testimonies: The Ruins of Memory,* Langer writes: "... humiliated memory negates the impulse to historical inquiry. Posterity not only can do without it; it *prefers* to ignore it" (79).

The victim is not the only one affected by amnesia; so is the jailer. Thus Roote is not certain about the date of 6457's death. There is a gap in his records. He seems to remember having had a conversation with the patient the previous day, yet, when he and Gibbs consult the file, it becomes clear that the interview took place on a Friday (the Jewish day of prayer preceding the Sabbath), a week earlier. It is Gibbs who amusingly points out the discrepancy:

> In your diary, sir. (*He moves to the desk.*) I must point out that you are in fact referring to Friday the 17th. (*He indicates a date on the page.*) There, sir. Yesterday was Friday the 24th. (*He turns the pages forward and indicates a date.*) Here, sir. You had a conversation with 6457 on the 17th. He died on the 23rd. (*Indicates a date.*) Here. (15)

This may be an extreme form of black humor—Grand Guignolesque in fact—but it also suggests the collapse of the ground of knowledge. Speaking of the testimony of a Leon H., Langer writes: "... humiliated memory is a prison" (96).

Although Pinter's close associates know that the mental hospital which provided the central image of the play is Maudsley, we find ourselves facing a complex metaphor: prison/insane asylum/laboratory/no-exit sanatorium/Russian-style psychiatric clinic/torture chamber, and finally the hottest of houses, a crematorium. This is a place where fires erupt and burn, where the heat cannot be regulated. Here life is extinguished, and all patients live under the threat of impending death. As to the hospital setting, it is falsely reassuring, a mask or lie, like the so-called showers of Nazi death camps, camouflaged gas chambers. Thus, this hospital is a mockery of the act of healing, as indeed was Nazi medicine. Nothing suggests that "patients" ever leave, except in a coffin or, as Primo Levi writes, "by way of the Chimney" (24). If buried, it will be in some unmarked mass grave, deprived of last rites and any ceremony. Here is a revealing exchange between Roote and Gibbs:

> ROOTE: Did he get a decent burial?
> GIBBS: Oh, very decent, sir.
> ROOTE: I don't see why I wasn't invited. Who said the last words over him?
> GIBBS: There were no last words, sir. (26)

The statement is ambiguous. It could mean that the condemned man was never allowed to utter a word, or that no speech was made over his grave.

At any rate, Gibbs is lying in typical fashion when he affirms that 6457 received "a decent burial."

This form of lying was built into what Robert Jay Lifton calls "the medicalized Nazi killing system" (5). The latter worked smoothly as the healers, forgetful of the Hippocratic oath of their profession, gradually turned into assassins. According to Lifton, a bureaucracy of killing was set up, based on "the visionary motivations associated with . . . a concrete medical ideology" (15). Basing his analysis on Hannah Arendt's celebrated judgment of Adolf Eichmann, "the banality of evil," Lifton explains that ordinary doctors performed "demonic acts." In so doing they were altered into men "no longer banal" (12). Once death camps were constituted, physicians "were given much of the responsibility for the murderous ecology . . . the choosing of victims, the carrying through of the physical and psychological mechanics of killing, and the balancing of killing and work functions in the camps" (18). Perhaps the most shocking aspect of this organization was its "perverse medical aura" (18). Doctors were present everywhere in the camps, from the arrival of the cattle trains to the selection process and the daily, hourly decisions as to who would be allowed to continue working and who would be sent to the *revir* (the death house) or directly to the gas chamber. In the chapter entitled "The Auschwitz Self: Psychological Themes in Doubling," Lifton deals with the elimination of the Hippocratic oath, replaced by another ritual, the oath to Hitler:

> That is why the Hippocratic oath, though a pledge to remain a healer and to disavow killing or harming those one treats, was all but abandoned in Auschwitz. The oath was perceived as little more than a distant and muted ritual one had performed at medical school graduation, and was readily reversed by the searingly immediate selections ritual, as well as by the array of direct pressures and rewards in the direction of a Hippocrates-free Auschwitz self. . . . (433)

Yet, as both Lifton and Lucy Dawidowicz point out, none of this could have taken place had this program not been preceded by the legalized sterilization of "unfit" procreators: the insane, the retarded, the crippled or infirm, those afflicted with hereditary maladies. Systematic annihilation in secret hospitals of "life unworthy of living" was carried out under "controlled" conditions, often with the complicity of parents requesting the mercy killing of brain damaged, deformed infants. These legal murders were perpetrated in the name of "euthanasia," a misnomer in this instance for a practice which puts an end to life only when the situation of the patient is deemed irreversible. From this program of the purification of the race there was only one step to the declaration that non-Aryans were germs in the body of the *Volk,* microbes to be eliminated for the greater health of the nation. The Nuremberg Laws of 15 September 1935 prohibited sexual contact between Jews and non-Jews, and ordinances regulating sterilization followed a month later. The Nazi "ideal" of the purity of blood paved the way for mass death for "inferior" races by the fastest and cheapest means: the Zyklon B gas.

In order to maximize the efficiency of mass killing, it was essential to achieve a technology for destroying large numbers of people by means of a highly poisonous gas. Administered at a distance by trained medical personnel, this procedure allowed for distancing. The death process was watched through a pane of glass, and subsequently the corpses were rapidly conveyed to the ovens. Thus, both victims and victimizers were utterly dehumanized and psychologically separated. In Pinter's play, Roote is so distanced from his patients, even those he sees regularly, that he is unable to recall their appearance. He questions Gibbs, first about 6457:

ROOTE: Which one was he?
GIBBS: You had quite a lot to do with him, actually, sir.
ROOTE: He was a man I dealt with personally?
GIBBS: Yes, sir.
ROOTE: Well, which one was he, for God's sake?
GIBBS: You knew him well, sir.
ROOTE: You keep saying that! But I can't remember a damn thing about him. What did he look like? (23)

Was he dark or fair, thin or fat, tall or small? The only features that come to mind are "a sharp sort of face" (24) and a limp on his left leg—in some folk tales a limp is characteristic of the Devil. It is also associated with some famous heroes: Oedipus of the pierced feet and Odysseus. However, in the context of the play, lameness does not differentiate 6457 from 6459 any more than the fact that one is male and the other female. Roote recalls that the woman had a sensual wobble "on her left buttock" (42), or might it not have been the distinguishing mark of a spy he met in Casablanca?[2] Could the two women be one and the same, products of Roote's erotic reverie? At any rate, the female spy, a movie cliché, must have been a nightclub dancer. She is indelibly marked by a tattoo, not a number but the image of a pelican upon her belly. As she moved, presumably performing a bellydance, the pelican waddled across the room "on all fours, sideways, feet first, arse upwards, any way you like" (125). This is no Marlene Dietrich "Blue Angel," despite her "blue dress"—ironically, blue is associated with the color of Mary's veil—but a prostitute willing to assume any sexual position, however grotesque or demeaning, the better to please her client. Roote recalls with awe her "superhuman" control. "Only a woman could possess it" (126).

If the web-footed pelican is distinguished by its waddle when out of its watery element, it is also associated in the mythic imagination with Christ's sacrifice, as well as with the Christian symbol of the fisherman. The self-sacrificial death is connected to numerous legends and folk tales portraying the male pelican as capable of ripping open its belly with its beak in order to allow its hungry progeny to feed on its entrails. Coming toward the end of act 2, just before Roote's sentimental evocation of a kind of German Christmas, "walls . . . hung with Christmas cards, knee deep in presents . . . aunties and uncles popping in for a drink, a log fire in the grate, bells on the Christmas tree" (126), the grotesquely erotic story of the pelican connects in some subliminal way with the birth of a male child on Christmas eve, a child whose father remains a mystery. Here Pinter would seem to connect the Christ figure as victim with the Jewish victims of the camps, suggesting as well that a supposedly Christian society's Christian ethos is in danger of annihilation.

What will become of this boy born in a hospital-jail? Will he be choked to death as were so many infants born in camp? Will he be cast, as they were, into the burning fire of "the hothouse"? All we know is that Roote wants to "get rid of it" (44). Gibbs explains that "the mother would have to go with it, sir" (44). This brief exchange evokes the selection process in camp, whereby mothers with infants and small children were dispatched at once to the gas chamber. Although his birth in this closed society is a kind of miracle, it can be nullified by the bureaucratic stroke of a pen. In the meantime, as one of the characters says: "The kid's got to have a name after all" (54).

From this point on, all dialogue assumes the form of double talk. The truth bursts out at the beginning of act 2, when Roote exclaims: "God, the heat of this place. It's damn hot, isn't it? It's like a crematorium in here. . . ." Later on he adds: "I'm suffocating" (94). The "hothouse" is finally revealed for what it is, not a place for healing, for restoring people in their community, but a death camp, complete with gas chambers, ovens, crematoria. We have been tricked into thinking we were looking at a hospital, much as the deportees were tricked into believing that at the end of an inhuman voyage without food or water, locked up in cattle cars, they were at last to be taken to a warm shower, given a change of clothes. More than the torture of Lamb which we are allowed to view, it is the vocabulary itself that unveils the hidden truth.

Clearly the mythical and religious references in the text are neither gratuitous nor used for ironic effect. They play an essential role in what Edith Wyschogrod describes as a "resacralization" project, a basic pattern of the Nazi system. Not only are the simple objects of daily life desacralized and mocked, not only are the truths we live by turned topsy-turvy, as in the motto inscribed over the portals of Auschwitz: "*Arbeit Macht Frei*" ("Work Makes One Free"), but ritual itself is vitiated. Evoking the pitiful piles of personal possessions, once meaningful to the owner, now ready to be recycled, Wyschogrod writes:

> Instead of the thing holding life and death in equipoise to create a microcosm of human meaning, death streams forth from these piled up, ownerless possessions. They become symbols of alienation, tropes for the pure annihilation of the death-world. (14)

They will be reused in some efficient manner, or passed on to the true Germans. Wyschogrod explains: "Thus new modes of efficiency—the bureaucratic and material means of technological society—are now the 'raw' stuff to be organized in the interest of resacralization" (28).

As ancient myths and rituals are discarded, new myths must be forged. This is evident in Roote's lyrical evocation of his charismatic predecessor, a man who might have "retired," but more probably "was retired" as the hesitation, the momentary silence before this word is uttered, indicates. Roote, the new leader, describes this personality, worthy of a cult, as an Aryan hero, with his "golden forelock, his briar burning, upright and commanding . . ." (38). The Colonel recalls how his predecessor looked down from the platform at "row upon row of electrified faces." If the word "electrified" is not a sufficient sign, we also hear that the house was packed to "suffocation" (38), hardly an innocent word in a post-Holocaust world.

Outside the gymnasium's window, the crowd is able to glimpse the equestrian statue of the predecessor's predecessor, "the predecessor of us all," as Roote puts it, the Mike "for the love (of whom) order" was called. It was he who "introduced the first patient," soon to be followed by many more, by the proliferation of "institution after institution . . . rest homes, nursing homes, convalescent homes, sanatoria" (38). We are a sigh away from the word "crematoria" which will surface in act 2.

In what manner do these sanatoria differ from one another? When the mother of 6457, unapprised of her son's sudden demise, comes to pay a visit at Christmas, she discovers that what she had taken for "a convalescent home" is actually "a rest home." He has been transferred, she is told, to "a convalescent home." Lush, one of the guards, launches upon a long explication of this terminology and its hidden meanings:

> In a rest home, you see, you do not merely rest. Nor in a convalescent home, do you merely convalesce. No, no, in both institutions, you see, you are obliged to work and play and join in daily communal activity to the greatest possible extent. Otherwise the concepts of rest and convalescence are rendered meaningless. (39)

What became meaningless in Nazi Germany was the difference between an institution for healing the sick and one for systematic destruction. In his book *Murderous Science,* Benno Müller-Hill traces the evolution of German psychiatric clinics to economically viable institutions of forced labor, the latter being practiced under the rubric of "work-therapy." He writes:

> The psychiatric institutions were very much like concentration camps. Once in, there was no way out for the inmate. He carried out forced labour, had no rights. If he remained uncooperative, a course of up to twenty treatments with leptazol, insulin or electricity would be prescribed as therapy . . . not as punishment. If the patient believed that this painful shock therapy was a punishment, the psychiatrists saw it as a further sign of insanity, which could only be cured by more electricity. Courses of sixty shock treatments were not uncommon. Broken bones and even deaths caused by the shocks were regarded as unavoidable accidents which were a normal consequence of the therapy. (38)

This description is eloquently illustrated by Lamb's torture, culminating in the play's final tableau: "*Lamb in chair. He sits still, staring, as in a catatonic trance*" (154).

The practice of forced labor by a new class of slaves, and slaves of slaves led inexorably to the systematic extermination of those who could not or would not work, undesirable social elements: Jews and Gypsies. The first had to be stripped of posts and possessions, the second, mobile, free, unpredictable, uncontrollable, had to be held in check for the sake of order, the keyword of National Socialism. It is also important to recall Paul de Lagarde's comparison of Jews with vermin, the very simile used by Lenin to denounce the bourgeoisie and the intelligentsia. Lagarde declared: "With trachinae and bacilli one does not negotiate, nor are trachinae and bacilli to be educated—they are exterminated as quickly and thoroughly as possible" (Dawidowicz 41). We recognize this vocabulary in Roote's Christmas toast, which is broadcast throughout the hospital; it is a salute to the "glorious dead . . . who helped to make the world clean" (98).

The Christmas festivities are also marked by a raffle to be held for the understaff. The objects to be raffled are unclaimed possessions. They are identified by numbers, just like the patients. Nor does the similarity stop there. For example, number 84 is a duck, "ready for the oven" (102). There are all kinds of goodies, Portuguese cigars, crockery, cookery sets, cutlery, china. Lush, the insidious guard, a spitting image of the concentration camp Kapo, or of the ordinary German criminals culled out of jails for employment as camp superintendents, speaks of a whole pile of "unclaimed stuff" (103). There is enough to hold another raffle at Easter. The only object that cannot be kept for a future religious feast is the duck; it is "as dead as patient 6457, if not deader" (104).

Those who will soon be "deader" still are the director and the hospital staff, slaughtered in an uprising staged by the patients whose cells remained mysteriously unlocked. Actually this neglect can be accounted for since the locktester, Lamb, supposed to be on duty, was and is forgotten in torture chamber/interrogation laboratory 1A, Miss Cutts's "favorite room in the whole place" (120). Gibbs, who reports the massacre to Lobb, the official come to bring special commendations from the ministry and news of succession, explains that he survived because he was "engaged on some research"—one wonders about the nature of the latter—and stayed awake. However "Lush, Hogg, Beck, Budd, Tuck, Dodds, Tate and Pett"—plain British names that nevertheless reveal some vices and a general grossness—were "variously hanged and strangled. Colonel Roote and Miss Cutts were stabbed in their bed." Lobb questions: "Excuse me, did you say bed, or beds?" (149–152). Gibbs confirms the singular.

Gibbs's assumption of Roote's post continues the succession by violence which must have started with Mike, went on with his successor, himself "retired" to make room for Roote. The modern reader is reminded of the Lenin/Stalin/Brezhnev line, but the underlying cyclical order is that analyzed by Frazer in *The Golden Bough*. In her seminal study, *The Dramatic World of Harold Pinter: Its Basis in Ritual,* Katherine H. Burkman speaks of the ambiguity of the nature of the victim who often plays "the double role of victim and victor." Power in *The Hothouse* cannot be transmitted peaceably; it is wrested by violent means, as in the ancient "sacrifice of the priest-king-god" (Burkman 21–22). This is indeed a basic pattern of Pinter's dramaturgy: "Beneath the daily secular rituals which Pinter weaves into the texture of his plays—the taking of toast and tea—beat the rhythms of ancient fertility rites, which form a significant counterpoint to the surface rituals of the plays and which often lend the dramas their shape and structure" (Burkman 10). Thus Gibbs is now the next "entrusted . . . appointed . . . delegate" (132). He is as proud of this as Eichmann was of having followed orders. For Pinter, tyranny is an ever-present threat, and dictatorship can never be finally defeated.

The writing of *The Hothouse* in 1958 coincides with the end of a political era dominated by Hitler and Stalin, announced in *Mein Kampf* and denounced in *The Gulag Archipelago*. Not only was this the end of the Stalin era marked by Khrushchev's revelations and his "thaw" of the mid-1950s, but on the political front West Germany was now beginning to be accepted as an ally, having gone through denazification and having made some official acts of contrition and reconciliation. It was at this transitional time that Holocaust literature was just starting to emerge.

The play, however, does not sound a note of triumph. It sounds, rather, an issue (as virtually all of his early plays do) and announces a style that Pinter has continued to elaborate in his dramas right to the present. Pinter did not need to keep on creating symbolic manifestations, as he did in *Hothouse*, of one particular if epoch-defining genocidal process, because he could see that various aspects of this dehumanizing process and way of regarding one's fellow humans were still going on in everyday life, even in civilized countries like England. Perhaps, however, the Holocaust more than anything else has forced us to recognize such dehumanization, which Pinter still dwells on in the highly political, sombre plays of his maturity: *One for the Road, Mountain Language,* and *Party Time,* which received an initial staged reading at *A Pinter Festival.*

If *The Hothouse* is as full of mystery and menace as these three short works, it is also infused with the bizarre wit that characterizes all metaphysical farces, one that elicits laughter through tears. *The Hothouse* is a play which surfaced from Pinter's Jewish origins, conveying by means of brilliant images and ambiguous, multileveled vocabulary a nightmare, particular yet universal, one from which it is almost impossible to awaken.

Notes

1. Pinter requires of his reader and audience a particular kind of attention. John Lahr points out that the Pinter audience is always aware "of the inherent mystery of people and objects" (xi). The dramatist also has suggested, though he denies that the remark has significance, that his plays are about "the weasel under the coctail cabinet" (Burkman, *The Dramatic World* 4). Both Katherine H. Burkman, in her book *The*

Dramatic World of Harold Pinter: Its Basis in Ritual, and later, Leslie Kane in her *Pinter Review* essay, "The Weasel under the Cocktail Cabinet: Rite and Ritual in Pinter's Plays," demonstrate how essential it is to decipher an allusive, often elusive subtext. John Lahr also states that we must listen carefully to whatever lurks "beneath the words" (xiv). But it is Pinter himself who provides us with a key to listening to his texts, or decoding them, when he suggests: "So often, below the words spoken, is the thing known and unspoken," defining language as one where "underneath what is said, another thing is being said" (Burkman 9).

    2. "Casablanca" also suggests the romantic World War II film. It is important to keep in mind the importance of the cinema for Pinter, the script writer of *The Quiller Memorandum, The Guest, The Servant, The Pumpkin Eater,* and *Accident.* Pinter is presently preparing a new film version of Kafka's *The Trial.*

FIVE

Disjuncture as Theatrical and Postmodern Practice in Griselda Gambaro's *The Camp* and Harold Pinter's *Mountain Language*

Jeanne Colleran

In its popular mythology, the Vietnam war is described as the "war fought in America's living rooms." Indeed this fact, that Vietnam was the lead story of every nightly news program for months, then years, as it ground to its final, desultory close, is cited as a factor in the ensuing national crisis of confidence, the self-doubt that would lead inevitably to a second round of international humiliation, the hostage crisis. The conflict in the Persian Gulf might also be described as a "war fought in America's living rooms," but with this crucial difference: it also can be *refought,* courtesy of such ubiquitous video cassette recordings as "CNN's *Desert Storm*" now on sale at supermarket checkouts across the United States, next to the candy, cigarettes, and disposable lighters. Available and inexpensive, *Desert Storm* can be inexhaustibly rewound, re-played, fast-forwarded. Carrying as it does the imprimatur of CNN, the cable network described as a "democratized" approach to news delivery with a "global clientele" and a "visual esthetic" that is "antistar" and "real people" (Green 56), *Desert Storm* claims for itself the authenticity, thoroughness, and objectivity associated with the production of historical documentary. Though it is manifestly obvious that this electronic bit of documented history has been packaged and made portable for mass consumption, the net/work, net/worth of this videoed war can be described as resulting from what Walter Benjamin has termed the "aestheticization of politics" (Polan 56). For just as the pro-duction of *Desert Storm* collapses distinctions between news coverage and entertainment, so too the reception of the video entails an arbitration between the generic expectations of history and of fiction. The considerable extent to which *Desert Storm* leans toward the latter suggests that its production is a kind of fictionalizing, aestheticizing activity in which the "instantaneity of sight" and the immediacy of observation supplant the more distanced critical approaches of analysis and commentary (Polan 56). In short, as a virtual emblem of postmodern culture, *Desert Storm* makes spectacle—live, continuous, localized spectacle—the equivalent of critical engagement. If Steven Connor is correct in his definition of "theatricality" as the "contamination of any artifact that is dependent upon conditions outside, or other than, its own" (134), a video like *Desert Storm* suggests that perhaps "spectacularity" ought also to be inscribed in our critical vocabulary as indicative of the inverse process: that is, of contamination of historical events as occasioned by their transformation into artifacts.[1]

One of the peculiarities of news coverage as practiced by CNN's reporting of the war in the Gulf is the degree to which the crisis mood is intensified and extended by the media until the television audience itself becomes a kind of hostage, bound to an inexorable onslaught of "just breaking" information. That this information proliferates exponentially, that it is immediate, visible, proximate, and instantaneous, suggests how far the media have moved away from a model of communication as analytical and recuperative to one which attempts to simulate a "pure performing present" (Connor 170). And because, as Guy Debord has pointed out, spectacle presents itself as something "enormously positive" and "indisputable," it says "nothing more than that which appears is good, that which is good appears" (12). The result of this relentless visibility is, according to Jean Baudrillard, an "obscenity of the visible, of the all-too-visible . . . of what no longer has any secret, of what dissolves completely in information and communication" ("Ecstasy of Communication" 131).

What then are the possibilities for political drama in a world more spectacular, more staged, more performed, more immediate, and more visible than the theatre itself? And given the collusion between representation and ideology, how possible is it for resistant theatre to enact both a critique of power relations and, no less importantly, of the act of representation itself? In reaching toward some assessment of the potency of performance as a political activity in an age of staged politics and media domination, it is critical to consider both the operation of the play in its particular social and political context and its relation to the system of information dissemination and control it necessarily opposes. Put schematically, the performance of the drama is circumscribed by other performances: the "bloody show" of politics, the bloodless show of information control, the showcase of theatrical venue.[2] In the first instance, the recognition that the drama is tied to a specific political and social framework is foremost a recognition of the extratextual invasion or destabilization of the text by its volatile historical moment. But the reception of this volatile historical moment has become, more than ever, an extraordinarily mediated process, mediated both by the manipulation which occurs via censorship in circumstances of absolute totalitarian control and by the hyper-reality of ubiquitous news coverage and "infotainment" which occurs in democratic societies. To the extent that political drama self-consciously offers itself as an alternative source of political knowledge and critique, it operates in opposition both to the practices of information censorship and to information commodification. The force of these dynamics—that of the particular political and social moment and, at work within this moment, the mechanisms of information exchange—is a demand that the dramatic work be extratextually situated. This insistence is made even more marked by the recognition that this extratextual invasion occurs within the confines of a given institutional structure. No performance takes place within a neutral, autonomous, or nonaligned space, and the reception of a performance is inevitably bound to the choice of dramatic venue, be it a trade union office or a National Theatre. Even when the choice of theatrical space is an act of subversion, it operates through, not outside, this institutionalized alignment.

More than twenty years ago, Martin Esslin claimed that the chief power of avant-garde theatre, by which he meant both absurdist and epic theatre, was its ability to stand in opposition to the "far greater potential realism of the mass media" ("Epic Theatre, the Absurd, and the Future" 191). As my introductory comments have suggested, Esslin's claim requires some modification: contemporary theatre remains in strenuous opposition to the media, but it is an opposition to the seeming "realism" that has actually been aestheticized, narrativized, or theatricalized for mass consumption. Seeking to establish itself as conspicuously different from the "realism" of media, contemporary drama charts its power and uniqueness in the same terms in which avant-garde, notably absurdist, drama claimed its own singularity: by virtue of forging a new *form* of dramatic expression. Thus, despite Esslin's own insistence on the "nonideological" nature of absurdist drama, several contemporary playwrights have stretched the sense of absurdist thematics and dramaturgy to accommodate a drama of political commitment.[3] Chief among these playwrights is Harold Pinter, whose work has moved from a conscious disavowal of political intent to one of a well-publicized political activism.[4] But while Pinter's most recent plays, *One for the Road, Mountain Language,* and *Party Time,* are politically engaged, they continue to rely upon the fusion of absurdism and naturalism that has become synonymous with this dramatic craft. Pinter has long maintained that horror and absurdity inhabit one another, but his latest works examine not the ontology of horrifying absurdity but the apparatus of those absurd and horrifying mechanisms of political repression.

Significantly, Pinter's political plays can be described as both overdetermined and underdetermined in their specificity, a fact which explains in part the bewilderment these plays have occasioned in theatre reviewers.[5] This complex issue of referent and specificity is in fact at the heart of Pinter's extension of absurdist practice into the political realm. Pinter's excursion into this new territory is not, however, an uncharted foray. In an odd but not unexpected set of circumstances, Pinter's latest dramatic endeavors have been anticipated by other writers—Jorge Diaz in Chile, Andre Brink and Chris Barnard in South Africa, Griselda Gambaro in Argentina—all of whom have adapted absurdist techniques, some explicitly associated with Pinter's dramaturgy, to the requirements of drama written in states of siege, emergency, or terror. One of the lessons taught by playwrights such as these is that in the framework of the social up-heaval in which they work, valorizing socially realistic drama over absurdist theatre is untenable. In fact, these writers would claim, absurdist figuration and nondiscursive representation exert a strenuous appeal to a kind of "hyper-real-ism" that is recognizable as characteristic of the skewed state of national affairs.

As valuable as it can be, then, to speak of absurdist elements in a Chilean, Argentine, or South African drama, less can be said about the effect of texts produced and performed in Third World theatrical venues on British, American or European playwrights. This is not to deny reciprocal influence, but it is to suggest that issues more powerful than literary influence or intertextual dia-logue have radicalized Pinter's dramaturgy. While it is tempting to frame this discussion in terms of dramatic precedent and indebtedness or in terms of reversed influence, ultimately it would be a mistake to reestablish lines of demarcation between national and international consciousnesses. What is a far more compelling notion is perhaps best expressed figurally: the shrunken world and the open stage. For while theatrical space is inextricably attached to its actual physical location and hence to a specific sociocultural milieu, it is easily penetrated by external, global forces. Drama, as Michael Hays has pointed out, "is always dependent on its institutionalized context, on the role the theater plays in giving verbal and spatial presence to the structures of meaning that organize the cultural paradigms defining the world and the sphere of the interpersonal in a given society" (105). That the theatre of the Empire is now susceptible to invasion by such unlikely "subjects" as mountain people indicates the extent to which the Empire itself has been overrun. That this theatre (and this society) continues to flex the flaccid muscles of Anglo-Amer-ican imperialism subjects it even further to forces of destabilization. Conse-quently, the degree to which Pinter's latest dramas resemble Gambaro's early works, which she herself has described as indebted to Pinter's craft, is less a measure of influence than of the playwrights' common task of enacting a political critique in a world resistant to notions of global interdependence and dominated by the fabrications of a media which practices—but denies—a kind of partisan narrativization. In response to these dynamics, Pinter has written *Mountain Language,* a twenty-minute play whose power lies in providing the British stage with a new kind of theatrical language, one which is at once deterritorialized and localized, which makes equivalencies of overt and com-plicitous acts of oppression, and which does so via a critique of the dominant, conservative impulses of media.

In the discussion which follows, I propose to examine some aspects of Pinter's extension of absurdist drama into the political realm, and I propose to do so by discussing two works which are arrestingly similar in dramaturgy but emphatically dissimilar in production and reception. These plays, *The Camp* by Griselda Gambaro and *Mountain Language* by Harold Pinter, are both describable as absurdist dramas, yet they are marked, ultimately, by the crucial differences which result from being works produced, performed, and received in radically different circumstances. In the terms already suggested above, these dramas are much differently placed in relation to cultural and political frameworks, to systems of information control, and to theatrical venue. Both plays represent an encroachment by theatre into the political realm that is undertaken with an awareness of theatre's symbiotic but adversarial relationship to the operation of information dissemination as managed by government and media. In each play, however, this incursion is differently motivated and differently received. In Griselda Gambaro's *The Camp,* the incursion is effected, in part, by a reliance on dramatic techniques borrowed from the Theatre of the Absurd, especially as practiced by Pinter, in order to establish on stage a theatrical disjuncture that is a recognizable replication of the social disjuncture characteristic of oppressive forces operative outside the theatre. In Harold Pinter's *Mountain Language,* absurdist disjuncture is also at work, but it is a disjuncture performed not to suggest immediate or direct correspondences, but rather to serve as an act of disclosure. Unlike Gambaro's play, in which the staged disjuncture is a replication of repressive forces, Pinter's disjuncture alludes in part to the normalizing practices of government management and media manipulation. In short, I propose to reach *Mountain Language* by a detour through *The Camp,* an excursion meant to chart what is partially unmapped: the place made for political commentary by absurdist theatre.

For Griselda Gambaro, a great work of theatre is one which belongs "ferociously" to its times.[6] Self-described as an Argentine writing for other Argentines, Gambaro's work has always had a very direct relationship with Argentine politics. As Diana Taylor has pointed out, in more than twenty plays written between 1983 and 1986, Gambaro has focused on themes of persecution and criminal violence resulting from Argentina's political factions, on the country's ongoing fascination with fascism, on its misogyny, its anti-Semitism, and on its racism (167). Significantly, Gambaro's dramatic oeuvre reflects the tumultuous changes in Argentine government from the sixties onward.[7] Throughout this time period, Gambaro received death threats, had her work censored or rejected for publication, and endured a two-year exile. During the run of one of her plays, *Saying Yes,* the Buenos Aires threatre where it was being performed was burned to the ground (Taylor 167).

Gambaro herself has acknowledged explicitly the influence of Pinter on her writing (Echague 13),[8] and certainly *El Campo,* or *The Camp,* is a work in which striking similarities can be seen.[9] Like Pinter's *Betrayal, The Camp* is a three-character play during which a number of betrayals occur as two men and a woman (whom both Pinter and Gambaro have named Emma) combine and recombine their roles as victim and victimizer.[10] In one sense, *Betrayal* is an inverted *Camp;* in Pinter's play the semblance of civilized life— a life of poetry reading in Torcello, teasing friends' children by tossing them in the air, squash-playing and postgame luncheons—can barely be maintained as primitive emotions of territorialism and violence threaten to break through. In Gambaro's play, the imitations of civility—the parlor games between Emma and Frank, the piano concert—interrupt the rampant cruelty; the rituals of manner and breeding are meant not to keep barbarism at bay but to keep visitors in check. Like *The Room, The Caretaker,* and *The Dumb Waiter,* the action of *The Camp* takes place in single settings, in a boxed set that underscores a sense of incarceration. And like the Pinter plays, the title of Gambaro's work has a double referent: ostensibly the camp is a kind of resort, a place where Martin has arrived to do some "accounting" work. The entrance of Frank, a "worker" at the camp dressed in a Gestapo uniform, immediately darkens the play's cryptic beginning, and suggestions of the compound as actually a kind of concentration camp quickly accrue.

Gambaro's play most resembles Pinter's early works in its use of two kinds of disjuncture: verbal/gestural rupture in the first instance and onstage/offstage disjuncture in the second. It is in recasting these techniques for overtly political purposes that Gambaro has moved her play away from an unspecified protest against totalitarianism to a more localized, but equally virulent, commentary on the peculiarly Argentine variety of political repression, especially as enacted through state-controlled information dissemination.

Much of *The Camp* depends on the rupture between verbal language and stage language; like Pinter, Gambaro seduces the audience with a seemingly naturalistic setting and with a dialogue that mimics rationality and logic. But working violently against setting and language is stage gesture, and Gambaro thereby creates the kind of hyper-reality typified by an Argentine newspaper proclaiming "Justice Takes Power" while thousands of *desaparecidos* remain unaccounted for. The disrupture takes place at various levels: semantic, tonal, kinesic, and proxemic. In the first scene, for example, Emma is coerced into seducing Martin, but her efforts to play the coquette are foiled by her appearance—her head is shaved and she wears a gray prison gown—and interrupted by bouts of scratching and scab pulling. Game-playing is metonymic in both Pinter's and Gambaro's plays and signifies in each case a more radical kind of disjuncture: the squash-playing and publishing rivalries (or the larger game known simply as capitalism) in *Betrayal* and boxing (and butchery) in *The Homecoming* operate in a manner similar to the references made to a hunt for unnamed prey in *The Camp.* In both Pinter's and Gambaro's worlds manly arts and tyrannical acts are made equivalent.

The second and perhaps more chilling aspect of Gambaro's adaption of Pinter's dramaturgy is her use of offstage action. Here, as in Gambaro's handling of verbal disjuncture, the effect achieved is more alarming, more grotesque, and more violent.[11] The offstage action in Gambaro's world is not just menacing, not only *potentially* harmful; it is a certain, though ambiguously rendered, act of torture. Outside the room of this bucolic concentration camp, dogs can be heard barking and a hunt is on. Outside the door where Emma and Martin speak, carcasses are piling up, and though we are not told what kind of carcasses they are, the characters speak of children crying out as they try and fail to climb over the camp's fence. It is in this handling of an unspecified but perceptible offstage presence that Gambaro has most succeeded in politicizing Pinter's dramaturgy. For like Emma and Martin, caught in a room of no-exit while bodies are piling up outside, threatre-goers are similarly caught and held during the play's duration, a duration which is itself an interval in the performance outside the theatre where other bodies pile up. The potency of Gambaro's drama depends crucially on an awareness by the audience that the disjuncture they are witnessing on stage is similar in both kind and manner to the life they know outside the theatre which is itself a kind of hyper-reality with a government declaring itself orderly, controlled, and just while thousands of its citizens disappear. It relies on a recognition that the offstage presence of the play is the real presence of the world which threatens to invade the theatre, and it precipitates an anxious awareness that the sacred space of the theatre is not at all inviolate. Theatre, too, is encamped.

But theatre is also resourceful. A theatre's strategic employment of disjuncture stands in opposition to a government's strategic employment of spectacle. Disruption, indeterminacy, contradiction, ambiguity—these disturbances in what is expected to be a smooth and seamless narrative—are exploited in order to subvert the easy superficiality of spectacle which is both *unable* and *unwilling* to mean more than it shows. The complexity of narrative and theatrical disruption is poised against the reductiveness and false coherence of spectacle. The disjuncture serves in part to suggest that political spectacle as an act of terrorism is as much a "strategy of containment" as an aesthetic production, but it is one meant to "contain" alternate readings of political reality (Jameson 53; Polan 62).

In a very direct sense, then, Gambaro requires her audience to supply a context drawn from outside the theatre to compensate for the purposeful indeterminacy of the performance they are witnessing. This action, undertaken by audience members attempting to arbitrate between what they have seen on stage and what they know of their world, is an operation which further subverts the boundaries between private and public. The "private" moment on the stage, the moment of staged violence and of theatrical manipulation, reproduces "public" experience. As the audience involves itself in supplementing the text of the performance, it becomes excruciatingly aware of the symbiotic relationship between both theatre and audience and terrorism and spectator. Neither can function without an onlooker; both performances, the one on stage and the one outside, are intimately bound to the reaction of the spectator. By randomly choosing individual victims, by making one's own people into human shields, for example, terrorists claim an invincibility that works on the basis of selected brutality transformed by the power of metonymy into a claim for absolute power. The atrocious and the unthinkable are welded together metaphorically on stage, literally in the world, until the melding of the figurative and the literal is entire, a molten image of the real. As the creators of these brutal acts, terrorists, like playwrights, remain largely invisible; they seem to operate everywhere at once, everywhere and nowhere in a "no-man's land" or "a kind of Alaska," which is impossible to predict in location, scope, or timing. As spectators, the terrorist's audience, like the playwright's, is forced to look upon *and thereby make possible* acts of barbarism. The power of terrorism and the potency of theatre are rooted in this shared dynamic: the establishment of a relationship with an audience which makes that audience complicitous with the act witnessed.

The crucial difference between drama and terrorism, of course, is that no one enters a theatre with a gun to the head; there is a consent to watch, and it is at this point that the issue of theatrical space or venue becomes important. Gambaro's drama is written for a specifically Argentine audience to be performed in Argentine theatres. Even when she wrote in exile, her frame of reference was Argentine. This specificity of audience and the reliance on an indigenous theatre is an act of concretizing the text, of establishing its meaning with a very conscious awareness of factors of production and reception (Pavis 2). Gambaro's dramatic text is enacted on a stage which can claim status as the center point of a circumscribed theatrical experience, the circuits of which include the site of performance, the intertextual relationship the text has with other sources of political information, especially state-controlled ones, and the historical framework of the present political moment. The use of absurdist techniques by means of disruption and disjuncture calls attention to these circles of mutual influence in order to elucidate their interdependence.

If political theatre and staged geopolitics do operate similarly by virtue of their relationship with spectators and by virtue of the powerful equation of the metaphorical and the literal, theatre, especially absurdist theatre, operates at once representationally and metafictionally. In calling attention to its own aesthetic strategies, it replicates the mechanisms of political manipulation. It exposes what it enables, undermining the very complicity on which it (and totalitarianism) depend.

But while Gambaro requires that her spectators complete the text in a manner which is specifically and directly related to Argentine politics, she clearly aligns herself with the audience. Ultimately, the operation of Gambaro's theatre as a demystifying act makes it a weapon of political and cultural transformation addressed to an audience bound together in a state of shared victimization.

An audience, however, can be differently implicated in what they are witnessing. They can become affiliated with the dominant, have their values exposed as belonging to and sustaining the practices of an oppressive hegemony. But in the complex world of geopolitics, the lines of culpability are seldom so easily drawn as they are in Gambaro's dramatic world. It is in this indefinite terrain that Pinter must work, but here, too, comparisons between the operations of political drama and those of terrorism are instructive.

Terrorism exceeds territorial boundaries; isolationist policies become effete as terrorist acts (or, alternately, revolutionary ones) are produced and packaged for a world stage, albeit with some members of the audience—frequently Americans—played to more than others. In this kind of political performance, no place is safe from invasion; the world is literally the stage, and every consciousness is liable to being raided, ravaged by that minority who clamor to be heard. The terrorist/revolutionaries known as the "H-block" or blanket prisoners of the IRA who attempted in the seventies to rouse international outrage at Margaret Thatcher's refusal to accord them the status of political prisoners is one example of a dramatic gesture with a far-reaching agenda, ranging from the very specific protest against equating political action with criminal activity, to the larger claims against Thatcher's refusal to consider the eventuality of a unified Ireland, to a protest against continued policies of neocolonialism. That in the eighties, Thatcher's economically ruinous defense of the Empire undertaken on behalf of the Falkland Islands occasioned an outpouring of British patriotism sufficient to divert attention away from Thatcher's attempt to dismantle as much as she could of the British socialist program is a measure of how deeply entrenched the imperialist urge remains in the British psyche. It is against this epoch of Thatcherite monetarism and imperialism, deflected by both jingoistic and isolationist rhetoric, that Pinter has positioned his own absurdist drama, stretching it to accommodate a new form of political commentary. It is one which, like Gambaro's political theatre, depends upon disrupture, disjunction, and indeterminacy and operates through its manipulation of historical framework, media operation, and theatrical venue. But unlike Gambaro's drama, Pinter's work is much differently produced and received; it configures its relationship with a complicitous audience in a manner more adversarial than Gambaro's theatre. Pinter's political theatre strips its spectators of their conventional invisibility and makes disinvolvement possible only as a conscious choice. In doing so, Pinter's drama, especially *Mountain Language,* makes dissociation, the act of psychic numbing, as offensive an act as hostage-taking.

For many British playwrights of the sixties, seventies, and eighties whose concerns were primarily political, a theatre of ambiguity was equivalent to the mainstream bourgeois-humanist tradition they wished to undo (Bull 211). Pinter's dramaturgy bore little resemblance to the work of such playwrights as Howard Brenton, David Hare, and Trevor Griffiths, who, in addition to often making known their political views and affiliations, crafted dramas which were more socially specified. The dominant view that the theatre's capacity for political demystification is best effected through a kind of social realism has yielded in the last decade, however, to include other, notably absurdist, forms of theatre. David Hare's 1982 play, *A Map of the World,* for example, anticipated Pinter's *Mountain Language* in several respects, notably in its displacement of character in favor of other issues (Bull 209); its insistence that a formal separation of the concerns of the Third World and the First is impossible; and its call for a critique of the reliability of any social analysis, including that offered by political theatre (211).

While there are several reasons for Pinter's conversion to a public practice of politics, one which surely must be included, then, is the greater receptivity on the part of the British theatrical establishment to his nondiscursive form of political drama. Pinter's great contribution in *Mountain Language* is to extend his earlier practice of elevating dramatic situation to theatrical metonymy, insisting as always that the figural has a power at least as great as the discursive. The difference between his recent political plays and the early "nonpolitical" work is that the dramatic situation which had heretofore been connected to the "existential adjustment" which ostensibly *precedes* and *predetermines* political attitudes (Esslin, *Pinter: The Playwright* 38) is now grounded in a configuration that is at once political and ontological and which accords neither privilege.[12] A second difference is that while Pinter continues to leave motivations unexplained and outcomes indeterminate, his critique encompasses not only a philosophical skepticism about certain and coherent knowledge but includes as well a critique of the semblance of certainty and coherence as posited by various sources of information dissemination. This latter concern is more apparent in Pinter's choice of montage or *bricolage* as the structuring principle of *Mountain Language*. In turning this most characteristic feature of mass media technology back on itself, Pinter's drama represents the fraudulence of electronic mimesis even as it preserves the integrity of its own practice of self-imposed strictures of containment.

Mountain Language is set in an unspecified totalitarian state but is insistently English in clothing, manner, and diction. Visitors and wardens have been given English names (Charley and Sara Johnson, Joe Dokes) and wear English clothing; references are made to Babycham, and the curses and epithets ("bloody," "Lady Duck Muck") are obviously British. In forcing these incompatible worlds together, in overlaying the brutal fascism of a prison camp with British mannerisms, Pinter violently dismantles—just as Gambaro seductively dismantles—distinctions clung to about the exclusivity of British civilization. Significantly, it is to this yoking that David Pryce-Jones objects in his review of the Lyttelton Theatre production. Pryce-Jones complains that "these English references do not make for a generalized condition in which compassion for the Kurds and all oppressed people is natural but only for implausibility and exaggeration" (1228). Pryce-Jones mistakenly views Pinter's use of disjuncture, by which actions performed on stage seem at odds with each other, drawn as they are from the seemingly irreconcilable worlds best exemplified by a Gestapo-garbed warden looking about for a glass of Babycham, and of dislocation, both in the play's refusal to specify locale and the audience's own sense of displacement, as a failing which could only be amended by relying on more socially realistic techniques. But Pinter has said quite specifically that *Mountain Language* is not primarily an account of the oppression of the Kurds, which in his estimation would "take longer than twenty minutes . . . and would take a great deal of historical research" (Gussow 17).

In devaluing disjuncture and dislocation, Pryce-Jones cuts the play in half, oblivious in his review of this great playwright of subtext to his own subtext: that any work written by a British dramatist about totalitarianism is necessarily an other-directed enterprise, an act of speaking on behalf of the voiceless other which could only be undertaken by a member of a just and equitable society. For Pryce-Jones, the central purpose of *Mountain Language* is to "show what an unspeakable horror it is when one human being has unrestrained power over another" (1228), and it is indeed true that the opening tableau of women waiting outside the prison wall is a searing image of an aspect of torture which can occur anywhere. But the insistence that the prison state of *Mountain Language* has no connection to the British system of jurisprudence is a dangerously narrow view of this play.

That such paternalism is indeed one of the objects of Pinter's critique is evident in the playwright's decision to mount a full-scale production of the drama with scene and costume changes at the National Theatre, the locus and, by extension, emblem of the authority and inviolability of British theatre and British civilization, the center, as Hays has termed it, of the cultural paradigm. In his choice of theatrical venue, Pinter insists that the unspecified state of his play be Anglicized. Thus, while it is not possible to see *Mountain Language* without thinking specifically of the Kurds, it also invokes historical comparisons to the oppression of the Welsh and the Irish, and in Pinter's own estimation, to the continued oppression of homosexuals, as inscribed by the passage of Clause 28, a law prohibiting English municipal authorities from allowing "anything that could be considered the 'promotion' of homosexuality" (Gussow 17). Performed in the United States, it might just as well call to mind the still-operative 1952 McCarran-Walter Act, by which "ideologically" suspect aliens are blacklisted.[13] In the institutionalized context of Gambaro's stage, disjuncture prompts a realization of correspondences; the mood of terror that permeates the camp despite all efforts to conceal, regulate, ignore, or live civilly in the midst of it, is directly connected to the strategies adopted within Argentina to manage life in a state of terror. In the institutionalized context of Pinter's stage, disjuncture serves a different purpose; it prompts an act of collocation; it seeks to make local that which has been distanced, to connect that which has been presented as irrelevant.

In order to allow disjuncture to make possible collocation, Pinter, unlike Gambaro, rejects narrative, relying instead on an aesthetic of montage.[14] In doing so, Pinter uses postmodern notions of fragmentation to oppose the fraudulent totality which constitutes current media practices. His drama is one of isolated, uncontextualized fragments which act as metonymy; joined together the fragments operate syntagmatically and announce themselves as an artificial construct which *posits* rather than *derives* meaning. Torn from any immediate, claimable frame of reference or meaningfulness, the individual fragments and the larger montage challenge spectators to find a frame of reference and to construct meaning. As a series of juxtaposed metonymies, the sense of meaning created by the montage depends on a performance of placement; by virtue of the drama's serial, fragmentary rather than narrative structure, meaning relocates itself, shifting by virtue of the dramatic text from one adjacent scene to the next, and shifting by virtue of theatrical performance from unspecified location to cultural context.

This dynamic stands in opposition to the "organic" method of information dissemination as practiced both by media and by government. Both media and government are invested in exerting claims to authority on the basis of "insider" information. For the media, this authority is maintained by insisting that the "immediate" is synonymous with the "real" and that the "fragment" completely reproduces the "whole." Despite the fact that media coverage of current events is intrinsically a piecemeal activity, the extraordinarily competitive and costly nature of saleable air time makes the impulse toward narrativization so compelling that incremental additions are nonetheless rendered as essentially *supplementary*, augmenting a story already in place. These additions are made to fit with a second kind of supplementarity: the invocation of issue experts and news analysts whose primary function is to smooth out the rough edges of the narrative. Similarly, governmental manipulation of information dissemination in places like the United Kingdom and the United States is obviously not controlled in the manner of Gambaro's Argentina; nonetheless it is a staged, aestheticized activity meant again as a claim to authority. Virtually every world crisis occasions some round of well-orchestrated public relations activities which move from the practical (consulting with advisors) to the symbolic (jogging at Kennebunkport). This staged response is essentially a performance meant to normalize public reaction, to provide a sense of wholeness and continuity in order to anticipate and to diffuse any suggestion that the government itself may be in crisis, in doubt, or in the wrong.

Because *Mountain Language* relies on metonymic fragmentation where bits are consciously uncontextualized, unelevated to paradigmatic status, it rejects the claim to authority implicit in organic structure and performs a self-critical, self-limiting act that is the inverse of media and governmental communication. While impelling political critique, *Mountain Language* does not impose it; the critique enacted depends utterly upon the spectator's decision to reject passive receptivity. In contrast to the "insider's" view of news coverage, *Mountain Language* moves the spectator from the "outside" of the prison wall "inside" to the visitor's room, then into darkness and back to the visitor's room again. The heart of this inside view is a pair of disembodied voices speaking in the darkness. It is a lover's discourse that we overhear, not a political critique, a fragment within a fragment. Its intimacy discomfits, just as the silence with which Pinter begins and ends the play unnerves; in the condensed brutality of the play, whose operative word is "fuck," the lovers' language exposes our voyeurism. We are, after all, as theatre-goers and as British or American citizens, merely visiting the sites of violence and tyranny. And as visitors, we are aligned not with the women who bring relief, nor with the lovers, nor with the mother and son. If there is, in fact, a viscerally felt connection, it is with the sergeant whose words, sounding very much like Americans weary of affirmative action hirings or Britons exasperated with the high costs of social welfare, end the play: "You go out of your way to give them a helping hand and they fuck it up" (47). More accurately, however, there is the sense that none of the speakers of the play speak for us, but that there is nonetheless a kind of hole inscribed within the place between the speakers, between the mother and the Sergeant, that we, however we resist it, are meant to inhabit.

If, as Philip Auslander suggests, presence as the matrix of power in the theatre is inevitably associated with charisma or salesmanship (26), Pinter's absent lovers perform a kind of theatrical deconstruction which resists the drive to authorial control but which establishes a kind of presence in order to enact a critique of other presences. This critique is done by means of nondiscursive, nonrepresentational juxtaposition; it is more than anything else *tonal* rather than verbal or visual.

Pinter more explicitly establishes the connection between presence and authority in the play's first scene in another instance of nondiscursive juxtaposition. In this scene, the Officer explains why the mountain language is outlawed. In a curious logic which recalls Lenny's explanation in *The Homecoming* of how he determined a woman was "diseased," ("I decided she was" [47]), the Officer declares in the midst of mountain people speaking their language that the language is "dead." This arbitrary, indeed false designation enables the next set of formulations: the mountain language is "not permitted"; it is "outlawed"; it is "forbidden." This prohibition is a "military decree." The decree is "the law. Then the logic is reversed: "Your language is forbidden. It is dead. No one is allowed to speak your language. Your language no longer exists" (21). The Officer's language relies wholly on an arbitrary but powerful establishment of presence which in turn becomes an establishment of power. Articulation becomes definition becomes decree. Equivalencies drawn linguistically (a military decree is equated with the law) become equivalences in fact. The end result is the desired result: the language described as dead becomes dead. In the fourth scene, an even graver consequence is revealed; definitions arbitrarily made on the basis of vested interest can be reversed arbitrarily, but lives lived on the margins of these kinds of arbitrations are not so flexible. The Elderly Woman who has been deprived of her native language has lost the ability to respond. Even as her imprisoned son importunes her to speak, the elderly woman remains silent. She can say nothing when her son falls to his knees, gasping and shaking violently (47).

Another instance in which linguistic equivalences are drawn arbitrarily but operate to sanction an act of brutality occurs in the first scene. The Young Woman who waits to visit her husband is not one of the mountain people, and as the Officer reminds the Sergeant, she has *as yet* committed no crime. The Sergeant responds by substituting legal langauge for religious language, objecting that it cannot be said that the women are "without sin" (23). Criminal activity is thus associated with congenital immorality, with a kind of barbarism, and hence it is not surprising that the Young Woman next is called a *fucking* intellectual and then is seen as one. The clichéd vulgarity becomes the mark of her character. By the third scene she is referred to three times as the "fucking woman"; she is "Lady Duck Muck" with an "intellectual arse" which wobbles lasciviously. Her lasciviousness is now an established fact; it is no longer possible to see it as the result of a string of correspondences drawn out so minutely that the beginning terms are no longer valid. Like the circular logic of a dead/forbidden/dead language, the woman's transformation from wife to whore is effected by the power of verbal assignation, an assignation which takes on the vested interest of those empowered to establish definitions, and by extension, laws. Surely, the system of British—or American—jurisprudence does not operate so differently.

In *Mountain Language,* Harold Pinter has established the power of post-modern absurdist theatre to perform a political critique that is global, complex, and self-critical. While other dramatists such as Griselda Gambaro also have recognized the ability of absurdist dramaturgy, especially that indebted to Pinter, to make political statements, their theatre ultimately produces a drama of correspondences, a theatre which employs disjuncture to propel an audience toward making immediate connections between the terrorism staged within the theatre and the terrorism performed outside of it. Pinter's theatre demands a framework that is both more global and more critical of its own generic, institutional, and national alignments. *Mountain Language* depends on a disjuncture which can be dissolved only by means of collocation, and this co-location, coplacement requires not only that a connection be drawn between the action of the stage and its immediate, national locale, but also that an alliance be forged between national and international consciousnesses. It requires, further, that a distinction be made between the kind of political commentary it is attempting and the kind rendered by alternate means of information dissemination, especially the government and the media. It insists on a self-critical stance that acknowledges its own complicity with the powers of representation. In its consideration of language and of silence, *Mountain Language* dramatizes that which most bars the meeting of national and international consciousnesses, that works most against the meeting of selves and others: it is the deformation of language into a device used to define, to place, and therefore to keep in place that which most allows the tyrant's voice to be heard above the lovers' whisper.

Notes

1. For a discussion of the collusion of presence and presentation with repressive power structures, see Philip Auslander, "Toward a Concept of the Political in Postmodern Theatre."

2. I have borrowed and extended Herbert Blau's term from *The Eye of Prey: Subversions of the Postmodern.* I am grateful to Professor Blau for his comments on an earlier draft of this essay.

3. Esslin suggests John Arden; other candidates might include Wole Soyinka and Athol Fugard.

4. In an interview with Mel Gussow, Pinter claimed that he is much more interested in his role as citizen than as playwright. In addition to his visit to Turkey as part of his activities with PEN, Pinter has traveled to Nicaragua, spoken frequently on politics and theatre at universities, taken up the cause of Salman Rushdie, and formed a

discussion group with other politically-active British writers. See Gussow, "Pinter's Plays Following Him out of Enigma and into Politics."

5. For reviews of *Mountain Language* see: Beaufort, Kennedy, Kirkpatrick, Pryce-Jones, Rich, and Speirs.

6. In an interview with Selva Echague, Gambaro says, "*Yo creo que un gran obra de teatro es aquella que pertenece ferozmente a su tiempo y que lo trasciende*" (13). ("I believe that a great work of theatre is one which *ferociously* belongs to its time and which reaches beyond it.")

7. Gambaro's works correspond to the changes in Argentine leadership occurring from the seventies to the present, including the struggle between the military and the Peronists of the 1960s; Peron's second ascension to power in the 70s; the military takeover and the "Dirty war" which took place from 1977 to 1983 after Peron's death; the removal of Isabelita Peron from the presidency; and the initiation of the new democracy (Taylor 167).

8. In her talk "Teatro de Vanguardia en la Argentina de hoy," Gambaro explicitly praises Pinter's work, especially recent productions in Argentina which were directed by Jorge Petraglisa, who also directed Gambaro's own work. She also acknowledges the influence of Pinter and Peter Weiss in the interview with Echague.

9. Translations of Gambaro's works into English are available in *Voices of Change in the Spanish-American Theatre,* edited by William Oliver. For a further discussion of Pinter's influence on Gambaro, see Laughlin's discussion of *El Desatino* and *The Birthday Party.*

10. Both Pinter and Gambaro are interested in the way in which women's bodies are the site of territorial claims, and they are interested in the manner in which subjects are objectified by means of semantic assignation. Gambaro makes this point in *El Despojamiento,* in which an actress auditioning for a role is asked to remove some of her clothes, is then stripped of them, and ultimately becomes a stripper. In Gambaro's theatre, roles assigned become roles internalized. As I indicate at the end of my discussion of Pinter's *Mountain Language,* Pinter demonstrated an interest in this same dynamic, particularly as it relates to gender issues in *The Homecoming* where Lenny "decides" that a woman is "diseased," and Ruth, in a counterstruggle, refuses to internalize the whore/mother label offered to her by her husband's family. For a discussion of *El Despojamiento,* see Boling.

11. Holzapfel and Cypess both discuss Gambaro's relationship to the Theatre of the Grotesque.

12. Carey Perloff's decision to pair *The Birthday Party* with *Mountain Language* in the production done by the Classic Stage Company was motivated by her sense that the early play was as political as the later. For a discussion of Perloff's production of *Mountain Language,* see Pittel.

13. Gabriel Garcia Marquez is one of several writers blacklisted by the McCarran-Walter Act; at the moment the law is being challenged by the case of Choichiro Yatani, a Japanese doctoral student detained without explanation by immigration officers for over 40 days. Yatani's case was reported by William Glaberson of *The New York Times* (21 May 1991: 1).

14. In an interview with Mel Gussow, Pinter acknowledged that his attitude toward dramatic structure has changed: "The whole idea of narrative, of a broad canvas stretching over a period of two hours—I think I've gone away from that forever" (17).

SIX

The Outsider in Pinter and Havel

Susan Hollis Merritt

My interest in Václav Havel began when I was writing about Pinter's support for the Czech dissident playwright during Havel's altogether over five years of imprisonment (see *Pinter in Play* 176–77). From fall 1989 through summer 1990, as I was engaged in the final stages of publishing *Pinter in Play,* the Berlin Wall was falling and the Iron Curtain rising on a new millennium in Eastern and Central Europe. Havel's role in the "Velvet Revolution" and Civic Forum culminated in his parliamentary election as president of Czechoslovakia. Daily news events led me to follow Havel's speeches and appearances all over the world. I began reading some of his plays and his other nondramatic writings. As he "took hold" of me, I recognized that, like him, whatever my actual circumstances, I have for most of my personal and professional life felt like an "odd man out," an outsider.

The lives and works of Pinter and Havel exemplify what Hans Mayer calls "existential outsiderdom." In *Outsiders* (*Aussenseiter*) Mayer "analyze[s] three types of existential outsiders: women who are exceptional because they ignore the rules; men who are outsiders on account of sexual inclination; [and] the Jewish outsider within bourgeois society" (xviii). In "What Is an Outsider? A Note for the American Edition" (xiii–xx), Mayer defines "outsiders" and "existential outsiderdom," highlighting an "antithesis between intentional and existential outsiders": "intentional outsiders" are "conscious and volitional outsiders, figures who consciously transgress boundaries"; whereas "existential outsiders" are "those who were, literally in their cradles, sung to of what they would one day be. They are those whose move into the margins and the outside was enjoined at birth through sex, origins, or psychic and corporeal makeup." An existential outsider is "no longer a single individual who is envisaged, a rebel, one marked man or woman. Existential outsiders are 'people who. . . .' They have become a genus. They can be lumped together as a minority with specific characteristics. The negative judgment stands" (xvi).

Since he completed the book in 1975, Mayer noted in 1981, the possibility of global self-annihilation "has become actuality for all of us. It becomes more and more difficult . . . to distinguish at all any more between outsiders and majorities. Everything can be turned around, so that the historical process that I attempted to sketch must perhaps be understood as the path from the intentional to the existential outsider that then ends with a virtual outsiderdom for everyone, of whatever origin, skin color, language, or tradition" (xix). Citing Jean-Paul Sartre's famous explanation to his fellow Frenchmen after World War II why "under certain circumstances everyone can become a 'Jew' to others," Mayer concludes: "More and more people . . . are beginning to recognize that to the question, 'What are outsiders?' there is no possible answer, or that there is an answer, which comes down to: 'Everyone, under certain circumstances'" (xx).

Mayer's section entitled "Judith and Delilah" analyzes briefly the ambiguous process of Ruth's alienation and self-alienation in Pinter's *Homecoming* (117–20), a play that Havel relates to what he considers the intrinsically theatrical "theme of human identity" (*Letters to Olga* 290–91; cf. *Disturbing the Peace* 53). A potent paradox of Pinter's and Havel's outsiders is what Havel terms "the power of the powerless" inherent in voicing the silence of others whose "identity" has likewise been absorbed into the "sphere of power" of "the post-totalitarian system" (*The Power of the Powerless* 36–37). Readers and other audience members (beginning with myself and you) are also outsiders whose personal experiences of the "unfamiliar but familiar" imaginary worlds created by both Pinter and Havel enable them to respond to new ways of seeing their own actual worlds.

Among many differences between Havel and Pinter, we must recognize their very different personal, social, and professional histories and cultural milieux.[1] While each was an "only child," Harold Pinter was the only child of a working-class Jewish family in the East End of London (Pinter's father worked as a "ladies' tailor"; at home his mother was "a good cook").[2] Václav Havel was the more "privileged" only child of a professional, "grand bourgeois" family in Czechoslovakia who owned a country estate, complete with "domestics," including a governess, a cook, and a chauffeur (Havel's grandfather and father were both builders and entrepreneurs).[3] A conscientious objector at sixteen, Pinter had some professional training as an actor before going on tour with Anew McMaster ("Mac") in Ireland performing Shakespeare; he had further stage experience in the English provinces, but he eventually subordinated his acting career to his success as a playwright, screenwriter, and director. Havel's desire for formal academic training in art history, philosophy, and film was thwarted by "the State"; he had studied at a technical university before being drafted in the army, where he cowrote a controversial play for the regimental theater company that he founded. Discovering Beckett, Ionesco, and "the other more or less 'absurd' playwrights," whom he found "extremely close to [his] own temperament and sensibility," made him a dramatist (*Letters to Olga* 248). He became a dramaturg and playwright rather fortuitously in response to his employment as a stagehand. But he was forced to work as a manual laborer before and during his imprisonments as a political dissident. His experience working in a brewery informs his 1975 play *Audience,* which he himself was unable to see performed until 1990. Since "[t]he theatre audience in Czechoslovakia is proportionately four times as great as that in Britain" (Day 251), potentially, until 1990, at least that many more people have *not* been able to see Havel's banned plays as have been able to see Pinter's admitted ones.

Pinter's current political goals in support of human rights and other issues in Britain, such as his establishment of the 20th June Society and support for Salman Rushdie, have at times been lampooned in the English press.[4] The current president of Czechoslovakia, Havel has been idolized as his country's most famous dissident author, respected as one of the first three signers (and originators) of Charter 77 (a national petition for human rights), and, at least when first elected, revered by university students as a "Godot" who had finally arrived (Garbus). Prophetically, it seems today, Havel conveys clearly a "politics of hope," which he has explicated at some length in many *samizdat* publications and interviews.[5] In contrast, Pinter's politics has not been so clearly phrased or analyzed; sometimes considered pessimistic or even cynical, it is still being actively debated, and so far Pinter himself has produced comparably little commentary on it (though see "A Play and Its Politics"; "Language and Lies"; "Oh, Superman!"; and "U.S. Elephant").

Despite these different backgrounds and vantage points, English "citizen" Harold Pinter shares with Czech President Václav Havel a "social emotion" (Havel's term) rising like a phoenix from the rubble of cultural oppression. Pinter's "social" and "political" experience as a Jew, the son of a ladies' tailor, facing gangs of Sir Oswald Mosely's Fascist boys, and his violence in response to anti-Semitic taunts like "filthy Yid" (Bensky, "The Art of the Theater"; Pugh; Esslin, *Pinter: The Playwright* 37) are analogous to the "oppression" Havel felt as a "fat little rich boy," the son of a "grand bourgeois," in a socialist environment that glorified the working class. Their circumstantial differences belie the strikingly similar intensity of their reactions to their own perceived crises of identity, their sense of personal ostracism, their deep "intimate affin-ity" with the work of both Kafka and Beckett, their unusual sympathies with others who have been oppressed, excluded, or expelled, and their abilities to create vivid characterizations of outsiders and paradoxical dramatic situations of outsiderdom—both in their own original creative works and their adaptations of those by others.[6]

"This is far from the first honorary doctorate I have received, but I accept it with the same sensation I always do: deep shame. Because of my rather sporadic education, I suffer from feelings of unworthiness, and so I accept this degree as a strange gift, a continuing source of bewilderment." President Havel spoke these words at the Hebrew University in Jerusalem on 26 April 1990 in a speech entitled "On Kafka," in which he confesses "my long and intimate affinity with one of the great sons of the the Jewish people, the Prague writer Franz Kafka."[7] "[I]n Kafka," Havel explains, "I have found a portion of my own experience of the world, of myself, and of my way of being in the world. . . . [T]he hidden motor driving all my dogged efforts is precisely this innermost feeling of mine of being excluded, of belonging nowhere, a state of disinheritance, as it were, of fundamental non-belonging." Pinter confessed a similar feeling in accepting the 1970 Shakespeare Prize in Hamburg, West Germany: "When I was informed that I was to be given this award my reaction was to be startled, even bewildered, while at the same time to feel deeply gratified by this honour. I remain honoured and slightly bewidered, but also frightened. What frightens me is that I have been asked to speak to you today. If I find writing difficult I find giving a public address doubly so" (*Complete Works* 4: ix). In other interviews Pinter has alluded to his lack of a university or Oxbridge education, paralleling Havel's embarrassment by speaking of his own "sporadic education." "Sometimes," the once ostracized Havel confessed to Marie Winn, "I wonder whether I didn't actually begin to write to overcome that basic experience of being an outsider" (81). Through such public confessions and preoccupations, Pinter and Havel reveal the profound interior sense of existential outsiderdom permeating their writings, which serve to exorcize this feeling.

As with Havel, among several influences on Pinter, critics often allude to Kafka and Beckett. Pinter told John Sherwood in 1960—"'When I read them it rang a bell, that's all, within me. I thought: something is going on here which is going on in me too'" (Esslin, *Pinter: The Playwright* 40). In October 1989 at the 92nd Street Y, discussing "his [then] current project of writing a screenplay of Kafka's *The Trial*," Pinter said: "the nightmare of [Kafka's] world is precisely in its ordinariness, and that is what I think is so frightening" (Merritt, *Pinter in Play* 189). The "ordinary" yet "frightening" experience that Pinter continuously dramatizes in his work epitomizes the "structure of feeling" of existential outsiderdom: social alienation and self-alienation.[8]

Granting the longevity of critical attention to themes of alienation, menace, and identity in Pinter's work, some renewed critical interest in these matters signals fresh perspectives on the importance and the function of the "outsider" in Pinter and provides a springboard for exploring further paradoxes of "outsiderdom" and alienation in both Pinter and Havel and in their work. Recalling Mayer in *Outsiders,* for example, Leslie Kane stresses the historical experience of the "the 'galut,' the exile" as a quintessentially Jewish source of Pinter's theatre. In an interview conducted by Donald Chase, "[Pinter said] that [t]he appeal of *Reunion,* Fred Uhlman's novella about the friendship between an adolescent Jewish boy and a Christian proto-Nazi in Germany of 1932 [which Pinter adapted for the 1990 film directed by Jerry Schatzberg], was 'simple: I'm Jewish.'" In *Reunion* the Jewish boy is sent by his parents to America, a safe haven kind of exile, from which, in the novel, he narrates his story thirty years later. Pinter introduced "the whole new element" of the man's return to Germany fifty years later, which adds another layer of outsiderdom to the already powerfully ironic structure of his "reunion." Several books that Pinter has read and recommended recently deal with the Holocaust and other forms of oppression of Jews and others (Knowles 26).

Though Pinter and Havel may engage parallel traditions of outsiderdom, these traditions are simply among their starting points. So as "not to suggest that Pinter is writing 'Jewish plays,'" Kane concludes, "Rather, we may postulate that Pinter finds that linguistic reticence and parody enable him to fuse identification with Jewish cultural and historical experience and his concern for the individual under arbitrary sentence of death. Always the Other, the Jew becomes the figure of universal experience in the contemporary world" (30). Similarly, extending the arguments of Marketa Goetz-Stankiewicz, I would not suggest that Havel is writing merely "dissident plays."[9] Rather, through his own brand of linguistic reticence and parody, Havel fuses identification with East-Central European cultural and historical experience and the same Kafkaesque motif that Kane still attributes to Pinter: his concern for the individual under arbitrary sentence of death. Both playwrights dramatize their characters' fear of death as a fear of ultimate outsiderdom.

In most of Pinter's work after *The Room* (1957), death is figurative.[10] In *The Hothouse* (1958, 1980) and *One for the Road* (1984), however, along with mental and physical rape and torture, death becomes literal (actual death, ultimate outsiderdom); characters "really" die. In both *One for the Road* and *Mountain Language* (1988), it may be that characters are being tortured to death. Death is the indirect referent of Pinter's dramatic sketch *Precisely* (1985), whose deferred subject is "precisely" how many "dead" people will result from bureaucratic decisions discussed quite casually over "drinks."[11] Though for some time I have thought that the sketch probably deals with the results of a nuclear war or some other nuclear catastrophe, after the war in the Persian Gulf, Sakellaridou's assumption in "The Rhetoric of Evasion as Political Discourse" that the subject is more generally "a secretly planned genocide" (45) seems more convincing than it did before. I can imagine the conversation about "how many" would be killed taking place in a bar near the Pentagon or State Department during and after this war.[12]

In Havel's plays death is figuratively a death of the human spirit and moral values (or virtual death) as demonstrated through the disintegration and "mendacity" of language and the vagaries of the time/space continuum. *The Garden Party* (1963) features the euphemistically named "Inauguration Office" and "Liquidation Office," bureaus of figurative life and death; the play's "main hero" is "the cliché": the "hackneyed phrase" (*Disturbing the Peace* 193; *Garden Party* 26); the "dead metaphor." The most self-consciously prominent "motif" of Václav Havel's writings about the effects of advanced or late totalitarianism on individual identity is "the loss of self" (*Disturbing the Peace* 196)—a figurative death of the individual resulting from suppression of freedoms, choices, and responsibilities. This concern may recall some recent critical perspectives on thematic issues of identity and individual responsibility dramatized by Pinter's plays (e.g., Prentice, "Ambiguity, Identity"). Yet Havel the philospher-dramaturg-playwright is temperamentally far more analytical and critical than Pinter the actor-playwright-director. Havel's letters and interviews explicitly define the absurdist tradition of his dramaturgy and his interest in "the meaning" and "meaningfulness" of the relations between such absurdist themes and life.[13]

As the "absurdity" of Havel's plays grows more subtle and less obviously imitative of Ionesco, the paradoxical philosophical implications of the motif of the "outsider" also become more complex. Since Havel models his characters rather directly on his own life, the outsider as a figure in Havel's work also grows more complex in proportion to his own political experiences and his analyses of them. Havel's three Vaněk plays—*Audience* (1975), *Private View* or *Unveiling* (1975), and *Protest* (1979), which was written after his first imprisonment—as well as (to a degree) the earlier *The Memorandum* (1965) and *The Increased Difficulty of Concentration* (1968)—and the other postprison plays, *Mistake* (1983), *Largo Desolato* (1984), and *Temptation* (1985), all present main characters modeled on Havel's own experience as an outsider. In the most simple of these, the sketch *Mistake* (Havel's only dramatic work set in a prison), three prisoners and a "trustie" have been berating a new arrival for not following the prison "rules"; his total silence provokes further verbal and then physical attacks, to which he does not respond. Finally, his muteness causes one of them to recognize that the strange newcomer is "some kind of bloody foreigner"—but, as another one says ominously, "Well, that's his bloody funeral" (14).[14]

Such silent or almost silent figures serve to expose the moral and social inertia—a "violence to humanity"—induced by totalitarian "entropy." Perhaps anticipating the "foreigner" in *Mistake,* Vaněk, like Havel, is "an alien in his own homeland" (Mel Gussow, quoted in Blackwell 109); but he is not Havel the man: Vaněk, Havel explains, is "not so much a concrete person as something of a 'dramatic principle'" through which Havel the playwright exposes the non-Vaněk characters as self-serving, greedy, and lascivious. The "politics" of their language—their tactical rhetorical cleverness—reveals that they are unable to comprehend the "truth" that Vaněk represents (through the way he lives, not speaks) because the world to which they have accommodated themselves has rendered them blind to it. In the non-Vaněk plays the main characters combine features of both Vaněk and these others to expose themselves through similarly complex rhetorical uses of language.

In "Light on a Landscape," Havel observes:

[Vaněk] does not usually do or say much, but his mere existence, his presence on stage, and his being what he is make his environment [including the characters in it] expose itself one way or another. He does not admonish anyone in particular; indeed, he demands hardly anyhing of anyone. And in spite of this, his environment perceives him as an invocation somehow to declare and justify itself. He is, then, a kind of "key," opening certain—always different—vistas onto the world in which he lives; a kind of catalyst, a gleam, if you will, in whose light we view a landscape. And although without it we should scarcely be able to see anything at all, it is not the gleam that matters but the landscape. The Vaněk plays, therefore, are essentially not plays about Vaněk, but plays about the world as it reveals itself when confronted with Vaněk. (238–39)

Havel adds parenthetically that the passage just quoted is "an *ex post facto* explanation. While writing *Audience,* I was not aware of this, and I did not plan things that way beforehand. It is only now that, removed in time and faced with Vaněk's literary and theatrical existence of several years, I have come to realize it" (239).[15]

Pinter played the role of Ferdinand Vaněk in a BBC Radio 3 production of *Audience* and *Private View* on 3 April 1977 (See *Sorry . . .*). Given Pinter's direct involvement in Havel's work, his attempts to get Havel released from prison, and Havel's acknowledgment of Pinter as one of his "masters" (Garbus), "the 'Vaněk principle'" might inform and be informed by Pinter's work.[16]

A paradigm of Pinter's drama is the "Matchseller" (who is wholly silent) in Pinter's play *A Slight Ache;* following Havel, we might call the structural function of this character the "Matchseller principle." Pinter's Matchseller and Havel's Vaněk are both outsiders on whom the other characters project their repressed insecurities and confusions about their own identities.[17] Variations on this "Matchseller" or "outsider principle" structure the character relationships in Pinter's other dramatic writing (including his screenplays) and most of his early prose fiction.

Structural configurations in games like Blind's Man's Buff in *The Birthday Party* and the even more spontaneous bag-tossing business in *The Caretaker* mirror the larger physical action and the analogous "Odd-Man-Out principle" structuring the character relationships and action in many of Pinter's other works; for example, *The Dwarfs* (play and novel), *A Night Out, The Caretaker, The Collection, The Homecoming, Old Times, No Man's Land, Betrayal, Family Voices, Victoria Station,* and *A Kind of Alaska* (*Other Places*). In several of these works, prominent outsiders are women. Women characters have been eliminated in early stages of Pinter's writing (the woman character omitted from an early typedraft of *The Caretaker* [held at Lilly Library, Indiana University] and Virginia's literal exclusion as a character in the play version *The Dwarfs*); distanced through and possibly even exiled along with love to memory and fantasies about the past, present, and future (in *Night, Silence, Landscape, Monologue, Old Times, No Man's Land, Betrayal* [through the play's structure], *Family Voices,* and *Victoria Station*); and figuratively excluded otherwise (Virginia in *The Dwarfs,* Stella in *The Collection,* Ruth in *The Homecoming,* both Kate and Anna—a literal as well as figurative outsider like Ruth—as well as Deeley in *Old Times,* Emma in *Betrayal,* and Deborah in *A Kind of Alaska*).[18] When the women in these works are silent, they function much as Vaněk and the Matchseller do: to display the verbal characters' moral and psychological weaknesses and preoccupations. Analogous to Pinter characters' well-known "two silences" are Vaněk's "true" silences counterpointing the non-Vaněk characters' false and "irrevocable" loquaciousness.

In *The Hothouse* and two of Pinter's more recent overtly political plays, *One for the Road* and *Mountain Language,* the characters are inmates and prisoners: existential outsiders. They are victims of what Havel calls totalitarianism's "criminalization of difference," suffering its destruction of "uniqueness" and personal "historicity" (as opposed to ideological "historical necessity" ["Stories and Totalitarianism" 16–18]). In *The Hothouse* the "patients" are never actually seen by the audience; reduced to numbers and merely talked about, they are ciphers indistinguishable from and easily confused with one another (Has Roote talked to 6457 or 6459? Has 6457 died and 6459 given birth, or vice versa?). Their very human muffled cries and whispers heard only during the darkened intervals recall Beckett's *Waiting for Godot:* "They gave birth astride of a grave, the light gleams an instant, then it's night once more." Like Vaněk, characters in *The Hothouse* and Pinter's most recent political plays, including Jimmy, the Young Man in *Party Time,* seem to have committed no specific crime against "the State" other than to think or to speak differently. Institutionalization or imprisonment keeps them, ironically, "inside" in order to keep them outside of and thus isolated from the rest of society, to keep them from "disturbing the peace," from causing "trouble" and altering the "status quo."

Havel's Dr. Foustka in *Temptation* and Professor Leopold Nettles in *Largo Desolato* both disturb the peace in their attempts to alter the status quo, but they function much more complexly than Vaněk does in the other plays in that they themselves are severely corrupted by their environments. The Mephistopheles of *Temptation,* Fistula, presents himself to the scientist Dr. Foustka as an outsider, "a cripple with a pension" (i.e., "retired"); but Fistula turns out to be an "external agent" of the Scientific Institute which Dr. Foustka betrays and thus actually an "informer," an insider.[19] Dr. Foustka's insatiable curiosity about outlawed magic makes him susceptible to Fistula's dubious devilish charms, but, like Faust, he tends to outwit himself verbally. Thus, when he expresses his views about "the basic questions of being" to Marketa, he tells the truth in order to get her to fall in love with him, in effect succumbing to the temptation of Fistula's promises by "ever so subtly . . . abusing his own truth" (*Disturbing the Peace* 194). Similarly Faustian is the "damned if I do, damned if I don't" trap which Nettles encounters in *Largo Desolato.* Nettles is "abusing his own truth" by subtly denying that he is the *same* Leopold Nettles who wrote an offending essay, in order to avoid punishment—being taken "there" by "them."

The existential dilemmas of both these characters were inspired by an actual dilemma experienced by Havel and years of painful self-reproach. His relentless critique of his own "tactical and cunning" rhetorical ploy in an ostensibly "honorable" request written while in prison in 1977 and then "misappropriated" by the officials led him to see how "the truth is not simply what you think it is; it is also the circumstances in which it is said, and to whom, why, and how it is said" (*Disturbing the Peace* 67).[20] To understand this multifaceted "theme," we must become as ruthlessly critical of the characters as Havel is of himself, all the while recognizing how their social and political environments make them both friends and victims of "the State": outsiders in a double sense.

Both Pinter and Havel stimulate analogous outsiderdom and feelings of (self-)alienation (bewilderment, confusion) in members of their audiences, who, like myself, may find ourselves in conflict. Instinctively, we may sympathize with the apparent "moral" or "true" content of Havel's characters' "absurd" speeches, while intellectually questioning these characters' "immoral" or "dishonest" motivations and thus our own responses. We may sense parallels between apparent "truths" (through "ethical lies") *spoken* by Havel's characters, Havel's own published statements about "*living* in truth," and our own values; yet we may not know how to "take" the parallels critically, whether or not to trust our emotional and intellectual responses.[21] Likewise, we may understand the tragicomic crises of Pinter's characters, indeed sympathize or even identify with aspects of them, and yet not want to see what they show us about ourselves, images of our own actual or potential outsiderdom. Like their characters, we ourselves become *both* "in" and "out" *and* neither "in" nor "out" of Pinter's and Havel's dramatic worlds.[22]

This reading effect or audience response—with ironically comic twists of further complexity—resembles what Lacan calls "the *vel* of alienation," the "lethal factor": "a Hegelian moment . . . called the Terror" (212–13). Unlike the apparently simple binary oppositions of such comic clichés as "When you're in you're in. . . . And when you're not in you're out. Or, more accurately, when you're out you're not in" (Pinter, *Dwarfs* [novel] 13), all at once, in the momentary flash of a "double" or "stereoscopic" perspective, we sense that we are *both* in and out *and* neither in nor out, *or both* "here" and "there" *and* neither "here" nor "there" (in the Kafkaesque sense of *there* in *Largo Desolato*). We feel as if we are in a purgatory of being/nonbeing.

Like many "others," we may be "quite raddled with" daily images of the terrible plight of Kurdish and other political war refugees trapped for weeks in an all-too-real, freezing, muddy no man's land in the mountains between Iraq and Turkey, a twilight zone of actual expulsion.[23] From the relative comfort of our armchairs and theatre seats, for perhaps only a few moments, we may inhabit an eidetic "no man's land" like that dramatized by Pinter—"Which never moves, which never changes, which never grows older, but which remains forever, icy and silent"—where the paradoxes of existential outsiderdom, of alienation and self-alienation, are "frozen" in place yet put in play, an imaginary but no less possible world where "the [individual] subject" both may and may not be "changed for the last time" (*No Man's Land, Complete Works* 4: 149–53), just as we both may and may not be changed "forever" by Pinter and Havel.

Notes

1. A possible East-Central European cultural history affiliates Pinter a bit more with Havel's background: "Pinter believes that his father's family might have come to England from Hungary; the name Pinter does occur among Hungarian Jews[.] But there is also

a family tradition that the name is of Spanish or Portuguese origin—Pinto, da Pinto or da Pinta—so that the Pinters were originally Sephardic Jews. There is no reason why both these theories might not be correct, as Sephardic Jews frequently settled in East and Central Europe after the expulsions of the Jews from the Iberian peninsula" (Esslin, *Pinter: The Playwright* 14).

2. See Esslin (*Pinter: The Playwright* 10) and Pauline Flanagan, as cited in Gordon (242).

3. Havel's extensive self-analytical autobiographical accounts appear throughout *Letters to Olga* and *Disturbing the Peace,* esp. chap. 1: "Growing Up 'Outside'" (1–33). See also Winn and Schiff.

4. See Merritt, "Pinter and Politics"; chap. 8 in *Pinter in Play;* and Knowles.

5. See, e.g., essays throughout *Václav Havel: Living in Truth* and *Disturbing the Peace* (180–86, 198–201, 204). Discussing his view on "hope" further, Havel admits that he still signs his literary works and playbills "with a green pen, the color of hope" and still adds "a little heart with a red fountain pen, so as to convey the idea of love, mutual understanding, tolerance—which accompanied our revolution and carried me to this high post" (Shinkarev 38).

6. All sixteen of Pinter's screenplays of others' novels and most of others' works that he has directed for stage and screen feature various kinds of outsiders. Havel wrote an adaptation of John Gay's play *The Beggar's Opera* (1975), whose hero is an outlaw; *Temptation* (1985) was inspired by Goethe's *Faust* and Thomas Mann's *Doctor Faustus,* both of which he read in prison. Mayer views Faust as a recurring "theme of emancipation in bourgeois literature" (54).

7. In *Letters to Olga* Havel discusses his "spiritual kinship" with Kafka in similar terms (126).

8. For extended definition of *structures of feeling,* see Williams (128–35).

9. Goetz-Stankiewicz questions the appropriateness of "'the dissident playwright' label" as it has been applied to Havel. She observes that "Havel never permits us to formulate a comfortably assured answer; rather, like Kafka or Beckett, he opens up a myriad of questions which seem to extend out of sight. Shades of implied shades of meaning mock and tempt the reader" (102). Havel is "a 'political' playwright in the sense that he is an eloquent critic of totalitarianism . . . because he defines, with intellectual and dramatic energy, the rigid social structures dictated by a totalitarian ideology which pulverize and absorb personal identity. . . . However . . . there is much more. By showing us how disturbingly close our most cherished linguistic formulations are to the dark realm of confusion and danger, Havel casts a giant question mark over the assumptions underlying the time-honoured patterns by which we are accustomed to live" (103).

10. While many critics assume that Bert kicks Riley to death at the end of *The Room,* the stage directions are rather ambiguous ("The NEGRO lies still" [Pinter, *Complete Works* 1: 126]), and Rose's psychosomatic blindness symbolizes her frightened identification with the outsider Riley's fate. Similarly, the gun never actually goes off in *The Dumb Waiter* (1957), and Pinter has recalled revising *The Caretaker* (1959) from having Davies killed to his probable expulsion. Though the wheelbarrow with which Stanley threatens Meg never comes "up the garden path" in *The Birthday Party* (1957; *Complete Works* 1: 34), critics have interpreted Stanley's breakdown and his removal in a large car at the end as the symbolic "death" of the maladaptive individual in society. They have also written much about the figurative "deaths" of Kate and Anna and Deeley in *Old Times* (1970) and the "death in life" of Hirst in *No Man's Land* (1974). In *Family Voices* (1980) the father speaks from the grave, as it were; we may assume that he has already died prior to the temporal setting of the play's voices, ironically, without the awareness of his son, for whom he is "dead" anyway. All the members of the titular family are alienated from themselves and one another psychically as well as physically.

11. Parenthetical dates here and elsewhere in my text are dates of composition supplied in chronologies in Pinter, *Complete Works* or of first publication otherwise.

12. I still do not find convincing Sakellaridou's assumption that *Precisely* takes place in a "totalitarian state," however. Mengel suggests important reasons for the unspecified settings of Pinter's recent plays.

13. For extended discussions of "the theme of identity" and "responsibility" in his own dramatic and nondramatic writings and in "[a]ll of modern art . . . and modern drama," see Havel, *Letters to Olga* (61–62, 290–93, 300–301), and "The Politics of Hope," *Disturbing the Peace* (190–97). In *Letters to Olga* (281–83, 284–86), Havel cites "the importance of structure . . . the space-time continuum. . . . The composition and development of motifs, the way they are arranged, repeated, reinvoked, combined, interwoven, connected, gradated and brought to a climax, their precise location—all these things—whether they be emphasized or disguised, whether they are more the result of conscious effort or 'merely' of a sensitivity to the matter—are what makes a play a play" (286). See esp. his analysis of "a circle of feelings . . . rather transparently connected with the tendency of my writing" and "the poetics" of his plays in terms of such a "structure" of "motifs" and "themes" (287–90) and his analysis of "[t]he mechanization of dramatic forms" in his work in terms of his "basic theme" of "human identity" (*Disturbing the Peace* 193–97). See also *Letters to Olga* (171–72, 177–78, 248, 290–92, 297–98, 300–303) and "Writing for the Stage," in *Disturbing the Peace,* esp. 53–57. In contrast, before his more recent political pronouncements, Pinter claimed not to "write from any kind of abstract idea"—"I wouldn't know a symbol if I saw one" (*Complete Works* 2: 10)—and not to "know" what the recurrent themes of his own work are—"I do in fact leave that to others to inform me" (1981 talk).

14. In "Many Thanks to Our Swedish Friends" Havel writes: "*Mistake* was not intended simply as a kind of snapshot of prison life; in its modest way it is meant to warn against the ubiquitous danger of the kind of self-imposed totalitarianism now present in every community in the world, large or small. Perhaps one can detect in this sketch of mine something more—namely, a reminder of our original exposure to the world and of the responsibility of every single member of the human race for what he or she is, including his or her membership of the nation in which they are born. There may, for all I know, be people who think it is a mistake to have been born Czech. As far as I am concerned, I see it as a special task, which I of course did not set myself; but I accept it and wish to make the best of it."

15. In the original Czech this essay is untitled; the translators, Milan Pomichalek and Anna Mozga, entitled it "Light on a Landscape" for *The Vaněk Plays.* For critical explication of the "Vaněk principle" in Havel's three Vaněk plays, see Blackwell. See also Baranczak (30–31).

16. Pinter and his wife Lady Antonia Fraser have also written essays for *Index on Censorship,* where an interview with Havel and some of Havel's works, such as *Mistake,* have first been published in English.

17. See Daniel Salem's recent intensive reading of the function of this very real "étranger" or stranger in *A Slight Ache* as the means through which Pinter exposes that Edward and Flora are "strangers" to themselves and each other.

18. On my own responses to what I call "the 'Odd Man Out' syndrome" in my experience of Pinter's plays through *Old Times,* see also Elliott, "Fantasy behind Play" (543), as discussed in Merritt, *Pinter in Play* (257–58). For extended discussion of the "outcast" status of women as Others in Pinter's plays and films, see Sakellaridou, *Pinter's Female Portraits;* cf. Hall and Rabillard.

19. Fistula's bad "smell" derives from "a certain unidentified fungus of the foot" (17), a festering sore apparently aggravated by constant visits to suspects like Dr. Foustka, during which Fistula repeatedly changes from his walking shoes to slippers. For derivation and definition of the name *Fistula,* see *Webster's New World Dictionary,* 2nd college ed., s.v. "fistula": "[ME. <OFr. <L., a pipe, ulcer] 1. [Rare] shaped like a pipe

or tube; tubular 2. an abnormal passage from an abscess, cavity, or hollow organ to the skin or to another abscess, cavity, or organ." When Fistula's actual identity as one of the "external agents of lying" employed by the Scientific Institute is revealed (99), this meaning of his name reflects pejoratively on the Institute itself as an "abscess, cavity, or hollow organ" of "the State" and, somewhat more ambiguously, on Dr. Foustka as either "the skin" ("body surface") or "another abscess, cavity, or hollow organ" of "State" society too. The *OED* points to a connection between *Fistula* and the Old French *festre* (FESTER). Ironically, the obsolete *Fousty,* or *fusty,* closest to Havel's name for Dr. Foustka, is "that which has lost its freshness, stale-smelling, musty" or "mouldy," while *Faust* (Dr. Faustus) derives from the Latin *faust-us,* meaning "Happy, lucky." Fistula observes that Dr. Foustka is a "victim" of his "own pride"—his own "tough luck" (99). Havel identifies Dr. Foustka and Fistula as of similarly questionable ("smelly") character.

20. Cf. *Letters to Olga* (347–56). In scene 6 of *Temptation,* Fistula tells Dr. Foustka: "My dear Sir, the truth isn't merely what we believe, after all, but also why and to whom and under what circumstances we say it!" (60).

21. See Havel, *Disturbing the Peace* (193–94), where he discusses his use of clichés or phrases (normal "lies") in *The Garden Party* and characterization of Dr. Foustka in *Temptation.* Goetz-Stankiewicz observes that "[a]lthough every single one of [Havel's] plays deals with a critique of language in one way or another, the playwright seems to have given it the most challenging treatment it has yet had in his Faust play, *Temptation*" (96–99, 101–103), and she considers the "rhetoric" of "Havel's gallery of language acrobats" in several other plays (98–101). Havel discusses the intended "ambivalent" experience of *The Mountain Hotel* and his plays generally in *Letters to Olga* (171–72). Cf. Goetz-Stankiewicz (102), as cited above (note 9).

22. Sakellaridou discusses "emotional distance" in response to Pinter's political plays in "Audience Control" and "The Rhetoric of Evasion as Political Discourse."

23. Pinter says that he was "quite raddled with these kinds of images" of "people . . . locked up in prisons all over the place, being tortured in one way or another . . . with the sense that these things are ever-present" (Gross 25; cited in Merritt, *Pinter in Play* 176).

III. Pinter's Poetics

SEVEN

The Betrayal of Facts: Pinter and Duras beyond Adaptation

Judith Roof

As Jerry and Emma sit in a pub in the chronologically penultimate, but premier scene of *Betrayal,* Jerry nostalgically rehearses his postpartum parting shot to all imaginary competitors for Emma's favors: "... she may be having the occasional drink with Casey, who cares, but she and I had an affair for seven years and none of you bastards had the faintest idea it was happening" (23). Emma's response to Jerry's boast is to call his claim into question: "I wonder," she says, "I wonder if everybody knew, all the time" (23). This question of who knows what when is central to Harold Pinter's play and film *Betrayal* (1978 and 1983) and Marguerite Duras's series of works: the 1959 play *Les Viaducs de la Seine-et-Oise,* the 1967 novel *L'Amante anglaise,* and the 1968 play *L'Amante anglaise.* More than just meditations on the power endowed by information or enactments of a dynamic of dramatic irony, the works reveal how facts constitute a lure of knowledge. Divulging both the desire for knowledge and the means by which knowledge is conveyed, the lure of knowledge not only shapes each work, but also structures the interrelation among the series' works in different media.

Premised around a core "crime" and the illusion of an "original version" represented by Pinter's return to the scene of primal seduction in the last scene of *Betrayal* and Duras's appeal to a supposedly "true" news story, both series suggest that the process—the desire, the looking—is more important than finding facts. Dangling the decoy of a knowledge that presumably solves the mystery of the text (as Oedipus's identity solves the mystery of Laius's murder), the works lock us into the illusion of an alluring oedipal certainty, while, as in magician's sleight-of-hand, they perform a different trick—provide a different understanding—elsewhere. The texts also expose the lure of knowledge as a lure, making a consciousness of the lure's operation an intrinsic part of the work. This consciousness shifts the location of knowing from the consumption of facts and the illusion of mastery to a comprehension of our desire for knowledge, the deceptive mastery such knowledge stands for, and the relations among desire, knowledge, and medium.

In the play *Betrayal,* for example, the play's achronological presentation of the revelation of "facts" flirts with the characters' illusory investment in the play's form and our desire to see the adultery confirmed.[1] The paradox of knowledge in *Betrayal* is that the apparent power endowed by the dramatic irony of our knowing the "central" fact of betrayal isn't power at all, since the fact of adultery turns out to be primarily a lure. Instead, the information sought by both characters and audience is essentially the knowledge of a knowing: we know that Robert knows what Jerry doesn't know that he knows. While the play moves fitfully backward and forward, producing a shifting dynamic of irony and finally revealing the first moment of Jerry's seduction of Emma—presumably the founding moment of betrayal—the betrayal turns out to have been only a minor treachery in the fabric of endless betrayals we have witnessed on the way. Instead of a final culminatory oedipal reaffirmation of an originary knowledge that would reassure us of our canniness (a recognition played out in scene 9 nonetheless), the betrayals of *Betrayal* have to do with when the characters know what: when Robert knows, when Emma knows Robert knows, when Emma tells Jerry Robert knows, when Robert tells Jerry Emma knew that he knew, and in our wanting to know any of it. Our desire for a founding authoritative origin for all of this knowing and for a knowledge of the history of this triangle which drives us to the beginning in the end is betrayed by the fact that what is worth knowing in this play is always already known—that knowledge is not "it" at all. Our desire for knowledge is betrayed, and in the process our fixation on the power of knowledge is exposed.

Betrayal's preoccupation with the knowledge, situated as it is in the microtheatrical configuration of an adulterous triangle, already performs a meditation on the relation among desire, knowledge, and the medium of theatre. The constantly frustrated possibility of direct communication among the characters reflects a mode of indirection that paradoxically conveys the knowledge the characters (and the audience) seek. Knowledge is rendered through the indirect "languages" of squash, the artistic success of their respective authors, the lives of their children, and the self-reflexive, but still indirect metalanguage of knowledge itself: by the approximation of experience in an inadequate language that, like the play itself, is out of order, fragmented, disjointed. Rather than by "indirection finding directions out," we find that at best directions are always only indirections; language, questions and answers, and theatrical representations are approximations of a knowledge whose shape and specificity is filled in by an interpretive process shaped by our desire to see and to know. The indirection of representation becomes more significant than the facts to which the characters allude.

Thwarting and delaying the confirmation of our knowledge leads to a consciousness of the play's form, the medium of theatre, and a more general question about the relation between medium and convention. In enacting the indirection of Eliot's mermaids or Blanchot's sirens, *Betrayal* relies in part on a metacinematic rearrangement of chronology; the play utilizes a temporal flexibility analogous to cinema's code of flashback in an overtly Brechtian episodic context reminiscent of Godard's film *Masculin/Feminin*.[2] These filmic techniques, one enabled by cinema technology, the other already a transposition of a theatrical practice, engage an unconventional vision of theatre by enabling the illusion of an oedipal trajectory in the play's pieced-together chronology, while temporal dislocations frustrate the recognitions and certainty associated with the oedipal solution of a crime-solving identity. That *Betrayal* renders itself via techniques imported from cinema recasts the theatrical medium of *Betrayal* as self-reflexive, a consciousness paralleled by the characters' concern not with knowledge itself, but with knowing knowing. The technique of timing imported from cinema raises a consciousness about the method of theatrical timing precisely at the heart of the knowledge game the characters play. It is not what but when that concerns them, a when whose certainty is reflected in the revelation of when that constitutes the apparent organizing principle for the temporal disarrangement of the play's metacinematic structure.

Just as the chronological dislocations and the questionable relevance of *Betrayal*'s "facts" lead to an increased consciousness of the operations of the medium, so Duras's decoy of a presumably true-life crime leads to a recognition of the dynamic of desire and media that drives both plays and novel in her series of works centered around *L'Amante anglaise*. Commencing with the report of an "actual" murder, *Les Viaducs de la Seine-et-Oise*, the first play of the series, begins with an explanatory note to be read before the curtain rises: "In 1954 various human remains were discovered in goods trucks at different railway stations all over France. Biological analysis showed that all the pieces had once formed part of the same body. A reconstruction proving this was so was carried out in Bordeaux" (118). As the facts intimate, a married couple living with a deaf and dumb relative had murdered her, cut her body up into pieces and dropped them one by one into the open cars of trains that passed under a particular railway bridge in Eparney-sur-Orge in Seine-et-Oise. By tracing the routes of all the trains, the railway company was able to track their common intersection and so provide a clue about the location of the crime. The head of the body necessary to certify the corpse's identity was never recovered.

The play *L'Amante anglaise* begins with a similar explanatory note, this time presented by a tape recording at the beginning of the play. It recites: "On April 8, 1966 a piece of a human body was found in a railway truck in France" (87) and goes on to elaborate nearly the same facts as *Les Viaducs*. The different date and location of the crime, however, suggest that these introductory recitations are not a "true-life" story serving as the premise for a literary rendition, but rather that the introductory material constitutes a performative recitation of apparent facts. The preliminary announcements in both plays are parts of the plays themselves, frames of apparent authenticity—

"biological analysis," reconstructive proof—that provide a presumably solid factual base for both plays' quests for motives. Because we never think to suspect this masquerade of facts and so are fooled by the plays' manipulation of the relation between documentary reality and stage illusion, the prefaces serve as lures or decoys, giving the illusion of something that is not what it seems to be, but at the same time appearing to provide an answer, the "reality" that the plays merely adapt. The alluring facticity of the plays' prefaces creates both the illusion that such facts can be ascertained and the illusion that the truth of the facts is somehow crucial to an understanding of the dramatic artistry of the pieces. But just as looking for the real news story of the facts is a red herring, so we learn that putting together the dismembered pieces of human bodies does not solve a crime, locate identity, or provide a motive. The answer is someplace else, not in finding the head or discovering the motive of the murderer, but in the process of the search itself—in the desire to know that motivates the inquisitions and in knowing that the question that drives the search never mattered in the first place.

Pitting theatre against the illusions of a documentary reality draws attention to the theatricality of the plays but does not suggest that the theatre is more illusory or less reliable than the news. Instead, the plays' juxtaposition of the news version and Claire, the murderess's version of the murder story emphasizes the relation among medium, expression, and desire by revealing that no version is completely reliable or complete. Foregrounding the characters' consciousness of the untrustworthiness of language, the investigative method, even of the news media, the plays situate the substance of the drama not in a reenactment of the crime, nor even finally in any murder investigation, but rather, as in *Betrayal,* in the indirect examination of who knows what when and how. Focusing on the slippages, approximations, gaps, and misunderstandings by which knowing knowing is conveyed, the works' consciousness of the uneasy relation between fact and medium brings into question any reliance upon an original fact or text. The lack of media reliability is akin to the essential ambiguity of language within the works. As Pinter observes in his speech on writing for the theatre, "Language . . . is a highly ambiguous business. . . . You and I, the characters grow on a page, most of the time we're inexpressive, giving little away, unreliable, elusive, evasive, obstructive, unwilling. But it's out of these attributes that a language arises. A language I repeat, where under what is said, another thing is being said" ("Writing for the Theatre" 13–14).

Because relations among media reiterate the capricious relation between language and thought in Pinter's and Duras's work, rewriting from medium to medium contemplates the ambiguity of media and the irrelevance of the originary text, bringing the relations between texts in different media into question. This differs from the traditional assumptions of adaptation generally employed to understand the relation among works in different media which presume the primacy of an original version and its definable, iterable essence, and which separate medium from and subordinate it to meaning.[3] Focusing

on omissions, additions, and changes in narrative elements and their arrangement, adaptation studies measure the effects of alterations made in the transition to another medium and draw conclusions about textual infidelities and
subsequent shifts of substance. To see Pinter's and Duras's series of works as
adaptations requires the presumption of a single, definitive, original text whose
translation into subsequent works grapples with elements of media analogous
to the vagaries of a second language. But how can Pinter's and Duras's series
of works be regarded simply as adaptations when the central paradox of each
work brings the basic assumption of an adaptation study—the certainty of
initial content—into question?

Within this complex intermedial, intertextual tangle, the medium of theatre
already operates on an assumption of multiple, layered texts associated by
indirection rather than by any transparent or direct depiction of a founding
core. This theatrical reliance upon indirection has as much to do with a distrust
of language as it has to do with the conventions of theatre as a medium that
relies upon the maintenance of two texts—a manifest discourse and a hidden
but discernible subtext—whose tense relation tends to result in a decodable
indirection. Both *Betrayal* and *Les Viaducs* reverse and draw attention to the
typical dramatic relation between latent and manifest texts by appearing to
present the latent text at the beginning of the play. Despite the revelation of
this normally covert latent core, the plays continue to treat it indirectly as the
anticipated "answer" to which the plays' clues lead. But unlike many post-
Ibsenian plays, the manifest dialogue does not flirt with the substance of this
latent subtext at all, but rather is preoccupied with knowledge or the question
of others' knowledge of it. In *Betrayal* and *Les Viaducs,* "The end is in the
beginning," as *Endgame*'s Hamm quips, and yet they continue, doubling the
alluring "factual" core into the facts and the play of knowing facts.

Because of the way Pinter's and Duras's texts play with the separability of
manifest and multiple latent texts, these works present at least three situations:
the original "facts," knowledge of the facts, and knowlege of the knowledge,
which all exist in a differing relation to the assumption of an underlying reality
on the one hand and to the media in which facts are expressed on the other.
The normally latent original facts aligned with an illusion of an underlying
reality turn out to be nearly irrelevant, enacting an ironical lure that instigates
the search for the knowledge of facts comprising the second latent core or
text that coexists with the first, but which is more aligned with a consciousness
of the relation of knowing and expressing. This second text draws attention
to the various media—language, image, theatre—by which the facts can be
only indirectly conveyed. The characters' knowledge of the facts in relation
to the plays' positioning of those facts as an illusory (but spectacularly certain)
knowledge—the relation between two latent texts—constitutes an alluring dramatic text that parallels and leads to the plays' third text of knowing knowing.
This third situation, allied as it is to a media consciousness, has always been
the manifest text; but its subtext, as it turns out, has always been someplace
else, not in the first two latent texts fixed to the facts, but in the characters'

motives and desires that ultimately found the power relations among them. The shift of subtext from fact to desire exposes the complex triangulated relationship between knowledge and desire these plays illustrate; knowledge and the desire for knowledge result in a knowledge of desire that also functions simultaneously as a metatheatrical comment on the theatrical habit of reading through the surface—a comment on the quest of the viewer.

Consisting of the complex interplay of layered texts, the plays suggest that similarly complex constructions exist among the works in different media. The core of facts continues to circulate, as does the construction of the lure— knowledge is not what it seems to be—as the enactment of the relation among facts, knowledge, and expression central to the plays. This germ of fact and lure along with the works' metatheatrical consciousness already comprise three different referents for the second work. Since the first text as a complete play in itself constitutes yet a fourth different referent, works subsequent to the first can never merely adapt either the germ of the first work or the work itself, but must negotiate subject matter, treatment, their interrelation, and the complete text along with the questions of media raised by the texts' metatheatrical (and in the case of *Betrayal*, metacinematic) gestures. Instead of merely adapting one work into another, the second text recombines and essentially rewrites or omits a surplus of referential material that demands a reenvisionment rather than a translation.

The works' central consciousness of medium multiplies the difficulties of adaptation, since the incommensurate terms of media cannot themselves be simply adapted one to the other just as facts cannot be simply expressed among characters. Because the terms of any medium comprise a system wherein specific practices perform certain functions only in (and because of their) relation to others, what appear to be isolated tactics—the use of an image, chronological arrangement—cannot be rendered in another medium without taking into account entire sets of structural relations. Like the system of relations present in language, but more complex, since any medium includes several systematically related media (language, image, sound), no single feature can be made the equivalent of a feature in another medium outside of the context of the medium's entire system. That media are systems means, for example, that an image on stage is not the same as an image in film; they occupy different positions and functions within their respective apparatuses. Shifting a stage image directly to film may appear to adapt a play since the elements are presented via an image in both, but such a shift actually situates the image in several completely different contexts, altering the stage image in immeasurable ways that are inherent to the sets of signifiers and structures embedded in the cinematic image and not present on stage. The relations among media (language, image) in different media (theatre, cinema) are also altered. The function of and the correlation of word and image in theatre is transformed (and also greatly limited, as Duras muses) in cinema with its runaway asynchronicity and its static inscription of ideologically charged viewer-image relations not present in the same form in the theatre. Or while we might be tempted to claim that the relative importance of language and image is reversed from stage to screen, the differences between stage and cinema are much more complex, since language in cinema is mediated by a sound track, image is constructed, projected, and produced through the self-effacing structuration of the camera and lighting, attention is riveted, and the scenario fragmented in relation to a theatrical scene which is constructed within its own different, equally complex apparatus.

Instead of searching for a vocabulary of equivalents misleading in their superficiality, working from medium to medium means rewriting from the beginning and establishing a new relationship between works in terms of the different dynamic represented by a different medium. And insofar as Pinter's and Duras's works draw attention to media and the medium itself inflects and defines the relation of desire and knowledge of the core of these works, the core itself must change in another work in a different medium. This suggests that working from one medium to another is less like translation or adaptation, which both suggest a modification or adjustment, and more like a version of what poet Olga Broumas calls "a politics of transliteration": the continued attempt to transcribe experience in the face of the ineffable failure of language to do more than "fragment" or "mangle" (23–24). The problems resident to transliteration, such as a complete lack of equivalents, are complicated by systemic incompatibilities. Media are rendered in other media only by a systemic process wherein the radically different but superficially similar features of media are negotiated by means of a rearticulation of systemic relations that recreate in terms of a new system, producing a new text rather than another version of the first.

Because of its multiple and ambiguous references to the first work, this second new text also exists in a series which itself embodies the politics of the lure played out in the original text. Even though these works may be new works instead of adaptations, they exist in an intertextual web, as new works that are also derivative. The works themselves inspire intertextual reception: the film *Betrayal* makes reference in its opening credits to the play, and both series of works draw attention to their serial relation through the repetition of the titles and the listing and cross-referencing of works in editions.[4] The series' appearance of derivativeness reconstitutes a lure on the serial level. Seeing the relation among works in different media as a transliteration and rearticulation—a new writing, a restructuring—instead of an adaptation permits the thwarting of desire on a more universal plane. While this assumes that we see these works in a series, a view that the idea of each as an original work would oppose, the lure works precisely because among works we still tend to privilege and believe in originality—in the source that founds it all. The original facts or text, as in the individual works, are never the point though they may instigate the search and inspire desire. As in *Betrayal* and *Les Viaducs,* the ultimate irrelevance of the original text creates a dynamic dialogue among characters and media where the referent is always difference—differences in knowledge, differences in expressibility. In *Betrayal* this difference inheres in the theatrical offer of visual proof through time, of going back (forward) to the event itself. In Duras's works, this dialogue is worked into the texts' appeal to the supposed news story which automatically pits theatre against a discourse of "authenticity" represented by journalism and police reports.

Between the play *Betrayal* and the film *Betrayal* questions of media arise not as a result of the inherent incommensurability of media in a poor adaptation, but rather because the questions of theatre posed cinematically in the play are rearticulated and transliterated into questions of cinema posed theatrically in the film. The relation between a self-reflective medium and knowledge is missed if the film is regarded as a visual record of the play. Instead, Pinter's film, like the play, toys with the interrelation of media, exploring the strange incompatibilities between cinema and theatre. While cinema shares many of theatre's investments in the correlation of knowledge, vision, and power, the film *Betrayal* retains a maddeningly theatrical frustration of vision that exposes the cinematic investment in direct image as purveyor of knowledge and certainty. Retaining the play's rhythm and timing, whose rather slow, deliberate pace defies cinematic conventions of tempo, draws attention to the film's timing and order and also emphasizes the gaps in knowledge and the shifts in power created by the film's disordered episodes. And even though film provides the convention of flashback, *Betrayal*'s perverse reversals draw attention to the convention, which remains metacinematic and self-conscious.

The textual changes between play and film pivot around the relation of vision and certainty the play frustrates. The play's transliteration into film seems to compel more visual confirmations of "fact," but like the language of the play, the images of the film again provide only decoys of knowledge. This is particularly true of the film's opening scene, an added view of domestic violence between Robert and Emma that seems to make explicit the deterioration of their relationship and whose presence at the opening of the film seems to make certain the ultimate effects of the initial betrayal. The film also adds a scene of Emma crying in her car after the breakup of the affair with her husband's best friend Jerry in scene three. This crying seems to specify Emma's feelings about the end of the relationship, a reaction that is missing in her cool reacton to its end in the play. But while the explication of these added images seems to provide an answer created by the addition of pointed images at otherwise ambiguous moments, what the scene really does is provide ambiguous images in a place and in such a manner as to bespeak denouement and climax. Does the initial scene offer a cause for Robert's and Emma's strayings, or is it the brutal result of years of infidelity? Is Emma crying out of grief or relief? Though we may be lured by the apparent certainty of the beginning or of Emma's crying at that moment, the view of it really tells us no more than the play's omission of the image. What they do reveal, however, is our reliance on the image as producer of knowledge. The film in general seems more visually explicit than the play, though like the play's language, the film's images provide only the illusion of knowledge, and like the play, what we think we know we don't, while what we do know—that the calm march of images and sound is the betrayal of our desire for mastery—we don't know we know until after the film is over.

Marguerite Duras's group of works *Les Viaducs de la Seine-et-Oise* and the novel and play *L'Amante anglaise* carries this problem of desire, knowledge, and the medium a step further. More prone to a continual reworking of material, Duras's oeuvre focuses on the processes of transliteration and rearticulation themselves. *L'Amante anglaise,* a novel published eight years after *Les Viaducs,* is based on almost the same facts. The transliteration from theatre to prose takes place through the imagined medium of the tape recording made at the bar in *Les Viaducs* and evoked at the beginning of the novel: "Everything that's said here is recorded. A book is starting to come into existence about the crime at Viorne" (3). Both the change of location from Seine-et-Oise to Viorne and the use of the tape recorder and the process of transcription configure the transition from stage to novel while situating the novel in the uneasy space of mixed media—or making it a novel about the mixing of media, since the evocations of tape recordings, of course, really are a part of the novel. Self-conscious of its predecessor (if not the play, the idea of the event of the confession in the bar) represented by the tape, the novel inscribes the uneasy, if impossible relation between prose and stage, word and image. Remaining the somewhat awkward record of a conversation, *L'Amante anglaise* is a novel that expresses and draws attention to the difficulty of transposing live action to the page. It presents itself as transitional—as the making of a narrative through self-conscious questioning of the key witnesses to Claire's confession.

Facts already presented, the knowledge produced in the text, as in *Betrayal,* is not manifest, but rather exists in textual interstices: in the discernible differences between language and its referents, between question and answer, text and reader, text and text, medium and medium. But not even this indirection is the knowledge of the play; as in *Betrayal,* consciousness of indirection leads to a knowledge of desire as that relates to expression. The method of indirection is self-reflectively provided in the novel's opening matrix:

> I have here a copy of the recording that was made there that evening without your knowledge. It gives an exact rendering of all that was said, but it just repeats the words blindly, opaquely. So it's up to you to set the book in motion. And when what you've said has given that evening back its real depth and dimensions we can let the tape recite what it remembers and the reader can take your place.
> —How about the difference between what I know and what I say
> —what will you do about that?
> —That's the part of the book the reader has to supply for himself. It exists in any book. (3)

The dynamic of indirection defined as a quest for sense and meaning, the novel nonetheless depicts the investigator's search for meaning—for the location of the head of the corpse as yet undiscovered. But Claire and the investigator don't want the same thing—the battle for knowledge becomes a battle of desires. While he looks for facts, Claire "seethes" through the objects and forms that have composed her life, looking not for meaning, but for recognition from the investigator. While his search is for a knowledge of her actions, her desire is for his recognition of her desire. Desire and the desire for knowledge are at cross purposes, exposing both, their investments, and their construction in relation to convention.

The same character Claire occupies the play *L'Amante anglaise* published one year later. Retaining the tape recorder which adds another medium to the theatrical production, the play consists of the interrogator questioning first the husband, then Claire. Filtered through the discursive medium of the novel that performs a removed analysis (the analysis of an analysis) of the more immediate investigation in *Les Viaducs,* this version of the crime investigation focuses on the inevitable misrecognitions and catachreses that accompany transliterations, even Claire's attempts to recall her own experience. Still working at cross-purposes, the interrogator seeks answers while Claire cooperates only in the pursuit of something else—the something else which is there all along in her apparently evasive listing, nonresponsive answers, and self-contradictions. Claire's final line, "If I were you I'd listen" (140), points to the real core of the drama: the point is to listen rather than to search, to receive rather than to acquire, to understand rather than to define. Consciousness of the medium here leads to a consciousness of a continual coexistence of media that reiterates the politics of the lure among competing senses. The medium itself has been elsewhere all along—in the ear instead of the eye. The transliteration from *Les Viaducs* to *L'Amante anglaise* has resulted in a greater consciousness of the relations among media produced by an increasingly greater decentering of the facts, less and less certainty, a greater consciousness of the decoy of knowledge, and finally a consciousness of the decoyness of the decoy itself as represented by the use of the tape recording and the interrogator's quest for the head.

Adaptation is never that: it is always a systemic new writing in reference to multiple preceding texts. In the works of Pinter and Duras, transliteration and rearticulation instead of adaptation become a recognition of the dynamic of desire at the heart of both, a desire premised upon the relation between the medium and the lure of the knowledge it might produce. But what is perhaps most important is the intrinsic recognition of each medium's intermediary context. No longer separable modes, media refer to other media both as media and as a means of defining their own processes. What this suggests is an end to the idea of discrete media and to generic categories of expression. Authors like Pinter and Duras, who habitually work among several media— stage, cinema, video—no longer confine themselves to discrete media, but rather work through several at once, intermingling and exploring how media and ideas change in relation to one another. As the work of both Pinter and Duras demonstrates, the art of the latter half of the twentieth century extends the ambiguity of language to media, questions knowledge and mastery, and enacts the instability of constantly transliterating expression.

In approaching both the necessity and the difficulties of transliteration, both authors enact the jolt of what Broumas calls "the suddenly possible shifts of meaning" (24), as the works layer knowledge and process and as process becomes the very knowledge it seeks. And in the interplay of desire, knowledge, and the ambivalent possibilities of transliteration, the works are like Broumas's "amnesiacs in a ward on fire" (24). With the language of no language and the memory of nothing significant, the very act of speaking becomes the knowledge that both saves and condemns them. But what they know and we don't is that even thinking we know this is itself beside the point. As Robert says in scene 2, the final chronological scene of *Betrayal,* "You don't seem to understand. You don't seem to understand that I don't give a shit about any of this" (41).

Notes

1. Several excellent articles discuss the relation between form, knowledge, and desire, including Alice Rayner, "Harold Pinter: Narrative and Presence," *Theatre Journal* 40.4 (1988): 482–97; Katherine H. Burkman, "Harold Pinter's 'Betrayal': Life Before Death—and After," *Theatre Journal* 34.4 (1982): 505–18; and Silvio Gaggi, "Pinter's *Betrayal:* Problems of Language or Grand Metatheatre?" *Theatre Journal* 33.4 (December 1981): 502–16.

2. In "The Love Song of J. Alfred Prufrock," T. S. Eliot refers to the indirection of the mermaids' song: "I have heard the mermaids singing each to each./ I do not think that they will sing to me." Maurice Blanchot uses the sirens as a figure of the difference between experience and expression in *Le Livre à venir* (Paris: Gallimard, 1959). Jean-Luc Godard's *Masculin/feminin* (1966) contains fifteen separate episodes in a conscious exploration of the virtues of Brecht's idea that "the episodes must not succeed one another indistinguishably but must give us a chance to interpose our judgment. . . . The parts of the story have to be carefully set off one against another by giving each its own structure as a play within the play" (from "A Short Organum for the Theatre," in *Brecht on Theatre,* ed. and trans. John Willett [New York: Hill and Wang, 1964], 201). See also Enoch Brater's analysis of *Betrayal's* cinematic qualities in "Cinematic Fidelity and the Forms of Pinter's *Betrayal,*" *Modern Drama* 24 (1981): 503–13.

3. Many "adaptation" studies examine the relation between a traditionally "literary" work and a film, assuming the first to be the "real" version and the film a way of reproducing that version. This approach is valuable in discerning what happens to literary texts when they are filmed as well as in studying the techniques of adaptation, particularly when the adapter is someone other than the author of the original work.

4. Duras's publishers have a habit of listing all of her published works in the later editions regardless of publisher. According to Madeleine Cottenet-Hage and Robert Kolker, Duras "affirms the arbitrariness of the link between signified and signifier— meaning and the sounds and images that create meaning—but goes somewhat further. She denies the 'natural' association between images and between sound and image in a film and takes the notion of asynchronicity further than had previously been imagined" ("The Cinema of Duras in Search of an Ideal Image," *The French Review* 63.1 [1989]: 89).

EIGHT

Image and Attention in Harold Pinter

Alice Rayner

O but they say the tongues of dying men
enforce attention like deep harmony . . .
More are men's ends mark'd than their lives before.
The setting sun, and music at the close,
As the last taste of sweets, is sweetest last,
Writ in remembrance more than things long past.

—Richard II, II.i.3–14

The Duke of York has just advised Old John of Gaunt not to waste his breath giving counsel to the profligate, wastrel king, Richard. Gaunt's response, however, insists that words in the final moments of life and breath are functionally more resonant than words "long past" precisely because they are the last. In this exchange, he suggests that a motive for such final speeches is to "enforce attention." If I extract that motive from Gaunt it might well describe the conditions of Harold Pinter's work where the tension between narrative and silence exhibits a like desire to "enforce attention." There is a significant difference, however, between Gaunt's means for calling attention and Pinter's, and that difference measures the shift away from a traditional narrative hermeneutic in which the "end" generates both the desire to "know" and the satisfaction of that desire. Roland Barthes distinguishes the function of a "hermeneutic code" in narrative as a structuring of an enigma such that an end (or solution) is both desired and delayed (S/Z 75). The resistance to that form of desire and its satisfactions indicates a profound dissatisfaction with the equation of desire and death in those narrative conventions and shifts attention from the end to the ongoing present. In Pinter, such dissatisfaction is often manifest as an inarticulate anxiety raised both between characters and between a play and its audience.

Pinter invokes the desire and uses delay, but he also refuses to offer any solution to the enigma. Where Gaunt is trying to correct the profligate habits of Richard by asking him to attend to death, Pinter seems to be trying to correct an audience's profligate desires for meaning through closure. Attention, in Pinter, is a way of describing what Heidegger called "dwelling" in the sense that it defies the closure upon singular meaning and replaces it with openness to multiple significations in process where being *is* becoming.

Pinter's various techniques for subverting narrative trajectories radically alter the epistemological forms for the kind of meanings that come from narrative and its attendant shaping of time, identity, and subjectivity. In other words, rather than an authorial coercion to engender and satisfy a desire for the end, Pinter's techniques might be described motivationally as a desire to create attention by which the present of the theatrical time and space, the here and now of the theatrical moment, is made to resonate. I have suggested elsewhere that the differences are aligned in most of Pinter's work by gender distinction. The male narrative is consistently subverted and brought to silence by the female presence that demands attention (493). But within those sexual politics, and in that resonance, resides the further tension between the finality of inscription and the ongoingness of enactment that is itself at the foundation of a tension between the written artifact and the theatrical performance. The result is an embodiment of the theatrical contradiction between a final, scripted form that creates a subject and the subjectivity that is in process of creating through the process of enacting. This embodiment further alters the form of causality that can represent an originating subject. It puts Pinter's plays in a radical form of play that is what Robert Schürmann names as an-archic (4). The interplay of characters thus becomes an alternation of modes between narrative drive and stasis which enables the complex act of making a play to appear.

In the final moments of Pinter's play *No Man's Land*, the character Hirst, sometime poet, essayist, and critic, says, "Let us change the subject. (*Pause*) For the last time. (*Pause*) What have I said" (91). Apparently, what he has said is what then happens. A certain panic sets in when he asks what it means. Foster replies: "It means you'll never change the subject again." And later: "If the subject is winter, for instance it'll be winter for ever . . . If the subject is winter, for example, spring will never come. . . . Summer will never come. . . . Snow will fall for ever because you've changed the subject. For the last time. . . . there is no possibility of changing the subject since the subject has now been changed" (92–93). And Spooner sums up what has happened: "You are in no man's land. Which never moves, which never changes, which never grows older, but which remains forever, icy and silent" (95).

The closing moments of the play seem to articulate and to enact the issues and problems connected with writing itself. In the briefest formulation those issues concern the status of the completed artifact—the play, the novel, the critical essay—in relation to both meaning and ongoing experience. I want to look at the closing moments of *No Man's Land* as an instance of that concern as it appears in many places through Pinter's work of the seventies and early eighties.

The completion of a piece of writing confers upon that piece the status of a work. That workly status then departs from the ongoing subjectivity of its writer who in process can keep changing the subject, so to speak, and keep the process of forming and articulating as a process. In a completed form, subjectivity becomes a subject that has changed in some degree for the last time. That this is a cause for some panic is evidenced in Hirst's fearful query, "What have I said?"—a fear manifest by anyone who both wants to finish the work of writing and is also unwilling to achieve closure and abandon the work to the world. In both saying and writing, the speaker/writer maintains an open, conditional process that is available to change as the process can indeed span winter, spring, summer, and fall. In finished form, the artifact resists the temporal force of "nature" suggested here by the seasonal changes. In finishing the story or the essay, and especially in constructing a narrative that appears to create coherence between beginning and ending, the speaker/writer surrenders the openness of subjectivity to closure of an object. As Paul Hernadi put it, "Discourse is an instance of doing and a thing done . . . a process of making and a thing made" (750).[1] Pinter dramatizes the moment at which the difference between the making and the made is perceived.

In the tableau at the end of *No Man's Land* an appalling anxiety inhabits the moment of the subject that will not change. The ongoingness of the play itself stops in an arrested image, but it is an image that calls for a final toast. Hirst says, "I'll drink to that" (95). The response to the closure, in other words, is a salute of recognition: a recognition not of meaning or coherence, but of the work itself, of the anxiety it raises, and perhaps even of the work as a thing made, whose status as a product or a production deserves honor, if not exactly understanding.

A similar tension occurs consistently at what Sheila Rabillard has called the level of "local ordering" in Pinter's plays. This local ordering of dramatic structure occurs by the formalistic means of "mathematical or perhaps syntactical and rhetorical repetitions, series, permutations, and combinations" (41). But that local ordering which she called a technique of dramaturgy in general can also be seen as Pinter's thematic obsession that describes the play of power between inscription and enactment and the particular alignment with gendered power play. Rabillard, for example, cites this speech by Kate in *Old Times:*

> I remember you lying dead. You didn't know I was watching you. Your face was dirty. You lay dead, your face scrawled with dirt, all kinds of earnest inscriptions, but unblotted, so that they had run, all over your face, down to your throat. (67–68)

Where Rabillard is interested in the permutations of exclusion in the two-to-one odds, I am concerned with how this speech correlates memory and the objectification of a human object through "watching," and the foul or filthy aspect of inscription with the force of Kate's speech act itself. The referentiality is "unverifiable" because it is embedded in a creation of memory whose truth cannot be recovered. That truth is only asserted through Kate's speech, such that its truth becomes not its reference but the force of the statement to overpower Anna (and Deeley) in the present. The "written record" suggested by those "earnest inscriptions" would conventionally be the artifact that would assure some persistent record, some document of authority. But Kate's speech has the power to make those inscriptions "run" down the face to the throat. Her speech enacts the power of speech as a here and now phenomenon to muddy the clarity and permanence of earnest inscription. Memory itself turns the past into an image in an act similar to the act of making a fictional artifact, but the speech act in the present tense has a "muddying," disruptive effect that has force with no reference.

As in so many of Pinter's works, it is difficult if not impossible to trace a narrative plot in terms of the relation between the initial moments and the closure. The so-called narrative desire that propels events toward conclusion is delayed if not subverted at every moment. The who, what, why, when, and where that generate a constructed understanding of acts and motives in time and space are undermined at virtually every opportunity. Are the four characters in *No Man's Land* poets, servants, or cricket players? Who serves whom; who is trapped by whom? Who had whose wife? Is this a reunion of old Oxford chums or a chance meeting on Hampstead Heath? What Pinter appears to do in *No Man's Land* is to resist, at every opportunity, the narrative coherence of agent and act. While giving the exchanges between characters the quality of a normative social behavior, he sends them and the audience through the equivalent of the Bolsover Street labyrinth described by Briggs: "easy enough to get into. The only trouble was that, once in, you couldn't get out" (120). The image of the labyrinth is one of Pinter's favorites, most recently shown in the film *The Comfort of Strangers,* where the two characters, Colin and Mary, get lost and wander in the back alleys of Venice looking for a place to eat before they are "rescued" by the stranger who is following them. The disorientation of following a path up dead ends and blind alleys becomes a visual correlate for the audience trying to follow Pinter's narrative paths to meaning. And like the ominous stranger, Robert, the playwright appears to be following as much as he appears to be herding and directing the way.

Pinter extends the dynamic of textual eroticism in the narrative desire for conclusion and protracts what Roland Barthes called the dilatory space (*S/Z,* 75), in which delay and indeterminacy serve to generate desire but not conclude it.[2] The effect of this subversion of a solution and labyrinthine exploration has many possible implications. On the one hand, it would be possible to say that Pinter is pointing at the very indeterminacy that belongs to the real as opposed to the fictional. In this measure, he is a "realistic" playwright who demonstrates that the unknown and unnameable desire operates within and alongside the mundane. At the same time, on the other hand, one could say he is pointing at the element of "agon" that occurs in the daily exchanges of politesse, most particularly in British rhetorical habits, where gamesmanship and one-upmanship are a way of both life and speech. Or in the terms he will never live down, that there is a "weasel under the cocktail cabinet." The implication I want to focus on, however, is not the comedy of menace or the model of indeterminacy or even the erotics of the text, but the narrative subversions that occur because of Pinter's self-conscious awareness of his own interventions in the work.

In *The Comfort of Strangers* narrative itself makes an appearance as an aspect of the violence and erotic demand of the stranger. There is a voice-over at the opening of the film that begins, "My father was a very big man. All his life he wore a moustache. When it turned grey he used a little brush to keep it black, such as ladies use for their eyes. Mascara" (3). The voice-over has no immediate relation to the scene. Later, after Robert takes Colin and Mary to his restaurant, where there is no food, and plies them with wine, he tells his story, which again begins, "My father was a very big man. All his life he wore a moustache . . . " (15) and ends with his humiliating description of having been forced by his sister to defecate in his father's study. In the final image of the film, after he has killed Colin and been arrested by the police, Robert speaks to the police: "My father was a very big man. All his life he wore a moustache . . . " (51). Robert's narrative is not only highlighted as a self-conscious device in the film, it becomes a manifestation of his "psychosis" or whatever clinical term one might apply. The narrative is in some sense identical to the brutal, obsessive eroticism between Robert and his wife Caroline and their fascination with and ultimate murder of Colin. The narrative act engulfs the relative innocence of Colin and Mary, who have become lost in the back streets of the Venetian labyrinth and is shown in some degree to be the instrument of brutality.

The idea of the brutality of narrative closure derives from the sense that narrative form is an intervention upon the "innocence" of experience. But in Barthes's terms, again, that intervention is an aspect of an "Oedipal" desire "to denude, to know, to learn the origin and the end" (*The Pleasure of the Text* 10). *No Man's Land* can be seen as a representation of the self-consciousness of the poet who makes an object and thereby closes the subject. Spooner is constantly articulating himself as such a poet. The play itself, however, transfers the temporal trajectory of narrative that has beginning and end into the spatial and atemporal image. The play thereby duplicates the transformation from process to object, from subjectivity to subject. The temporal unfolding of events through time tends to circle back upon itself so that the unfolding appears to present a refolding and appears at the end of the play as a tableau (cf. *Homecoming, Caretaker, Old Times*). Closure thus arrives not as an aspect of coherence between beginning and end but as an arrested image in the theatrical space. It is manifest by Pinter's penchant for the final tableau as a conclusion without closure.

This transformation from process to object occurs in enough of Pinter's plays and screenplays to appear as an identifiable aspect of his work. It says something not only about Pinter's interests but about how the friction between temporal and spatial forms can identify (1) differences in forms of knowledge and (2) the dynamics of creating those forms as a three-way negotiation among a playwright or screenwriter-author, an audience-reader, and the desires generated by means of a text.

The form of knowledge presented by a narrative construction of events presumes that it is possible to know both when an event begins and when it ends. That narrative form shapes an equation between linear time, meaning, and knowledge. It creates an artifact out of experience. In Pinter's plays, a reverse process seems to occur: that is, he creates an experience out of an artifact. Pinter pays explicit attention to failed narratives, to desiccated forms of knowledge, and to temporal disorientation as his characters seek to undermine each others' narratives. In place of narrative coherence, he forces his characters and his audiences to focus on spatial rather than temporal constructions of meaning.

In the final moments in *No Man's Land* the matrix or space of the event disorders the equation between form, time, and meaning. Hirst's imaginary narrative or image of a past conflicts with the assertion by the other characters that "the subject has changed for the last time," leading to Spooner's verbal assertion of an atemporal space and a final silence. The dominance of the space over the narrative forces the audience/critic's attention toward the qualities in the performance of the present. The consequent form for experience, asserted by the characters and felt by the audience, might thus best be characterized not as "knowledge" of the play's meaning but as "knowing," the gerundive that indicates knowledge is simultaneously a thing and an act derived from the simultaneity of space. Grammatically speaking, the gerund is a verbal noun that is used as a noun (i.e. an object) but maintains certain characteristics of the verb (i.e. action, motion, and time). Significance thus occurs as a participatory sense of presence—of being in the same space at the same time—a space that is loaded with a perceptible but unnameable charge. Time is in some sense spatialized as an event, which nevertheless resists reification and makes the final silence of *No Man's Land* not an empty stasis but an alternative form for meaning that has the dual characteristics of action and thing.

That alternative form, however, leads to the questions that have plagued Pinter. At first it was "What do the characters mean by what they say?"; then it was "What do you mean by these characters?" The very openness of the ending, in other words, opens a space to ask questions not just of the work but of the author.

In a discussion of Samuel Beckett, St. John Butler says, "While there are kites and cars, pubs and prostitutes to think about we think about them, but where there is nothing but mud or greyness or breath to think about we are rapidly thrown back to the conceiving mind, the creator" (184). Now the difficulty with Pinter is that he has given us pubs and prostitutes to think about in many of his plays. The realistic scenes of the plays tend to put focus on the representations rather than on the representer and to deflect attention from the producer to the product. But the very indeterminacy of the open endings in the context of social relations puts authorial intervention if not authorial intent into relief.

In Pinter's later work, and perhaps most explicitly in several screenplays, he becomes more and more of a metadramatist, who illustrates the fact of intervention and the act of making. In the films, especially *The Proust Screenplay,*

The Last Tycoon, and *The French Lieutenant's Woman,* the act of the author's intervention in the dramatic structure is obvious. In *Betrayal,* too, the conspicuous artifice of a narrative that proceeds backward in time as the play develops forward exaggerates both narrative desire for cause/effect coherence and the authorial power to provoke that desire. In all of these works, conspicuous intervention of the maker modifies the perception of the story being told. That process of making furthermore becomes the "subject" of the work: the problem then focuses on how the making of the work, in which the things said and done are simultaneously the thing made, closes the work, highlights its nature as a "made," not a discovered object. What occurs is the "slippage" between the work and the act of making it. The hiatus itself becomes the subject. In the hiatus meanings proliferate, desires engage and disengage, and the knowable itself becomes fluid. In film particularly, images both entrap and release, consume and regurgitate all the aspects of the making of images: the flow of time, the dynamics of desire to possess and release, the desire to complete and to continue. The fluidity of images on the screen is difficult to create on the stage, though Pinter's plays come close. But it is that very quality that defines the technology of power that belongs to the film makers and marks their intervention.

One of the clearest images for this oscillation appears in *The French Lieutenant's Woman.* Jeremy Irons, portraying an amateur paleontologist, is *"examining a fossil"* (1). He is scraping at it, and gradually the shape of a chambered nautilus appears. What is impossible to determine visually, however, is whether he is sculpting it or simply uncovering it. I like to think of this image as Pinter's own self-consciousness, particularly when he is adapting the work of other authors to the screen. For he is doing both: making for the first time and uncovering something that is already there. The ambiguity of the image contains the ambiguity of the process of making art.

Both *The Last Tycoon* and *The French Lieutenant's Woman* intercut images of films "made" and the film being made, of actors and their characters, with the result that the next step is implicated: the very characters we are watching are also being made into images by the same process by which the film within the film is made. This interplay in fact becomes the "subject" of *The Last Tycoon,*[3] in which we see Robert DeNiro as Monroe Stahr, captivated by the real woman who is the image of his dead wife, who was a movie star herself. Stahr's desire for the real woman—his desire to recover the real—is what could be called an occluded desire for an image that was his wife. He attempts to recapture the real, which has become an image, in terms of an image that is itself a constructed image. In a moment of filmic self-consciousness, Stahr berates a screenwriter for "writing his own fantasies." He says, "You've distorted the girl. By distorting the girl you've distorted the story. . . . I'm not interested in your fantasies. . . . You've given her a secret life. She doesn't have a secret life. You've made her a melancholic. She's not a melancholic." When the writer asks how he knows, he says, "because I paid $50,000 bucks for that book and because that's the way I see it. If I want a Eugene O'Neill play

I'll buy one. The girl stands for health, vitality, love. You've made her a whore." When the writer asks how he wants the girl, he replies, "Perfect." And of course, this perfect girl is exactly who appears to remind Stahr of his wife. The first shot of her is atop the studio prop of a gold head of a generic Indian-looking goddess, floating down the waters of the flooded sound stage. The actress looks somewhat like a Botticelli Venus on the half-shell. As it turns out, she does have a secret life, she is vaguely melancholic, she briefly does act like a whore, and she finally marries and disappears from the film and his life. She was perfect.

In the same film, a studio tour guide, played by John Carradine, explains to a group of young women how earthquakes are produced. A short time later, there is indeed an earthquake in the film which as part of the narrative instigates the flood on the sound stage where Stahr first sees the young woman who reminds him of his wife. The seduction of narrative is such that I must confess it required two viewings for me to recognize the duplication and to become conscious that the earthquake which served the narrative was indeed filmed with all the techniques that are described by the tour guide. In another instance, Stahr is explaining the making of images to a writer, played by Donald Pleasance, who complains that his work is being "buggered" by the screenwriter. Stahr enacts an elaborate scenario which the film later reenacts. It supplies the reenactment with the characters of Stahr's own story. The further irony is that for both the bottom line is the nickel that the audience pays for the movie. When the writer asks Stahr what his little enactment means, he says, "I don't know, I just make pictures." In the final shot of the film, having lost both the girl and his job, Stahr walks into the black space of a sound stage. Instead of the camera fading out the image, in other words, the character walks into a blackout in a final conflation of a narrative in which agents appear to enact their own willful deeds and the image which spatializes events through the technology of the camera.

The makers of the movie, who include the writer, Fitzgerald, the screenwriter, Pinter, the director, Kazan, the actors, DeNiro, Mitchum, Pleasance, Milland, Nicholson, the unknown girl who remains unknown, even the cameo by Angelica Huston, the unseen technicians and cameramen, all are seen to intervene in the temporal development of the story. At the same time, they create a product. And that product is an economic object that is the result of those interventions. You pay $50,000 for a story and charge a nickel for admission. The meaning is indeterminate because they just make pictures. It is a product in which the subject has changed for the last time: the film that "never moves, which never changes, which never grows older, but which remains forever, icy and silent." The writer, like the Donald Pleasance character, wants to control his meanings but the images resist such control. At the same time, however, they exhibit the absolute control of the technicians who determine the image. The fact that the screenplay is based on Fitzgerald's unfinished novel further precludes any ability to refer to an authoritative closure, making the film an instance of a kind of "feedback loop" that feeds on its own incompleteness and multiple creators. As in Fitzgerald's novel,[4] the filmic narrative cannot be confirmed or denied, cannot be verified as a truth except in terms of the truth of the image: that it is there; that it has emotional force; that it commands our attention and our desires; that it has been produced as a work by the workings of its makers. The status of the work as a work means that within that limited field, as Foster says of Hirst, "nothing else will happen forever. You'll simply be sitting here forever" (152).

At the point where the narrative is disrupted, the image appears and enforces attention. Unlike the writer who wants control of meaning and significance, the image maker allows the indeterminacy to persist in the images. The subject that changes for the last time is the subject of making, not the object. What we "know" as viewers is only the fact that it was made. We come thereby to know what it is to make something and be caught up in the desires it creates as well. In the films *The Last Tycoon* and *The French Lieutenant's Woman* an audience sees backstage: it is in on the production and is both receptor and voyeur of the processes of making. The work is thus, as in *The French Lieutenant's Woman*, "archaeological" by layering the subject and objects of perception. It is not sequential, not referential, but a compression of accidental discoveries, poor memory, and incomplete knowledge of significance. Yet by attending to it, an audience is forced to acknowledge the presence and force of the work in the world, forced to acknowledge, as Gaunt would have Richard do, its own limitations and to attend to how desires are generated.

Notes

1. The context for Hernadi's statement is more complex than this quotation indicates. He is making a case that links discourse to "action, creation, and signification." "Whenever we 'say' something—whether in speech, in writing, or in silent deliberation—we thereby do, make, and mean something at the same time" (749). My notion of the artifact is related to his idea of "writing" which, he notes "is primarily making rather than doing not only because it results in lasting physical objects (say, black marks on white paper) but, more important, because it enables speech and thought to remain effective beyond the scenes of their initial occurrence" (751). In the dramatic world of action, the text is "made" and the material production is an instance of "done." Both elements, in my view, "have the potential of removing discourse from the writer's subjective mind and from his or her intersubjective lifeworld" (753) but are also available to further interpretation. Pinter, in *No Man's Land*, seems to look at the issue from the position of the subjectivity which is appalled by experiencing the said and done as irrevocable.

2. In outlining his terms for the "hermeneutic code," Barthes says, "just as rhyme (notably) structures the poem according to the expectation and desire for recurrence, so the hermeneutic terms structure the enigma according to the expectation and desire for its solution. . . . between question and answer there is a whole set of stoppages:

between question and answer there is a whole dilatory area whose emblem might be named "reticence," the rhetorical figure which interrupts the sentence, suspends it, turns it aside. . . . Expectation thus becomes the basic condition for truth: truth, these narratives tell us, is what is *at the end* of expectation. . . . To narrate (in the classic fashion) is to raise the question as if it were a subject which one delays predicating; and when the predicate (truth) arrives, the sentence, the narrative, are over, the world is adjectivized (after we had feared it would not be)" (*S/Z* 75–76).

3. I wish to thank David Saltz for reminding me of this film and its appropriateness to my topic. I have relied on the videotaped version of the film. For her discussion of the film, however, Joanne Klein used a copy of the shooting script made available to her by the American Film Institute.

4. In Klein's chapter on *The Last Tycoon* she points out: "The preeminence of the imagination and illusion, as a corollary to this condition [in which "choices, decisions, recountings, must transpire without the facts"] also forms a major theme in the novel. . . . The very backdrop of the movie business supplies a tension between fact and fiction that mirrors the self-recriminations of the narrator" (131).

In Fitzgerald's novel, the narrator is Cecilia Brady, daughter of the head of the studio, who, as Klein points out, "must frequently admit her penchant for fantasy in order to excuse accounts of which she could have no conceivable knowledge" (130). The self-consciousness of the narrator's position as fabricator and failure marks the modernism of both Fitzgerald and Pinter and twentieth century formalist studies of narrative deriving from Roman Jakobson and Victor Shklovsky.

Pinter and the Ethos of Minimalism

Jon Erickson

In 1967 Michael Fried, a follower of the formalist art critic Clement Greenberg, published an essay, "Art and Objecthood," in *Artforum* magazine, attacking the new art movement known as minimalism. Fried, a defender of the high modernist idea that each particular art seeks to locate and manifest its most essential nature, saw the progress of both painting and sculpture (as distinct genres within modernism) as movements of gradual reduction to their essences. This is most clearly seen when one looks at the essay in the light of his later book, *Absorption and Theatricality: Painting and the Beholder in the Age of Diderot.* In the book he begins to trace a progression originating in the emerging autonomy of the easel painting in the eighteenth century toward the fundamental and unique characteristics of modern painting as a pure art form. They consist of a unity of content and form such that the entirety of the painting could be taken in at a glance (instantaneity, "alloverness"); a flatness that reinforces the painting's meaning as a picture, and not an object; and finally, in its utter integrity, an autonomous existence that registered an indifference to the viewer. But what was most important about all these elements to Fried was the experience they were supposed to induce in the viewer, what he called "absorption," or self-forgetting, in an experience that united the beholder and the painting. Minimalism attempted to defeat that relation and thus provoked Fried's criticism of it.

At the time of the essay the painters championed by Fried were known as "postpainterly abstractionists," since they rejected the thick painting methods of abstract expressionism, preferring to stain unsized canvases. Their styles were varied although they all attained a flat, pictorial "alloverness" in their work: Paul Jenkins poured his paint in veils across canvases, Morris Louis painted spectral stripes across the width, Kenneth Noland made large circular targets and chevrons, and Jules Olitsky sprayed fine mists across the entire picture plane.

What upset Fried about minimalist (or what he called "Literalist") art is that (1) it disrupted the distinction between sculpture and painting, being a category that shared characteristics of both, (2) due to their scale and spatial imposition upon the viewer, minimal objects disrupted the absorptive quality of the experience of painting and added a third element: situation or context, which made the viewer's experience of the work depend upon his/her physical position relative to it, and (3) finally, the emphasis on context, in separating the viewer as subject from the artwork as object, created an estrangement, an alienating theatrical consciousness that made the viewer aware of his or her participation in the perceptual process. In other words, the artwork lost its autonomous existence as soon as its meaning relied upon the relative positioning of the viewer, creating an ambiguous or indeterminate contingency of value threatening to the modernist autonomy of either subject or object. Fried would say that "the concepts of quality and value . . . are meaningful . . . only with the individual arts. What lies between the arts is theatre" ("Art and Objecthood" 142) and that "Art degenerates as it approaches the condition of theatre" (141).

This "theatrical" art that Fried derided had an anonymous, industrial, architectural look. Donald Judd arranged identical galvanized aluminum boxes along the wall vertically and horizontally. Tony Smith made a blank six-foot cube called "Die" which prevented the average-sized viewer from seeing the top. Robert Morris constructed three large identical right-angled plywood boxes called "L-Beams," whose shapes were understood according to whether they were placed on their ends (forming an upright triangle relative to the floor), on one side (forming an "L"), or flat on their sides. Rosalind Krauss had this to say about the meaning of the shape of the "L-Beams" being contingent upon placement:

> Morris seems to be saying, the "fact" of the objects' similarity belongs only to an ideal structure—an inner being that we cannot see. Their difference belongs to their exterior—to the point at which they surface into the public world of our experience. This "difference" is their sculptural meaning; and this meaning is dependent upon the connection of these shapes to the space of experience . . . Morris's work addresses itself to the meaning projected by our own bodies . . . He is suggesting that the meanings we make—and express through our bodies and our gestures—are fully dependent on the other beings to whom we make them and on whose vision of them we depend for them to make sense. He is suggesting that the picture of the self as a contained whole (transparent only to itself and the truths which it is capable of constituting) crumbles before the act of connecting with other selves and other minds. (267)

Strangely enough, the very concept of absorption that Fried uses he took from the theatre itself. In line with his idea of absorption, it is the "nature" of painting not directly to address, but effectively to ignore, the presence of the beholder. In the theatre, of course, this is the "fourth wall" effect of naturalism. In this sense the absorptive power of the dramatic is opposed to the self-assertive and declamatory nature of the theatrical. Fried seems to agree with Diderot in his assumption that what is theatrical is synonymous with that

L-Beams by Robert Morris © 1992 Robert Morris/ARS, N.Y.
Photo by Rudolph Burckhardt.

which is *false,* while what is absorbingly dramatic is synonymous with truth
(*Absorption and Theatricality* 100). In other words, he says that the dramatist
and painter should do their best to *"detheatricalize beholding* and so make
it once again a mode of access to truth and conviction." Just prior to this he
makes it clear that "the very condition of spectatordom stands indicted as
threatrical, a medium of dislocation and estrangement, rather than of absorption, sympathy and self-transcendence" (*Absorption and Theatricality* 104).

Against this argument it should be made clear that the dramatic presentation
of *anything* is founded upon a convention that is always already theatrical,
even if that theatricality is self-effacing. Therefore, seeing such dramatic absorption as a means of attaining *truth* (conviction is another matter), while
considering theatricality—something that admits the truth of its own falsity—
as basically *false,* is patently absurd. This is by now a familiar argument posed
by deconstruction as well as other theoretical positions against positivism,
problematizing the simple or univocal truth-value of representation. That ideological position had already been critiqued by Marx, and in modern theatre
by Brecht, although there has been a sneaking suspicion about it in theatre

at least since Shakespeare. What Fried can't accept is that the indifference of the art object to the spectator is a conceit already ideologically charged, in the same way that the rectangular frame or flatness of the picture plane is itself a conventional conceit signifying "painting." Where he sees a sign he wants an essence, and he is disturbed when that essence is broken down by its sign-value's reliance upon a contextualizing difference; to paraphrase Wittgenstein, "A sign's value is its use." It may seem odd that *where Fried locates truth and conviction is where self-effacing theatricality achieves the height of illusion.* Yet it is possible, in his diatribes against literality, that the truth he seeks is immutable and poetic, not contextually specific.

What has all this to do with Pinter? It began for me when, in rereading the play *Old Times,* Deeley's description (44) of his modular beds, or divans, as being "susceptible to any amount of permutation"—paradigmatic of the whole question of subjectivity in the play—reminded me of nothing so much as Robert Morris's L-Beams, whose shapes are all essentially the same, but whose meaning depends upon how they are positioned in space. From that point on, it became clearer to me that the entire play was founded upon a dialectic between absorption and theatricality, quite similar to Fried's argument with minimal art. To draw a larger conclusion, this represents an interface between the autonomous subjectivity and absorptive interaction of modernism with the contingent and relativistic construction of subjectivity in postmodernism.

Old Times is about a couple, Deeley and Kate, and the reunion in their country house with Anna, an old friend and roommate of Kate's. The reunion's mood is complicated by Deeley's memory of picking up a woman at a movie called *Odd Man Out,* which might have been Kate, and his staring up the skirt of a woman in a tavern, which might have been Anna. As the play progresses, however, remembered distinctions between the two women become indeterminate and one could be confused for the other. Indeed, toward the end of the play the originally extroverted nature of Anna and the highly introverted nature of Kate switch, so that Kate becomes more active and Anna more passive. Deeley may or may not figure in Anna's memory as a man she discovered one night with Kate in their apartment. When Anna and Kate reminisce about "old times" in their flat, the absorbing power of memory is so strong that time itself becomes indeterminate and seems actually to move from present to past events, excluding Deeley in the process.

The indeterminate nature of the three characters' memories results in a conflict of interpretation that alienates them one from another, even while evoking a desire for unity. Neither the characters nor the audience can know the real truth of the situation, which at any moment is always contingent upon the discursive *position* of each character. From the absorbing dimness of the beginning scene to the theatrical brightness of the last scene—which seems quite like an example of minimalist installation art—the dialectic proceeds apace, now affirming through absorption an integral unity of personality, now denying that integrity through the theatrical disruption of contextual reminders.

One of the most obvious examples is Anna's reference to Kate's personality as being "completely absorbed," floating from the bath, unconscious of anyone holding the towel for her (50). Kate herself, in her love of the country and dislike of the city, describes her dislike of "edges" and "harsh lines," the exception being when rain in the city blurs things such as the lights of the cars; it "blurs your eyes" (55). This seems to describe nothing so much as the absorptive experience one might get from the soft alloverness of a painting by Olitsky.

The question of absorption also evokes the possibility of seduction, as in the scene in which Deeley gazes up Anna's skirt. Even the term "gaze," remarked upon by Deeley as seldom used—this was before Laura Mulvey—contrasts with the less absorptive "look at," as in the song "Lovely to Look At, Delightful to Know" (22). Jean Baudrillard has remarked that it is only the object that can seduce.[1] In keeping with Fried's idea of the art object's indifference to the beholder as a prerequisite for absorption, Anna's seeming indifference, which Deeley interpreted as allowance, might be heard in her laconic "I was aware of your gaze, was I?" (47).

Theatricality as a self-conscious interruption of dramatic absorption in a narrative is nowhere more evident to the viewers of musicals than when the song emerges with only the slightest contextual provocation. Thus Anna and Deeley are united in their theatricality over against their chosen audience and subject of their song, "Lovely to Look At, Delightful to Know": Kate.

There are moments when theatricality and absorption occur at the same instant and reflect the distinct positions of the characters. Anna relates how, after returning home, she would tell Kate about her night out, in the dark:

> But of course it was never completely dark, what with the light from the gasfire or the light through the curtains, and what she didn't know was that, knowing her preference, I would choose a position in the room from which I could see her face, although she could not see mine. She could hear my voice only. And so she listened and I watched her listening. (62)

In this way, Kate in her own darkness, becomes absorbed in Anna's story, while Anna herself maintains the theatrical split consciousness of telling the story and watching Kate's reactions at the same time.

Absorption, for Fried, requires two elements: the beholder and the painting. Minimalist theatricality is always created by a disruptive third element—the awareness of the context of beholding. It is thus not fortuitous that there are three characters in the play. In any interaction between two of the characters the third character is always a reminder of the context of their interaction, whether in the present or the past. (This is true of other Pinter plays, such as *Betrayal* and *The Collection,* as well as crucial moments in *No Man's Land.*) The third character disrupts the integrity of any character's particular memory, proving it unreliable when seen from another position. Thus for any absorption to take place in an exchange between two characters, the third character has to disappear.

So when Anna and Deeley speak of Kate in the third person and past tense, Kate replies: "You talk of me as if I were dead," with the word "were" itself ambiguously caught between past tense and present subjunctive. When Anna and Kate shift into a conversation that seems to be taking place in their former shared flat, Deeley seems to disappear; when Anna asks Kate if she is hungry, they are in the space of "old times," while Deeley, still in the "real time" of the play, comically tries to insinuate himself into their privacy by asking "Hungry? After that casserole?" (40). In the end, when Kate speaks about her encounter with the man (Deeley) lying in, or on, Anna's bed, Deeley asks her who had slept in that bed before him and she replies, "no one. No one at all," which ends up excluding Anna as well (69).

Another way of making the third party disappear is to make him or her merge with, or be absorbed by, his or her opposite. Thus Anna is identified with Deeley when Kate imagines Anna dead with dirt on her face and then remembers preparing to make love to Deeley by putting dirt on *his* face (68–69). Kate and Anna merge in Deeley's memory of the woman in the Wayfarer's Tavern (65). For Anna, Kate and Deeley merge in the act of looking down at her, one "shyly poised" in the present (31), the other in the past, ominously bending over her bed (28). If one takes this perspectivalism far enough, the argument could even be made that at any moment two of the characters could be seen as split projections of one character's mind: that what goes on in the play is happening only in the mind of Kate, Anna, or Deeley—although it is indeterminate as to whose mind it is.

This reading would appear to make the play thoroughly postmodern. The ethos of theatricality, aware of its own artificial, "arbitrary," and contingent nature, is a postmodern mode of understanding. It recognizes that the idea of essence and autonomous existence is always an ideological ruse, a convention disguised as nature, a contingent formation disguised as an eternal verity. What theatrical self-consciousness offers, in opposition to dramatic absorption, is a critical vision, unwilling to be fooled or to be used—a basic premise in Brecht's theories. When Fried uses the word "theatrical" he is at the same time saying "contingent," nonessential; but is that the same thing as "false"?

What interests me in Fried's argument, however, has little to do with its implied metaphysics or faulty logic, but with the moral impulse behind it: the question of "absorption, sympathy, and self-transcendence." This, to my mind, is the crux of the entire modern/postmodern debate about the subject. The ethos of dramatic absorption centers on faith, existential engagement with and in the world. The autonomy of the painting as a category reflects the autonomy of the subject as being in the world. At the same time the *identification* of the subject/beholder with the painting demonstrates a power of empathy necessary for efficacious communication with the world or the other, a communication that transcends mere self-interest or self-concern. The unity of the painting assures its absorptive power, eliminating distracting influences, and at the same time insures that the viewer beholds it as an end-in-itself, what

Kant proposes as the necessary condition in one behaving morally toward other *people*. This relation delineates the modernist position toward art and the individual subject.

From an ethical standpoint, the modernist ethos seems necessary to establish the possibility of a nonalienated experience of communion, even if predicated on an illusion. The postmodern ethos is necessary to establish the particularity of context in the determination of personal choice, in ethical judgment. It is easy, within the historically anterior position of postmodernism, to scoff at the naiveté of the modernist position of essential qualities. At the same time, the radical postmodern position of contingency would be meaningless without reference to the modernist position. The drive for modernist purity and essence, and the fragmentation that resulted when the self-defined minimum conditions of being were reached is what created postmodernist relativism in the first place. Yet postmodernism's own self-definition depends upon implicitly sustaining the modernist position, just as deconstruction depends upon the reiteration of an ontotheological metaphysics of presence. This is simply because the meaning of contingency itself is relative to an understanding of a possible absolute, just as the meaning of difference depends upon the notion of identity and self-presence.

The breakdown of the autonomous, essential position of painting into the contingent values of minimalist installation can be read as roughly analogous to Pinter's own forcing of the conceits of naturalism to the breaking point of theatrical self-consciousness. The role of memory in Ibsen, for instance, is central to his tragic vision, in its overwhelming determination of present consequences. In this sense, memory has an "essential" role and its truth-value is never questioned. Pinter, on the other hand, by calling into question the truth of individual memory, forces the characters into the radically contingent situation of constant self-construction on the basis of a highly indeterminate past, the truth of which is inaccessible. This is an important trait that Pinter shares with Samuel Beckett.

What is quite clear to me as the difference between what might *appear* to be the postmodernist works of Beckett and Pinter, and the postmodernist works of, say, Robert Wilson and a variety of highly "theatrical" performance artists, is that Beckett and Pinter's works, even if formally on the cusp of the postmodern, still retain a modernist sense of loss, of anguish, that in the wake of theoretical denials of subjectivity (even if that denial is hedged by the term "decentered"), more glib postmodernist works don't address. Or I'd like to say *won't* address, for I think that in the age of Reagan it is more likely a matter of self-concerned repression, while the unraveling movement of the nineties might result in a return of the repressed. If I may be so bold: a distinctive trait of postmodernism may be the *repression of the tragic,* quite unlike Brecht's *resistance* to tragic overdetermination, because radical indeterminacy is hardly conducive to the social choices that Brecht would like his spectators to make. To paraphrase Eliot somewhat cynically, only those who can afford unthreatened subjectivity are those who feel at ease in "ridding" themselves of it.

The end of *Old Times* is hardly a celebration of relativism, but is rather a tragic confrontation with the reality of alienation. The very last scene consists of movement and positioning. Anna walks to the door, standing with her back to the others. Deeley sobs. Anna switches off the lights, returns to her divan and lies down. Deeley stops sobbing, stands, looks at both divans, walks to Anna and looks down at her. He walks to the door and stands with his back to the others. He then returns to Kate's divan and lies across her lap. After a moment he slowly rises, returns to his chair and slumps in it. The lights come up brightly (69–71). As in Moris's L-Beam installation, the meaning of each figuration appears purely relational, not only spatially but temporally, for these positions are recapitulations of memories that had been recounted before. Absorption is not possible: Deeley cannot retain the piéta of the death of the subject in his object's arms for long before returning to a position that sadly affirms an alienation from experience due to the overwhelming consciousness of the contingent and indeterminate nature of both perception and memory.

Rather than repressing a sense of loss, a move could be made within the modern/postmodern debate not simply to limit ourselves to a choice between absorption *or* theatricality, but to recognize the necessity of establishing some dialectical coherence between them.

Note

1. *"Le sujet ne peut que désirer, seul l'objet peut séduire"* (163).

IV. Pinter and Influence

Chekhov, Beckett, Pinter: The St(r)ain upon the Silence

Alice N. Benston

To begin the odyssey implicit in my title, I need to stop a moment with Strindberg. (As Ibsen said, there is always Strindberg.) Although he did not contribute to the formal, theatrical device of pauses and silence in modern and postmodern dialogue, he articulated the first cause of invention of the technique by others. In the preface to *Miss Julie,* he lists a whole series of changes in theatrical strategies that will be necessary if the past is to be defeated and a new drama, reflecting new world views, is to come to be. His list covers everything from decor to concepts of character and, in discussing the latter, he describes the changes he has made in creating dialogue:

> In regard to dialogue, I have departed somewhat from tradition by not making my characters catechists who ask stupid questions in order to elicit a smart reply. I have avoided the symmetrical, mathematical construction of French dialogue, and let people's minds work irregularly, as they do in real life, where during a conversation, no topic is drained to the dregs, and one mind finds in another a chance cog to engage in. So too the dialogue wanders, gathering in the opening scenes material which is later picked up, worked over, repeated, expounded and developed like the theme in a musical composition. (68)

Strindberg, of course, is describing the means of modern realism/naturalism, and while this doctrine seems contrary to the purposeful artificiality of absurdist or postmodern drama, its applicability to Chekhov and Pinter is obvious. The theatricality of modernism requires real pots and pans, Stringberg says elsewhere in this same essay, and the kitchen sinks must have this same materiality in the world of Pinter as the samovars do in Chekhov's. But there is also a far-reaching metaphysical assertion in Strindberg's remarks. Although he is noting the means of psychological realism in this document, the implicit proposition is that our inner world as well as the universe do not present themselves to us in mathematical formulae, regular and predictable. In referring disparagingly to the French dialogue, he obliquely, I would argue, defies the basic concept of a Cartesian world view. (I feel safe in that assertion, with the hindsight afforded by the knowledge of what is to come in his own oeuvre, namely the dream plays!) But what is most striking for the topic I've chosen to explore are three propositions: the avoidance of "mathematical regularity"; "no topic drained to the dregs," hence the "wandering dialogue"; and the reference to music. All these objectives are enhanced or, in some cases, dependent upon the strategy of pauses and silences.

While Strindberg articulated the reasons for the need to change the quality of dialogue for a modern theater, neither he nor Ibsen, the other great progenitor of the movement, used breaks or hiatuses. Speech is often interrupted in Ibsen and connected metaphorically rather than logically in Strindberg, but it was Chekhov who first employed pauses as a means to represent the struggle of each character to represent a self to another or to connect herself or himself to a world of structured meaning. Chekhov, then, in contrast to Strindberg, uses pauses to *displace* rather than to avoid logic. Although Chekhov uses the device in numerous ways, marked and unmarked, the pauses are predominantly ironic.

My first example is from *The Seagull,* where an unmarked pause must be observed by the director if Chekhov's irony is to be felt by the audience. Trepleff has just finished an outburst against his actress mother, which includes the following tirade against the theatre: "The Theater today is nothing but routine convention. When the curtain goes up, and by artifical light in a room with three walls, these great geniuses, these priests of holy art, show how people eat, drink, make love, move about and wear their jackets; when they try to fish a moral out of these flat pictures . . . ; when they serve me the same thing over and over, and over and over, over and over—it's then I run and run like Maupassant from the Eiffel Tower and all the vulgarity about to bury him" (7). We must have new forms, he asserts. Just then Nina, his beloved, who will perform his piece, arrives and expresses her nervousness: "It's hard to act in your play. There are no living characters in it." Trepleff responds: "Living characters! I must represent life not as it should be but as it appears in my dreams." Nina continues: "In your play there's no action; it's all recitation. It seems to me a play must have some love in it" (11).

The pair exits upstage and, with no rhetorical connection, another couple, Dorn and Paulina, enter from the wings. The first line is hers: "It's getting damp; go back and put on your galoshes" (11). There follows a dialogue between them, in which she expresses her frustrated love, throughout which he hums a tune, avoiding her overtures. Without a *pause* between the moment in which we hear Nina's last assertion, "a play should have some love in it," during which the audience can associate her remark with Trepleff's previous condemnation of his mother's theater and connect it to Pauline's line, "go back and put on your galoshes," the audience would not be able to perceive the comic irony and the implied self-referentiality that the two separated pieces of dialogue constitute. For the play by Chekhov that we are watching is full of love, drinking, eating, and attention to correct clothing, particularly in the way much is made of Trepleff's need of a new suit. Thus, in this play in which art is the subject, Chekhov, rather than presenting a debate about new and old forms, puts the opposed propositions side by side so that it is the *audience* who infers the ironic contrast between Trepleff's and Chekhov's theatrical styles.

The activity required by the audience in the absence of dialogue or mimetic action is one of the most important effects of the modernist's gesture of creating pauses or palpable silence. In these interstices—the very absence of "recitations" that Nina complains about in Trepleff's piece—the play is the work of the receptor. Here we are required to piece together the comic irony. Elsewhere a pause may evoke pathos, as it sometimes does in Chekhov or, later in Beckett and Pinter, varieties of anxiety. In any case, we, the audience, construct the poetry of the theatre in the work of these dramatists, as we carry across the echoes in these moments of silence. Thus, between Nina's question to Trepleff after he has placed a dead seagull at her feet, "What's the matter with you?" a pause makes us wait and thus hear with emphasis his answer, "It's the way I'll soon end my life" (30). The way in which Chekhov creates his dense poetic texture requires a long discussion in itself, but here we can see how he allows us to take note of the act of signification and to work with the associations, so that, when the bird reappears, stuffed, early in the final act, we are prepared to bring back the remembered statement, which causes a sense of foreboding.

The Three Sisters provides rich examples of the use of dialogue interrupted to signify the characters' struggle to express their unhappiness. Indeed, the great number of verbal spaces indicates that the main action of the play is an attempt, through articulation, to discover by naming the cause of their suffering. There are nine pauses, one silence, and one stage note *"not listening"*, in the first act. There are fourteen pauses in act 2, nine in act 3 (and one "not listening") and twenty-two in the last act. There are other disruptions in the flow of the dialogue as well—discontinuities between sets of characters and interruptive laughter. The script also indicates silent moments when a character is engaged in an activity, such as laying out cards, poring over papers, or lighting a candle. The last moments of *The Cherry Orchard* have to be one of the most poignant and powerful examples of such nonverbal moments. Fiers, the aging servant, has been left behind when all the others go off to the railroad station. After some mutterings about life having gone by, the stage directions read: *"He lies still"* (Chekov 296). Finally, as the directions indicate, we hear the sad breaking of a string and the sound of an axe as it hits the first cherry tree. Surely, if those sounds are to affect us forcefully, the director has to space the last word from Fiers and the offstage sounds with an utter silence.

Equally interesting as the great number of marked pauses in *The Three Sisters* is the fact that two thirds of them (thirty) are internal to a character's speech. Also, these moments of reflective concentration are experienced only by the "sensitive" characters, Olga, Masha, Irena, and Vershinin. The sisters' brother, Andrei, has a reflective moment only once, after he recognizes that he is a failure and begins to long for Moscow, the floating signifier of his sisters' unfulfilled desires. Fighting through their boredom, lack of purpose, and growing fatigue, these characters are given what amounts to broken soliloquies in which their failure to make sense of their lives communicates a world without definition and signposts. The pauses hardly mark inarticulateness in these highly educated and verbal characters, but rather the gropings of the thoughtful modern person who needs to know why and suffers for the unavailability of codes and answers in a world where past orders are dissolving, created for this purpose by a playwright who was the perfect agnostic.

At the end of the play, as the three sisters stand huddled together, all illusions stripped, they are past the time of waiting for the future but confirmed in their acceptance that they must go on. Waiting, being stuck in place and having to go on—there is much in the rhythm of this plot to tempt us to see *Waiting for Godot* as an elegantly stripped and therefore heightened rendition of the same theme. The comparison between the two playwrights has been made frequently, and John Russell Brown makes the explicit comparison between the two in the use of silences. However, the pace of the silences has increased, for, as he notes, "there are six silences in the space of fourteen lines [in the opening dialogue of *Godot*] and elsewhere five within ten lines" ("Beckett" 27). Bert O. States observes:

> Out of Ibsen will come Pinter; out of Chekhov, Beckett. In other words, if stage conversation is filled with innuendo, with subterfuge, with intrigue, silence— when it falls—will emit these same energies. Silence is the same warfare by other means. But when stage conversation is filled with emptiness, as it is in Chekhov, or with a form of emotion and anguish that has no specific derivation and no promise of surcease through the possibilities in the world of action, silence— when it falls—will be the "negative equivalent" of emptiness. (74)

States's description of the similarity between Chekhov and Beckett is beautifully put and accurate as to the source of the tonal equivalences. However, the differences are important to note, since there are implications for both the actors and the audience. The world has changed, and hence even the possibilities for action are changed when we get to Beckett. As Brown observes, there are three individual stories in the Chekhov play, and the possibility of the continuation of the biographies is left to the audience. In contrast, he notes that in Beckett's theatre "the audience is left in possession of little more than what happened at each moment of the play" ("Beckett" 31). Quite so and more. If the sisters are stuck in place, they at least know where it is. Very early in act 1 of *Waiting for Godot,* after the first time Estragon suggests, "let's go," and just after the first time we hear the line, "We're waiting for Godot," Estragon asks despairingly, "You're sure it was here? That we were to wait?" Vladimir responds, "He said by the tree. Do you see any others?" (10). The avenue of trees in *The Three Sisters,* the cherry orchard, and the woods of *Uncle Vanya* have dwindled to a single Giacometti object on a barren plain.

Since the Chekhovian character is built within the richness of a social and personal fabric (the recall of a golden past in Moscow, or a prize-winning orchard), there is still a reference that is both the distance of realism and the arc of recognition. (They are like but not us.) After two wars the sense of scorched earth is omnipresent in Beckett's world. References to occupations are vague or nonexistent and a character's past is as unreliable as projections of a future. Hence, when Pozzo reappears blind in the second act, we never learn what caused him to lose his sight. What the change effects is an intensification of the relationship between slave and master, which is the essential characteristic represented by these characters. Nostalgia itself is questionable in the world of Beckett—a part of the play of self-creation. For example, Nell's "Ah yesterday" (*Endgame*), while according to the stage directions is to be said "*elegiacally*," is followed by a recall of how she and Nagg lost their legs. The one memory of the past, far from creating a sense of better former times, defines their present condition as decaying elders confined to ash cans (15–18). It is this stripping away of the before and after that brings the vivid nowness and, hence, the quintessential theatricality of his theatre works.

Once again, but in a new context, the concept of the world as theatre, with its two-way ambiguity, returns, cleansed and refreshed, to begin again. It is because the character is not re-presenting, but creating being, that pauses and silence are indeed "the key markers of Beckett's work," as Tom Bishop has observed, but not, as Bishop goes on to infer, "because silence is the counterpoint of language, the failure of language" (24). I would argue that there is no failure of language in Beckett, but rather a brilliant paring down to a poetic forcefulness. Characters do not fail to communicate or misunderstand or fail to hear one another in his world. (There is more of that in Chekhov's or Pinter's drama, understandably, given the social texture of their theatres.)

Silence, then, in Beckett's work, sets out the theatrical moment when, in language, character is created. The counterpoint between silence (the empty stage) and dialogue makes us aware of the coming to be of the drama. Ruby Cohn reports that the first audiences of *Godot* thought that the actors had forgotten their lines (17). It may be that we can never recover the innocence of that first encounter, given the intervening critical overlay, but I would argue that their response was on the mark. In Chekhov's plays, it is the characters who are uncomfortable and embarrassed; in Beckett's world, the audience bears the anticipation and anxiety, because, equipped with preconceived ideas and accustomed to traditional theatrical conventions, we are also waiting to encounter, to be told, to come to know (We to play!). Hence, while Chekhov's pauses and silences are ironic, Beckett's are mimetic. But as with Chekhov, Beckett's palpable silences can be filled with or cause pathos or laughter. It's all in the timing, as they say, and Beckett's meticulous care for duration shows his intent, as McMillan and Fehsenfeld have documented in *Beckett in the Theatre*. And it is important to stress that pauses and silences differ in duration within a play and from piece to piece. For example, Beckett was distressed when directors failed to give the silences in *Godot* sufficient time, but he agreed with Billie Whitelaw when she felt that the directors were dragging the pace of *Play* (Whitelaw 81–82). And, as with Chekhov, there are pauses within a character's speech and both pauses and silences between characters within the dialogue. Understandably there are more of the latter in Beckett.

Thus, as with Chekhov, the silences in Beckett are the means for creating the poetry of the theatre, as we bring the highly etched content of one episode over the silence to another patch of dialogue. Here we can recall Cocteau's definition of poetry *of* the theatre as made with ropes, rather than the lace of lyric poetry *in* the theatre (97). But there is another difference, one that marks a transition from the modern to the postmodern theatre. As we have seen, Chekhov's pauses cause disconnected juxtapositions, but Beckett's underscore a complete discontinuity. Chekhov's disjunctions are a theatrical parataxis, while Beckett's are totally without rhetorical connections. One speech does not motivate the next. Hence Beckett has taken Strindberg's desire for a rupture with the rhetorical structure of dialogue a large step further. Asymmetry has become a-linearity, even circularity. To echo Brown, we cannot speculate on the fictive future of the characters; we can only return to the play, to play again.

Brown goes on to trace the same lineage I am working with, ending with Pinter as Beckett's chief heir, citing examples from the endings of *The Caretaker* and *Old Times.* The charged tableaus of their final curtains do indeed have a resemblance to *Godot* in their lack of conclusion. But he does not, in this article, stop for the differences between these two playwrights, who are tonally worlds apart. To chart the full comparisons, we have to return to States's thesis that Pinter is more akin to Ibsen than Chekhov, since Pinter's silences emit similar energies to those of Ibsen because they are the product of "innuendo," "subterfuge" and "intrigue" (74).

However, I want to take slight exception to States's comparison of Pinter to Ibsen. Take *Ghosts,* for example, where one might claim that we are left with a silent tableau at the end, as inconclusive as any cited so far, for we do not know whether or not Mrs. Alving will administer the poison to Oswald. True, but Ibsen's manipulation of the audience here is to force a political and moral question onto us, which is very different from the effect or purpose of Chekhov, Beckett, or Pinter. Further, there are only three pauses throughout the play up to the final curtain with its "freeze action." Instead we have, as we do throughout Ibsen's middle period, much interrupted dialogue, characters intruding on the speech of one another. Thus, there is very aggressive inter-action among the characters, and I suspect that it is this sense of conflict and power plays that States had in mind.

Pinter's silences, then, have multiple sources and different effects. With Beckett, in contrast, we are *not* involved with the *non-dit.* Characters do not withhold; they struggle in the silence to face the challenge of the need to speak, their need to be. In fact, aggressive argumentation in the works of Beckett is explicitly a game to establish interaction between characters. Didi and Gogo are contestatory, but Pozzo and Lucky never argue. Pinter alone uses silence as a menacing gesture. Perhaps we have to add Ionesco to the melange of Pinter progenitors. His is a comedy of menace, particularly in the

Berenger plays. For example, *The Killer* ends with a long monologue during which the killer refuses to answer Berenger. It is this refusal of dialogue that carries the terror of the play. This is not an emptiness, a marker, to denote a struggle for expression, but a withholding of something submerged. Pinter, himself, aptly describes the difference between two kinds of silences:

> One when no word is spoken. The other when perhaps a torrent of language is employed. This speech is the speech locked beneath it. That is its continual reference. The speech we hear is as an indication of what we don't hear. It is a necessary avoidance, a violent, sly, anguished or mocking smoke screen which keeps the other in its place. When true silence falls, we are still left with an echo but are nearer nakedness. (Jacket copy to *Landscape and Silence*)

Silences, then, are not the absence of speech but the true, raw, and frequently brutal or vulnerable self. Spoken (heard) dialogue is but a cue to the subtext, which itself is the pure unadulterated thing. And if the spoken word is there to hold the "other" at bay, we are back in the world of social interaction. For this menace to be felt by the audience, we must feel that something is being withheld. An example from *The Caretaker,* which clearly pays homage to Beckett with a tramp concerned about shoes, who cannot find ones to fit, illustrates how Pinter takes the convention, as used by Beckett, and adapts it to his own means. Davies, the tramp, has asked for a pair of shoes. While Aston rummages under his bed looking for the pair that he will shortly proffer to Davies, the latter talks about his failure to get a pair at a monastery. Aston says, "You've got to have a good pair of shoes." Davies exclaims: "Shoes? It's life and death to me. I had to go all the way to Lutton in these. (He is wearing sandals.) Aston asks; "What happened when you got there, then?" After a pause, Davies replies: "I used to know a bootmaker in Aston. He was a good mate to me." A pause follows. "You know what that bastard monk said to me?" (23). To Aston's simple, direct question, "what happened, then?," we never get an answer. This is outright refusal of information, which suggests to the audience that there *is* an answer. The question of identity continues in the dialogue that follows concerning the real name of the tramp, who has no identity papers. When Mick surprises Davies, the tension erupts in violence, and it is Davies's turn to ask repeatedly, "who are you? I don't know who you are" (40). Davies's avoidance is a feint to guard his nakedness. Mick's prolonged avoidance of the question, as he humiliates and knocks Davies about, is, to quote from Pinter's list, "a violent smoke screen to keep the other in its place."

Pinter's avoidances and feints create a disjunctiveness as startling to the audience as Beckett's, but since they are a withholding instead of an absence, our reaction is different. We do not work across the text, as I suggested we do in Beckett, but we are teased to work vertically with the subtext. There are important implications for the actor as well as the audience, marked by these differences. Whether menacing, as in *The Caretaker* or *The Dumb Waiter,* or poignant, as in *Silence* or *Old Times,* the pauses fall between the characters as markers of interpersonal and social relations. Because there seems to be information not stated, the actor has an implied story or biography to call upon in handling these silences with content. Alice Rayner links this seeming omission to the suppression of narrativity in favor of the aesthetics of presence, especially in the "early comedies of menace." As she says, "The realm that Pinter explores is the verge of collapse for a narrative value-system but the collapse is not total. A tension occurs because the plays give indications in narrative terms that they still may mean something, that there may be a way of 'mastering' the events if one can find the right context or reconstruct the right story" (494). From this perspective, the Chekovian irony has shifted from differing expectations among the characters to a tension between what the dramatist teases the audience to expect and what he gives. Some of the menace, then, is directed toward us, as we are forced to recognize the Beckettian nowness, the essential presence of the act of theatre. As Rayner puts it, "... Pinter's fragmentation of coherence manifests not simply a negative erosion of narration but a positive enlargement for temporal formations" (485).

The very tension between audience desire and what the playwright delivers opens a space for those critics who note the importance of the phenomenon. John Lutterbie describes the modification of the Chekhovian silence by Beckett and Pinter as a recognition that unity of character represents a unity between consciousness and unconsciousness and is, hence, an illusion (469). For Lutterbie, the content of silence is subjectivity, which, he says, "cannot be located by language nor isolated by memory; rather it is at the moment when memory fails, when language betrays itself; in silence" (473). Thus, metaphysical and psychological meaning is supplied for the absence in the dialogue. Rayner, in moving to a feminist analysis, contrasts narrative linearity with spatial imagery (the former the sphere of masculine desire and the latter the province of female nonlogical awareness of being-in-itself). She finds a "meaning" in the absence of linearity, suggesting that the feminine Ruth, in *The Homecoming*, is the origin of masculine desire for meaning expressed through narrativity (493).

Such interpretations are richly suggestive and consistent with the texts. But there is a profound irony in that they represent the putative audience's desire for a meaning that is referential. In filling the gaps based on contemporary psychological and metaphysical premises, these critics are asserting a mimetic drama for Pinter, even as they attempt to show how radical he is in breaking with the western tradition of linearity, narrativity, logic, and meaning. Since meanings, finally, are the construct of the audience, there is nothing wrong with this representation of Pinter's world. It may well be that such pieces merely prove that all drama is mimetic; it is only the worldview that changes. But, although these commentators note the crucial role of Pinter's pauses and silences, they do not explore the systematic way in which silences are deployed by the playwright. Such an analysis shows, I believe, that Pinter is more rigorous than the critics are in maintaining a poststructuralist openness.

The person who has paid the closest attention to the use of pauses and silences in Pinter's work is Martin Esslin. In "Language and Silence," he carefully annotates the relation between this device and the quality of the dialogue in Pinter's work. Noting the changes in tonality that occur with changes in diction, he observes that this essential musicality is further aided by the pauses and silences that mark a rhythm in Pinter's dialogue. Esslin thus documents just how Pinter is a poet-of-the-theatre. Silence functions as the cesura in poetry or the pause in music (55). Esslin also makes the extremely important point that there is a difference in Pinter's use of the pause and silences: "When Pinter asks for a pause, therefore, he indicates that thought processes are continuing, that unspoken tensions are mounting, whereas silences are notations between the movements of a symphony" (56).

If we take Esslin's observations and stress theatricality, we find that Pinter is, indeed, forcing us to relate to presence rather than allowing us to relax with the conventional expectations provided by the narrative structures of classical drama. In this respect Pinter's strategy resembles Beckett's, since he forces us to concentrate on character in the making. Despite the implied stories in the subtext, we are made to concentrate on the moment on stage when a character becomes his or her story in the performed interaction. The musicality, as observed by Esslin, is also a refusal of rhetorical conjunction, without which narrative is impossible. *The Homecoming* provides a good example of both the rigor and the pattern of Pinter's pauses.

The play has a Chekovian flavor in the way it is bounded by arrivals and leave-taking. Further, its inner architecture is built along the shifting of relationships just as Chekhov's plays are. Particularly because this dynamic leads the audience to familiar territory, it is interesting to observe how Pinter thwarts us. Charting the first act, where normally we would expect narrative and character exposition, we find that the process is interrupted repeatedly. Over the course of the act, there are over one hundred marked pauses and twelve silences. Two blackouts indicate the act's division into three scenes. All but two silences occur when there is a change of personae, typically when a new character appears. Of the pauses, all but thirteen occur within a character's speech. Only thirteen are used to space the dialogue between characters. If the typical purpose of the pause were to indicate a failure of communication, we would expect the numbers to be reversed. Rather, we find that it is within a character's moments for self-revelation (character exposition) that we find hesitation or fragmentation.

Further, where we would expect the narrative exposition of a time past (story exposition) at the outset, we find the greatest number of pauses. There is a decelerating pattern, with fifty-three in the first scene, thirty-six in the second, and twenty in the last. If one counts the sections between silences where new characters enter, it is interesting to observe that the as yet unknown person has the greatest number of pauses within a speech. Thus Max, the patriarch of the menage, has all but two of the pauses in the opening scene where he is alone with his son, Lenny; Uncle Sam has six of the nine pauses after he first comes on; and Joey, the younger son, has but two of the six in a section with three others on stage. When Teddy, the returning son, arrives with his wife Ruth in the second scene, all the pauses are in his speeches. Thus, the dialogue is patterned with interrupted monologues that not only repress exposition but make us concentrate on the character's attempt to define his being. Max moves disjointedly from exhortation to threat to claim his authority. As the play opens, he asks for first a pair of scissors and then a cigarette. Lenny ignores both requests, and Max attempts to get to Lenny with a portrait of his former self.

> MAX: You think I wasn't a tearaway? I could have taken care of you, twice over. I'm still strong. You ask your Uncle Sam what I was. But at the same time I always had a kind heart. Always.
> > *Pause.*
> I used to knock about with a man called MacGregor. I called him Mac. You remember Mac? Eh?
> > *Pause.*
> Huhh! We were two of the worst hated men in the West End of London. I tell you I still got scars. We'd walk into a place, the whole room'd stand up, they'd make way to let us pass. You never heard such silence. Mind you he was a big man, he was over six feet tall. His family were all from Aberdeen, but he was the only one they called Mac.
> > *Pause.*
> He was very fond of your mother, Mac was. Very fond. He always had a good word for her.
> > *Pause.*
> Mind you she wasn't such a bad woman. Even though it made me sick to look at her rotten stinking face, she wasn't such a bad bitch. I gave her the best years of my life, anyway. (24)

The failure of the other, here Lenny, to move into the spaces and confirm the biographical statement casts doubt on their veracity at the same time as they fail to confirm or activate Max's power over Lenny. In futility, Max wields his stick throughout the act. The stick seems to function as the authority symbol much like the "speaking staff" of the archaic Greek world. In a similar vein, Sam tries to assert a biographical relationship to connect himself to his brother:

> SAM: I want to make something quite clear about Jessie, Max. I want to. I do. When I took her out in the cab, round the town, I was taking care of her for you. I was looking after her for you, when you were busy, wasn't I? I was showing her the West End.
> > *Pause.*
> You wouldn't have trusted your other brothers. You wouldn't have trusted Mac, would you? But you trusted me. I want to remind you.
> > *Pause.*
> Old Mac died a few years ago, didn't he? Isn't he dead?
> > *Pause.*
> He was a lousy stinking loudmouth. A bastard uncouth sodding runt. Mind you, he was a good friend of yours.

Pause.

MAX: Eh, Sam.
SAM: What?
MAX: Why do I keep you here? You're just an old grub. (34)

Max's refusal to confirm or deny his brother's self-portrait leaves Sam inchoate. Further, the memory of the past differs between the brothers. Did Max honor Jessie? Was Mac a tall man, over six feet, or a runt? Was he a fierce man to be reckoned with or merely a loudmouth? The very facts and details that promise to ground a narrative and a "real" past are put in question. So, too, the stories the men tell to create portraits of masculine power are claims that are momentary, never confirmed. Lenny's long story about his brutal treatment of a woman he picked up is particularly interesting for its self-conscious assertion that things are as he sees them, that he has control over the facts.

Lenny tells of how he picked up a woman at the docks and, having decided that she was diseased, proceeded to beat her (46). The story is the longest uninterrupted narrative in the play. When he finishes, Ruth responds without a pause by asking, "How did you know she was diseased?"

LENNY: How did I know?
Pause.
I decided she was.
Silence.
You and my brother are newly-weds, are you?
RUTH: We've been married six years.
LENNY: He's always been my favorite brother, old Teddy. (47)

"I decided she was." The answer comes after a pause, an answer that is chosen for the context. The story need not be true to carry the menace when he tells her that he will create character, the ultimate power over a person. The silence that follows is one of only two internal to a speech in the act. It not only marks the change to an opposite tone and a switch in topic, but lends significance to his refusal to accept her correction of his assumption that Teddy and Ruth are newlyweds. Hence, when he goes on to claim a fondness for his brother, we do not take it as fact, but relate it to the way he shifts his persona from a portrait of cruelty to a would-be sensitive man as another stratagem for control. Such shifts in persona are as menacing as the story is, if more subtle.

In Alice Rayner's view, the desire of the male for linear narrative is centered around the female as source and object of that desire. If pauses are markers of this male desire, we should find that Ruth never is given pauses. It would also mean that Ruth never becomes a character in the sense that I am describing here; that is, she never takes a role in the present by representing herself. But, when we look at the second act, we find that Pinter sees her as a character as well, although her description of her life before marriage as a "model for the body" and her recall of the places where she has modeled do not bear

a sense of factual past. As Rayner observes: "Dream like, it [her story] invokes
a distant 'other' place from a past that may never have existed. . . . The quality
and effect of the description have the quality of myth; impossible, unlikely,
appealing, erotic, hypnotic" (493).

If Ruth's stories of the past in the second act are erotic and appealing, they
are her means not only of responding to the male characters she has met in
the first act, but of controlling them in the second. If we have been watching
carefully, we should not be altogether surprised when she sends Teddy away
and decides to remain with the father and brothers as wife/mother and income-
earning whore. The irony within the play, and one Pinter very carefully pre-
pares, is that the manipulating men are in her power at the end. It is fascinating
to find that her only pauses occur when she is bargaining with the men:

RUTH: How many rooms would this flat have?
LENNY: Not many.
RUTH: I would want at least three rooms and a bathroom.
LENNY: You wouldn't need three rooms and a bathroom.
MAX: She'd need a bathroom.
LENNY: But not three rooms.

Pause.

RUTH: Oh, I would. Really.
LENNY: Two would do.
RUTH: No. Two wouldn't be enough.

Pause.

I'd want a dressing-room, a rest room, and a bedroom.

Pause. (92)

As Ruth names the rooms, the naming punctuated by spaces, she is imagining
and creating her role. Warming to her position, she goes on to wrest control
of the financial arrangement and make further demands for a personal maid
and a wardrobe. She has begun to create her future self. The final vignette
finds Joey with his head in Ruth's lap, Max groveling, asserting still, as he did
at the beginning, that he is still virile, and Lenny, once again silent, but standing
and observing. Husband, son and pimp; wife, mother, whore. The roles are
written as the play ends. But the instability of even this finale is underscored
by Max's lament that he doesn't know what the future will bring.

Thus, we come to realize that all character is factitious, and the contrast
between artificiality and the seemingly naturalistic texture is where Pinter's
self-consciousness or overt theatricality becomes part of his theatre. The tension
we feel between our desire for a sense of a stable reality which traditional
narratives provided and the insistence on the illusory nature of that demand
recalls yet another founder of modernism, Pirandello. In fact, there are moments
in Pinter's later plays that recall Pirandello. For example, in *No Man's Land,*
in which the central characters are poets and the dialogue concerns language
and creativity, the first act closes with a purely Pirandellian gesture as stage
and audience merge. We are in the middle of a typically Pinter moment, here,
that involves a story that fails to emerge:

FOSTER: Do you know what I saw once in the desert, in the Australian desert? A man walking along with two umbrellas. Two umbrellas.
Pause.
SPOONER: Was it raining?
FOSTER: No. It was a beautiful day. I nearly asked him what he was up to but changed my mind.
SPOONER: Why?
FOSTER: Well, I decided he must be some kind of lunatic. I thought he might confuse me. (*Foster walks about the room, stops at the door*). Listen. You know what it's like when you're in a room and then suddenly the light goes out? I'll show you. It's like this. (*He turns the light out.*)
BLACKOUT (114–15)

With self-conscious theatricality, the character puts out both the room's light on stage and the house light.

In *Landscape* and *Silence,* Pinter uses spatial relationships as well as the customary pauses and silences to isolate the narrative and separate the characters. While in Pirandello the characters struggle to make their version of a character dominate, Pinter underscores the futility of the desire to dominate by preventing interaction altogether. In *Landscape,* a memory play written all in the past tense, the monologue never becomes dialogue. Scraps of memory, which surface as each of the two characters in the play recall what is significant, only serve to separate the lives they live. The details of the one character's memories never confirm or deny those of the other character. In *Silence* the characters' disjointed and segmented memories are juxtaposed as the three, Ellen, Rumsey, and Bates, move in doublets and triplets over the three defined spaces of the set. Interestingly, there are no pauses within speeches; they only occur in the dialogic passages when the characters are interacting. The episodes of contrapuntal thought are punctuated by silences, which accelerate as the play closes on bits of separate lines, which repeat thoughts already spoken. These repetitions are not unlike Beckett's, creating a similar lack of closure, reinforcing the sense that the game goes on. The game here is the attempt to create a character, a self, in the absence of confirming interaction. The silence, in this play, is the isolation. Self-consciously this point is articulated, on stage, by Ellen:

ELLEN: Around me sits the night. Such a silence. I can hear myself. Cup my ear. My heart beats in my ear. Such a silence. Is it me? Am I silent or speaking? How can I know? Can I know such things? No-one has ever told me. I need to be told things. I seem to be old. Am I old now? No-one will tell me. I must find a person to tell me these things. (211)

In his most recent political plays, Pinter's use of silence is both a summation of his previous strategies and a new manipulation. In addition to the usual rhythm of pauses and silences, we find the return of the totally silent character like the matchseller in *A Slight Ache,* but now, as in *Mountain Language,* in an explicitly political environment. Throughout his work, Pinter has used pauses to make the point that the command of language is a question of power. It is hardly surprising, then, that he would choose to focus on the suppression of a group's native language or dialect as the touchstone of tyranny. However, when, at the end of *Mountain Language,* the ban has been lifted as arbitrarily as it seems to have been promulgated and the mother is invited to speak in her native tongue to her son, who is a prisoner, she fails to do so. She remains silent as he pleads with her, and he finally collapses. The moment is the denouement of the play, and it is highly ambiguous. Since the son pleads in English, perhaps we are to conclude that the tyrannous prohibition has alienated him from his own language and he can no longer reach his mother. Or is it that she has lost her ability to use the language? Or is it that she cannot trust this arbitrary reversal? Or have we come back to the personal, that is that the mother has nothing to say to the son?

With Pinter, we have returned to Strindberg, to a realistic, modern dialogue that, in avoiding continuity, imitates how people think and how they avoid relatedness or fail to make contact in the contemporary world. This proposition would suggest that Pinter's work is an amalgam of the strife that characterizes Strindberg's world with the devices of Chekhov's theatre. What I have been suggesting is that Chekhov created a major theatrical device that has enabled modern playwrights to accomplish the new theatre toward which Strindberg was working. It has been deployed with great variety of effect and carries much of the sense of loss that we feel about our world.

ELEVEN

"That first last look..."

Martha Fehsenfeld

> That first last look in the shadows after all
> those in the light to come—wrings the heart.

I first heard that sentence in an interview of Pinter on BBC Radio 3 in July 1980. Or at least part of it. Pinter revealed to the interviewer that Beckett had sent him a letter after he had seen the first draft of *Betrayal* and in one sentence summed up the play. In recalling the sentence Pinter was able to retrieve only "the look in the shadows" and "the light to come." I wrote and asked Pinter for permission to quote the sentence after receiving Beckett's approval. Pinter gave his, with the one instruction that Beckett concur. When I told Beckett about the letter, he said, "he hasn't finished it. Write him again and say I asked him to finish it." So a month later Pinter's second letter arrived with the missing phrase restored, "wrings the heart."

I have mulled over Beckett's statement ever since. He has always taken great pains to avoid sentimentality in his own work as Pinter has in his. However, quite clearly the play had touched a nerve in Beckett and he responded, restoring the priority of sensibility with his reaction to the image of the look that compelled, held, and finally moved him.

I admit I've been bothered by Pinter's *Betrayal*. And I have found this disappointment and frustration is shared by several Pinter critics who have written about the play. The situation is a triangle of two men and one woman involved in what seems to be a nasty little affair that really doesn't matter very much. I remember when I first saw the play in London in 1979 that I felt cheated. And it seemed to me that that was the tenor of the play: Emma and Jerry cheating on Robert, who was cheating on Emma, and Jerry cheating on Judith, who may or may not have been cheating on Jerry, etc., etc., and my final reaction was, frankly, so what? A subject for the gossip columns, but for a play? As *La Ronde,* a game of love, I had seen it all done before and better, I thought. The infinite possibilities in the complications of relationships. Who cares? And why does Beckett care?

Then I considered, well, what's interesting is not what is being said but how Pinter is saying it. The mechanics of it all, the manipulation of time as

Pinter reels it back, plays with it, loops it in and over as he does several times when he stretches a time before to a later time before. But again, I thought, Pinter does not seem to give us a chance to care what happens to these people. We see them playing off one another or one against another in an empty game. If we are involved at all in the play, it seemed to me it is when we are willing, like his characters, to be manipulated into taking sides, to be willing to be cast by Pinter in the role of examiner, inspecting his characters against an antiseptic white set under white light.

The play begins in the light. It is spring, the beginning, the time of renewal. The time is noon—the middle of the day when the sun is at its highest point. It takes place in a pub, a public place. Emma and Jerry meet after the end of their affair. They are used up, finished.

The final scene is during a winter evening. It takes place late at night, perhaps close to midnight. (We know the guests are leaving the party given by Emma and Robert.) It takes place in darkness, in the private space of Emma's bedroom.

Certainly, this is ingenious manipulation of time, but what is it that "wrings" Beckett's heart? What is it about that "first last look in the shadows . . ."?

"That first last look," of course, refers to the initial encounter of Jerry and Emma in scene 9 of *Betrayal*. It is the poignant exchange between two people who will become lovers. We, the audience, are looking through a keyhole at a very private meeting. This look is the recognition of what is and perhaps of what will be. It is the beginning. Everything else that comes from it, played in reverse, is dependent upon that look. But it is also perhaps the inevitable ending of the relationship that is seen by both lovers, the foreshadowing of the end that must come of such a relationship (the end that we have already seen), that Beckett found so moving. This is more important than time past or present because it is the catalyst of everything that follows, that has followed. The image of the look is the still point when time stops for the two lovers as they discover their attraction; it is the turning point around which the wheel of time within the play revolves; it is the fixed point which is the center of the play. The last scene is both the beginning of the story and the end of the play. The look is perhaps the beginning and the end of the affair.

Perhaps this silent exchange between lovers was a recognition of the impossibility of the relationship, together with the inevitability of it—the clashing of the "can't go on" and the "must go on," with the resulting "go on." Certainly Beckett's reaction is not that of an examiner or an inspector but that of an involved reader.

Reading and rereading the text of *Betrayal*, in the context of the Beckett statement, I was struck by something in scene 9. In this last scene, Jerry declares his passion for Emma; he says, "You. You're lovely, I'm crazy about you. . . . All these words I'm using, don't you see, they've never been said before. Can't you see? I'm crazy about you. It's a whirlwind . . ." (265–66). When I read, "It's a whirlwind," it triggered a memory in me, and the memory brought me to the fifth canto of Dante's *Inferno* with its pairs of lovers damned to the eternal storm of their passion, principally Paolo and Francesca da Rimini. Of all the lovers in the canto, it is Paolo and Francesca who are singled out by Dante as *"due che'nsieme vanno,/e paion si al vento esser leggieri"* (translated by Charles Singleton as "those two that go together and seem to be so light upon the wind" [Singleton, *Inferno 1* 50, 51]). "This suggests that these two spirits are more violently tossed by the wind than the others are" (*Inferno 2* 82).

I suddenly realized that there were other echoes in Pinter's play that might be allusions to this canto. First, Dante describes its setting, *"in loco d'ogne luce muto,"* "a place mute of all light" (*Inferno 1*, 48, 49). Second, there is the reference to Jerry as Robert's best man, as he reminds Emma in scene 9 in a passionate outburst; "I should have had you in white before the wedding. I should have blackened you, in your white wedding dress, blackened you in your bridal dress, before ushering you into your wedding, as your best man" (265). Paolo, according to the legend Dante used for the canto, was proxy for his brother Gianciotto's betrothal to Francesca. Further, the shocking introduction of "blackened" by Jerry may have an echo from the blackened air of Canto 5, *"l'aura nera"* (*Inferno 1* 50, 51), here indicating a soiling of the atmosphere, rather than the rape of a bride, but both attesting to the violent and unnatural climate of the images.

Earlier (and later) in scene 5, Emma and Robert are in a hotel in Venice, and Emma is lying on the bed reading a book by a man called Spinks that has been recommended by Jerry. After Robert tells Emma he has read it, and has decided not to publish it, she asks why and Robert replies, "Oh . . . not much more to say on that subject, really, is there?" Emma asks him, "What do you consider the subject to be?" and Robert answers, "Betrayal" (216). This exchange leads directly into the accusation of betrayal by Robert, who has intercepted a letter from Jerry to Emma, and subsequently to Emma's confession of her betrayal to her husband. In the *Inferno* canto, the dramatic importance of the book of betrayal by Guinevere and Lancelot of King Arthur is central to the climax of the passion of the lovers Paolo and Francesca as they secretly read it together, during an assignation, when their eyes meet: *"ma solo un punto fu quel che ci vinse"* ("but one moment alone it was that overcame us" [*Inferno 1* 54, 55]). It is also the source of discovery of their deception by Gianciotto which leads to their death and subsequent eternal torment.

In scene 7, at a time described by Pinter only as *"Later,"* Jerry meets Robert for lunch at an Italian restaurant. Robert, who has been told about the affair by Emma, brings up the matter of the Spinks book and ironically confides his wife's reaction to Jerry, who is still unaware of Emma's confession: "Emma read that novel of that chum of yours. . . . She seemed to be madly in love with it." And later, his bile includes his former best friend; "You know what you and Emma have in common? You love literature. I mean you love modern prose literature, I mean you love the new novel by the new Casey or Spinks. It gives you both a thrill" (248, 250).

Ultimately, the most resonant echo of Dante in *Betrayal* is found in the fifth canto's most universal and most universally applicable lines: "*nessum maggio dolore/che ricordarsi del tempo fellice/ne la miseria,*" translated by Singleton as "there is no greater sorrow than to recall in wretchedness the happy time" (*Inferno 1* 54–55). This could be a description of *Betrayal,* which begins in sorrow and follows with memories—albeit often faulty ones—of past happier times, at least some of the time.

Finally, Pinter's own words on a related aspect of the writing process provide a fitting last word on the Dantean underpinnings of *Betrayal:*

> I am aware, sometimes of an insistence in my mind. Images, characters, insisting upon being written. You can pour a drink, make a telephone call or run round the park, and sometimes succeed in suffocating them. You know they're going to make your life hell. But at other times they're unavoidable and you're compelled to try to do them some kind of justice. And while it may be hell, it's certainly for me the best kind of hell to be in. (*Complete Works: 4* xiii)

TWELVE

A Rose by any other name: Pinter and Shakespeare

Hersh Zeifman

The Ruffian on the Stair, the title of Joe Orton's 1964 radio play which he later revised for the stage, could just as easily have been used by Harold Pinter for the title of his first play, *The Room* (1957). Its source is the opening stanza of a poem by the Victorian writer W. E. Henley:

> Madam Life's a piece in bloom
> Death goes dogging everywhere:
> She's the tenant of the room,
> He's the ruffian on the stair. (87)

Rose, the central character of *The Room,* is, as her name indicates, indeed "a piece *in bloom*"—"the tenant of the room" who, in at least one reading of the play, is constantly dogged by Death.[1] Even the apparently "unruffian" couple Rose encounters on the stair outside her room embodies this threat of Death. It's present in their very surname, Sands (the sands of time?), as well as in their given names: Tod (German for "death") and Clarissa (from the Latin *clarus,* "clear"—the clarity promised by the apostle Paul in the life to come: "For now we see through a glass, darkly; but then face to face . . ." [1 Cor. 13.12]).

Characters' names are almost always of special significance in Pinter's plays. Clarissa, when complimented by Rose on the "prettiness" of her name, responds: "Yes, it is nice, isn't it? My father and mother gave it to me" (112). Who else gives us our name, our identity? Pinter, ultimately both "father and mother" to his characters, chooses his "offsprings'" names carefully. By naming the protagonist of *The Room* Rose, for example, Pinter subtly evokes her essential vulnerability: the transience of her life, the inevitability of her death. "As for man, his days are as grass; as *a flower* of the field, so he flourisheth," the Psalmist informs us. "For the wind passeth over it, and it is gone; and the place thereof shall know it no more" (Ps. 103.15–16; my emphasis).[2] The Bible, however, is not the only source of echo sounded in Rose's floral name. For Rose has another name in the play, one conferred on her by Riley—"the ruffian on the stair" who ascends from the damp basement where he has been waiting, as Mr. Kidd so redundantly phrases it, "in the black dark" (121). When Riley finally enters Rose's room, he is Mr. Kidd's "black dark" made flesh—"a blind Negro" (122), and therefore doubly dark. "Your father wants you to come home," Riley tells Rose. "Come home, Sal. . . . I want you to come home" (124–25; my emphasis). Is Riley, then, an incarnation of Rose's father? Is Rose really Sal? Rose can change her name and thus symbolically her identity, can hide from her father (earthly or heavenly), can try to cheat Death, but to no avail; whatever identity she takes on, Death will sniff her out. To Riley, a Rose by any other name still smells of Sal.[3]

What's in a name? For Pinter's characters, the answer—like the question—can often be found specifically in Shakespeare. Rose is only the first of many Pinter people who carry an evocative Shakespearean resonance in their names, a resonance that subtly focuses the audience's attention on the key issues of the play. Pinter comes by his knowledge of Shakespeare honestly. Being taken on a school outing to see Donald Wolfit act Lear and Macbeth proved to be a major turning-point in Pinter's life (Gross 37; Bensky, "Harold Pinter" 22); later, in one of his earliest literary efforts, he wrote an essay praising Shakespeare's skill as a dramatist (Esslin, *Pinter: The Playwright* 58–59).[4] As a fledgling actor, Pinter deepened his love of Shakespeare by appearing in many Shakespearean roles—Macbeth and Romeo while still in school; Pistol in *The Merry Wives of Windsor* during his abortive study at RADA; Abergevenny in his first professional performance of Shakespeare, a BBC radio production of *Henry VIII*. In the early 1950s Pinter toured Ireland with Anew McMaster, playing nine different Shakespearean characters; in 1953 he briefly joined Wolfit's company at the King's Theatre, Hammersmith, where he added six more Shakespearean roles to his repertoire.[5]

Not surprisingly, perhaps, a number of critics have been tempted over the years to try to "read" Pinter's plays through a Shakespearean lens (with at least one intrepid critic attempting, ingeniously, the reverse!).[6] The temptation is understandable and potentially rewarding, but also rather risky. Unlike the work of Samuel Beckett, say, which he so admired, Pinter's dialogue, while equally spare and elliptical, is almost totally devoid of direct Shakespearean allusion. It's possible, I suppose, to hear an echo of *Macbeth* in Len's paranoid observation in Pinter's stage version of *The Dwarfs* (1963): "There is my hundred watt bulb like a dagger" (96; cf. *Mac.* II.i.33ff.). Or, more amusingly, an echo of Hamlet's disgust with his mother's o'erhasty marriage in Davies's bathetic account, in *The Caretaker,* of abandoning his bride after discovering a pile of her unwashed underwear in a saucepan: "That's why I left my wife. Fortnight after I married her, no, not so much as that, no more than a week . . ." (18; cf. *Ham.* I.ii.138). But one has to reach a bit to make those connections; while Browning may have been right that a man's reach should exceed his grasp, *over* reaching, in literary criticism as in life, often goeth before a pratfall. Leery of falls, I want to make only the most modest of proposals—that Shakespeare leaves his mark on Pinter's drama not so much through direct allusion as through subtle resonance, a faint echo most frequently sounded in Pinter's characters' names. And that echo has continued to sound throughout a now lengthy theatrical career: each of the Pinter plays I have chosen to examine is from a different decade.

In *Landscape* (1968), Pinter introduces us to Duff and Beth, a middle-aged couple, presumably husband and wife, seated in the kitchen of a country house. But though they share the same theatrical space, the landscape of their lives is in fact sharply divided: "DUFF sits in a chair at the right corner of the [kitchen] table"; "BETH sits in an armchair, which stands away from the table, to its left" (175). (This division was emphasized in John Bury's brilliant set design for the original RSC stage production: a fissure in the stage floor, to the left of the table, further separated the couple, isolating Beth on her own little "island." The split in the stage floor thus mirrored a more profound split between the two characters, a visual reminder of the deep chasm separating them.) When they ultimately speak, neither seems to hear the other; though Duff normally refers to Beth, "BETH *never looks at* DUFF" (175). As divided as the two are physically, they are even more so emotionally: the landscape of their inner lives, reflected in their speeches, charts very different terrain, a landscape of memory and desire that never fuses into one. Like the kitchen table that simultaneously both joins and separates them, their apparent "dialogue" is in reality a series of monologues, two alternating voices—Beth's gentle and lyrical; Duff's coarse and violent—running along separate tracks. The couple's presence in a unified physical space is thus a particularly cruel *trompe-l'oeil:* they appear to be linked—a shared kitchen table, a shared marital history—but in fact are alone, together. Divided they sit: the family cell has ironically turned into solitary confinement.

At one point in *Landscape,* Beth recalls being taught the basic principles of light and shadow in drawing:

> Objects intercepting the light cast shadows. Shadow is deprivation of light. The shape of the shadow is determined by that of the object. But not always. Not always directly. Sometimes it is only indirectly affected by it. Sometimes the cause of the shadow cannot be found. (196)

A huge shadow looms over this couple, the shadow of their painful estrangement; can its cause ever be found? A possible clue may lie in the specifically Shakespearean resonance of the couple's names. Beth and Duff are as joined together as Macbeth and Macduff, and ultimtely as deeply divided.[7] Macbeth and Macduff begin Shakespeare's tragedy as blood brothers, brave Scottish noblemen fighting to protect Duncan's kingship; they close the play as bitter enemies, blood brothers in a far different sense: Macduff ends up slaying the tyrant Macbeth, proudly bearing aloft "[t]he usurper's cursed head" (V.viii.55). The seeds of their enmity are planted by the witches' warning Macbeth to beware Macduff, to which Macbeth reacts by slaughtering Macduff's family. The two characters are linked, then, by the death of children. Macduff's response to the news of his family's slaughter focuses precisely on this point:

He has no children. All my pretty ones?
Did you say all? O Hellkite! All?
What, all my pretty chickens. . . . (IV.iii.216–18)

Perhaps what separates Pinter's Beth and Duff is this same absence of children; the missing link that might join them, as it joins their names in the Shakespearean original, is "mac" Gaelic for "son." Clearly Beth has always wanted a child; almost the first words she speaks in the play, addressed to her "man" asleep in the sand, concern children: "Would you like a baby? I said. Children? Babies? Of our own? Would be nice. . . . Our own child? Would you like that?" (177). So urgent are these questions that, a few moments later, she repeats them: "I lay down beside him and whispered. Would you like a baby? A child? Of our own? Would be nice" (185). If the man on the beach is in fact Duff, as Pinter has intimated,[8] then the gulf separating Beth's lyrical hopes of the past from the stark reality of her present is placed in particularly bold relief. Late in the play, Beth recalls sitting in her kitchen one beautiful autumn morning: "The dog sat down by me. I stroked him. Through the window I could see down into the valley. I saw children in the valley. They were running through the grass. They ran up the hill." Significantly, this reverie is followed by the stage direction "*Long silence*" (195), the only such direction in a play studded with "*Pause*" and "*Silence*." The loss of children thus appears to be the shadow separating Beth and Duff, as it separates their Shakespearean counterparts; the tenderness and life symbolically associated with children are precisely what's absent from their barren marriage.

The geometry of marriage is also the subject of Pinter's *Old Times* (1971), where the parallel lines that never meet of *Landscape* are replaced by an onstage triangle. The subtext of *Old Times* dramatizes a struggle for the "possession" of the heart and soul of Kate, a struggle between her husband Deeley and her old friend (and possibly ex-lover) Anna. Through most of the play Kate sits and watches passively, seldom speaking, as the two woo her with memories of old times, each memory designed to annihilate the other's claim on her. Cast by them as an object, a "thing," Kate becomes the glittering "prize" for which Deeley and Anna are fighting. And it *is* a fight, a no-holds-barred boxing match replete with fancy footwork, wicked little jabs, clever feints, and the occasional knockout—all of which an audience is encouraged to "score." "It's nice I know for Katey to see you" (19), Deeley begins his offensive, subtly attacking Anna with a carefully aimed punch, immediately establishing, through the diminutive "Katey," the intimacy of his relationship with Kate. Anna, however, is no easy pushover; a few minutes later, in recalling an incident from her past with Kate, she counterpunches with an identical claim to intimacy: "This man crying in our room. One night late I returned and found him sobbing, his hand over his face, sitting in the armchair, all crumpled in the armchair and *Katey* sitting on the bed . . ." (28; my emphasis). The battle lines have been neatly drawn; which of these two skillful opponents will "win" Kate?

The answer, of course, is neither, for Kate is not an object, a "prize" with no mind of her own. Unlike her Shakespearean namesake in *The Taming of the Shrew*, Pinter's Kate cannot be "tamed."[9] Petruchio's goal in *Shrew* is clearly spelled out: "For I am he am born to tame you Kate, / And bring you from a wild Kate to a Kate / Conformable as other household Kates" (II.i.278–80), a goal in which he presumably succeeds; Kate winds up conceding defeat, subjugating her will to his: "What you will have it named, even that it is, / And so it shall be so for Katharine" (IV.v.21–22). Anna and Deeley have a similar goal: both of them want Kate to accept their "visions" of the past—their "naming" of reality—but Kate proves far more self-possessed than Shakespeare's heroine. She has never been the domesticated "Katey" they fondly imagine; she remains Kate, that monosyllable with no soft edges which might allow others a way in. They have chosen the wrong pun on her name: she is not, as Petruchio maintains, "my superdainty Kate, / For dainties are all Kates" (II.i.89–90)—i.e., cate as "delicacy," a comestible to be "eaten up" by them. ("You have a wonderful casserole," Anna informs Deeley when they first meet. "I mean wife. So sorry. A wonderful wife" [16].) Rather, she is the "wild Kate" (wildcat) incapable of being tamed—elusive, inscrutable, her relative silence her greatest strength.[10] And when she finally breaks that silence, in the play's concluding speech (by far the longest speech in the play), her victory is complete. If truth is what is not forgotten, as the etymology of the Greek word for "truth," *aletheia*, implies, then Kate triumphs by establishing *her* memories as the "truth" ("But I *remember* you," her final speech begins [67; my emphasis]), by "naming" both Anna and Deeley "dead." The rest is a *"Long silence"* (69)—again, the only such direction in the entire play. The taming of Shakespeare's Kate has been reversed by Pinter; the battle of *Old Times* has been won by its most unlikely combatant.

A Kind of Alaska (1982), the last Pinter play I want to examine, was inspired by neurologist Oliver Sacks's *Awakenings,* a collection of case histories describing survivors of *encephalitis lethargica* (sleeping sickness) brought back to life after more than 40 years with the wonder drug L-DOPA. Specifically, Pinter chose to dramatize the case history of the patient Sacks calls "Rose R." (67–79)—and so, coincidentally, we end where we began, with another Rose. Sacks's Rose becomes Pinter's Deborah; as the play opens, the 45-year-old Deborah has just been awakened from a "sleep" of almost 30 years by her doctor, Hornby. This miraculous metamorphosis is compared in the text, implicitly or explicitly, to various celebrated literary transformations. Thus Deborah describes her years spent "asleep" as dancing in very narrow spaces: "[I] [k]ept stubbing my toes and bumping my head. Like Alice" (24). Being restored to life strikes Deborah as a sort of fairy tale, like "Sleeping Beauty": [D]id you wake me with a magic wand?," she asks Hornby, adding " . . . you are my Prince Charming" (19).[11] But the most cryptic, and ultimately the most significant, literary echo concerning Deborah's transformation comes from her sister Pauline, informing Deborah of how her illness first manifested itself:

> You were standing with a vase of flowers in your hands. You were about to put it down on the table. But you didn't put it down. You stood still, with the vase

in your hands, as if you were . . . fixed. . . . Then Daddy tried to take the vase
from you. He could not . . . wrench it from your hands. He could not . . . move
you from the spot. Like . . . marble. (30–31)

Deborah had become, in effect, a living statue.[12]

The presence of Pauline standing constant vigil through the years over
a statue-like human being—in the text, Pauline simply "materializes" in
Deborah's hospital room, with no indication of when, or if, she entered (26)—
recalls another "statue" come to life, and another Pauline: the Paulina of
Shakespeare's *The Winter's Tale,* guardian of the "statue" of Hermione. *The
Winter's Tale* is likewise a kind of fairy tale, a Christian romance in which
faith and repentance bring redemption, in which that which was lost is found
again (III.ii.135–37). Time, the great redeemer, acts as Chorus in the play,
effecting the transition between the two "worlds" of the play—from the tragedy
and death in winter of the courtly world of Sicilia, to the comedy and rebirth
in spring of the pastoral world of Bohemia. As the earth is reborn through the
wonders of nature, so humanity is reborn through the act of generation, and
still further "reborn" into everlasting life through God's forgiveness of its sins.
"Oh, she's warm!," marvels Leontes when the statue of his wife suddenly
comes to life. "If this be magic, let it be an art / Lawful as eating" (V.iii.109–
11). But Hermione's resurrection is neither magic nor art; it's the result of
divine grace, as Paulina reminds us when instructing the "statue" to move:
"Bequeath to death your numbness, for from him / Dear life redeems you"
(V.iii.102–03).

Pinter's Pauline, by contrast, stands guard over a very different "resurrection," a very different "statue." Sacks's Rose ("a Rose by any other name")
becomes, for Pinter, not Hermione but Deborah, the Old Testament prophetess
who helped deliver her people from captivity, for which she offered praise to
the Lord: "Awake, awake, Deborah: awake, awake, utter a song" (Judg. 5.12).
But when Pinter's Deborah awakes, she is ironically still a captive. Hornby
tries to explain to Deborah that she has not been dead but merely suspended
in time: "[your mind] took up a temporary habitation . . . in a kind of Alaska"
(34). Yet her awakening is also into "a kind of Alaska"—our first sight of
Deborah is of a woman in a *white* bed (6), and her response to Hornby's
statement is, significantly, "I'm cold" (35).

"A sad tale's best for winter," the young prince Mamillius informs us in
The Winter's Tale (II.i.25); *A Kind of Alaska,* as its wintry title suggests, is
indeed a sad tale. For Deborah, there is no divine reversal of this winter's
tale: no Bohemia, no spring, no regeneration; her "awakening" is as nightmarish as her "sleep" has been. As Hornby states, "No-one wakes from the
dead" (15); in *A Kind of Alaska* what is lost *stays* lost, never to be recaptured.
Time marches inexorably on, like the "drip" Deborah keeps hearing (38–39).
Awake or asleep finally makes no difference; we're always "asleep," always
ambushed by the ravages of time, always overcome by the suddenness of loss.
One minute we're children; the next minute we're parents, or not parents;

the next minute our parents are blind, or dead. As Pozzo notes in *Waiting for Godot:* "... one day we were born, one day we shall die, the same day, the same second, is that not enough for you?" (57). For Deborah, it's too much; mechanically repeating the "facts" of her situation at the end of the play, she carefully filters out the most painful of them. Who can blame her for resisting belief in the horrors of the present, for clinging instead to the false comforts of the past, for refusing to accept the steady erosion of time which, in *A Kind of Alaska,* can never be redeemed?

In the essay on Shakespeare he wrote when he was in his late teens or early twenties, Pinter observed: "Shakespeare writes of the open wound. . . . The fabric breaks. The wound is open. The wound is contained. The wound is peopled" (qtd. in Esslin, *Pinter: The Playwright* 58–59). In many ways, this is at least as apt a description of Pinter's plays as it is of Shakespeare's. Pinter too writes of the open wound, a wound that is memorably peopled. In *A Midsummer Night's Dream,* Shakespeare has Theseus describe the poet/playwright as one who "gives to airy nothing / A local habitation and a name" (V.i.16–17). The "airy nothings" who people the wound of Pinter's drama are indeed given a local habitation, and often a highly evocative name. Significantly, that name frequently turns out to contain a ghostly—though usually subversive—echo of Shakespeare, adding a further level of weight and texture to a Pinter play. In a body of work celebrated for its surprises, this may be one of the greatest surprises of all: for Pinter, a Rose by any other name smells, more often than not, of the "sweetness" of a specific Shakespearean source.

Notes

1. I am taking Henley's lines slightly out of context in order to make my point. In Henley's poem, Madam Life is imaged as a whore; our "embrace" of her inevitably extracts a price, collected by her "pimp," Death.

2. "A flower of the field" is a biblical text frequently cited in the work of Samuel Beckett, a major influence on Pinter's writing. To quote just one instance, in *Endgame,* Hamm laments over the deceased Mother Pegg, "She was bonny once, like a flower of the field" (31).

3. The allusion, of course, is to Shakespeare's *Romeo and Juliet:* "That which we call a rose / By any other name would smell as sweet" (II.ii.43–44). See also my article "Ghost Trio."

4. Some of the material from this essay was later used by Pinter in chapter 23 of his novel *The Dwarfs* (written 1952–1956), where Pete and Mark debate the merits of Shakespeare over many drinks in a pub. Unusually for Pinter, this early novel also contains some direct Shakespearean quotation—for example, Mark's questioning the whereabouts of Virginia: "Who had seen the mobled queen?" (139). Cf. *Ham.* II.ii.524ff.

5. See Esslin (*Pinter: The Playwright*) and Thompson. Surprisingly, in a book attempting to trace the "links" between the plays in which Pinter appeared as an actor and the plays he would later come to write, Thompson almost totally ignores the

influence of Pinter's frequent appearances in Shakespeare. See also *Mac*, Pinter's memoir of Anew McMaster.

6. A relatively early example was Nelson's attempt to link *The Homecoming* with *Troilus and Cressida;* one of the most recent is Gillen's tracing of Shakespearean "patterns" in Pinter's plays back to the discussion of Shakespeare in Pinter's novel *The Dwarfs*. The critic who reversed the process and tried to "read" Shakespeare through Pinter was Brown.

7. In addition to playing Macbeth in a school production, Pinter also played Macduff with Anew McMaster's company and the Second Murderer with Donald Wolfit's company. See Thompson (6, 14). Interestingly, Macduff is referred to as "Duff" at one point in Shakespeare's play (II.iii.94).

8. In a letter written to the director of the first German production of *Landscape* (Hamburg, 1970), and subsequently printed in the program, Pinter stated: ". . . the man on the beach is Duff. I think there are elements of Mr. Sykes in [Beth's] memory of this Duff which she might be attributing to Duff, but the man remains Duff." Cited in Esslin (*Pinter: The Playwright* 180n).

9. Pinter played Hortensio in Anew McMaster's production of *The Taming of the Shrew,* and Nicholas, one of Petruchio's servants, in Wolfit's production. See Thompson (6, 14).

10. Cf. Stella, whose silence in *The Collection* is also her greatest strength, and whose inscrutability is specifically linked to the cat lying with her in the play's final tableau (157).

11. Cf. Sacks's conclusion of Rose R.'s case-history: "But she is a Sleeping Beauty whose 'awakening' was unbearable to her, and who will never be woken again" (79).

12. Cf. Sacks's description of Rose's nightmares during the onset of her illness: "she dreamed that she had become a living sentient statue of stone" (68).

THIRTEEN

From Novel to Film: Harold Pinter's Adaptation of *The Trial*

Francis Gillen[1]

Harold Pinter told BBC Producer Louis Marks that *The Trial* was the screenplay he had been wanting to write since he was seventeen years old.[2] This is not at all surprising, for Pinter has acknowledged reading Kafka's novels and short stories as a young man, and many interpretations of *The Trial* are similar in a number of ways to interpretations of Harold Pinter's own early plays. Josef K. may be seen as a victim either of society or some organization similar to the Vehmic courts of the late middle ages, just as some see Stanley in *The Birthday Party* as the victim of a society or a nameless organization. The opening lines of the novel—"Someone must have been telling lies about Josef K., for without having done anything wrong he was arrested one fine morning" (K 1)—seem to support this interpretation.[3] Others see the Court itself which destroys K. as existing threateningly and menacingly just outside the intellectual, moral, psychological, and social orders and structures within which, as in Pinter's rooms, the individual seeks illusory security. In *The Nightmare of Reason: A Life of Franz Kafka*, Ernst Pawel writes of "Joseph K.'s struggle to discover the nature of his guilt, the identity of his judges, the letter of the law, and his stubborn efforts to pit reason and common sense against the flawless logic of a sentence based on a verdict beyond rational comprehension—" (322). Other critics see a correspondence between the inner world of K. and the external events which lead to his downfall. Meno Spann, for example, writes: "The secret Court which has initiated criminal proceedings against K. is as real and as unreal as the beetle Gregor Samsa. . . . The giant metaphor 'Secret Court' seems to illustrate the trial in K.'s soul. His innermost feelings, which are offended by the life he is leading and initially silenced, repressed, and ridiculed by K.'s mind, win out in the end and call forth in him a growing desire for purification through punishment" (96). Kafka himself wrote in his diary on 10 December 1910, "I have continually an invocation in my ear: If you would only come, invisible tribunal" (36). Finally, for some critics, the minions of the law are not wholly negative, but have the potential for redemption, depending on how K. views them.[4]

These interpretations of *The Trial* indicate the difficulty in attempting to translate to the screen the many levels of a novel which remain essentially ambiguous because everything is perceived through the mind of the protagonist. In *Making Pictures: The Pinter Screenplays,* Joanne Klein suggests a correlation in Pinter's works between such ambiguity and the limits of film itself. "Like the camera Pinter manipulates not reality, but the mechanisms through which we glimpse it. The imperfections of these mechanisms receive frequent accentuation by various emblems in Pinter's work; the incidence of blindness, eyeglasses, and telescopes, for example, signifies both a desire and a failure to yield the secrets in our picture of the world" (4).

In his film adaptation of *The Trial,* Orson Welles saw K. as both a collaborator and a victim. He made this point in a 1965 interview published with the text of the screenplay:

> Q: In *The Trial,* you seem to be making a severe criticism of the abuse of power; or perhaps it's something more profound—Perkins appears as a kind of Prometheus . . .
> WELLES: He's also a little bureaucrat. I consider him guilty. (9)

Welles changed the ending of Kafka's novel, allowing K. to defy his executioners because he felt that was the way Kafka himself would have written *The Trial* in a post-Holocaust era. For all his protestations, however, and despite its many cinematic virtues, the Welles film with its gigantic sets, hundreds of desks at the office, all seeming to dwarf the individual, and with the often stupefied, boylike performance by Anthony Perkins as K., does make K. seem primarily a victim.

The political bent of Pinter's recent plays, as well as his work with Amnesty International and his public statements about arrest and torture, must have made such an interpretation appealing to Pinter, although in a somewhat different manner. At the time he was working on the screenplay, Pinter said in a conversation that he considered Welles's interpretation far too melodramatic, making K. too singular.[5] His words echoed Hannah Arendt's in *Eichmann in Jerusalem* about the very banality of evil that allows it to become so pervasive, or his own in the interview with Nicholas Hern that arrest, torture, and the complicity that allows them are everywhere.[6]

Pinter's screenplay does open the film to political interpretation, but it goes beyond that to indicate an inner correspondence between K. and what happens to him. Pinter accomplishes this in part by remaining extraordinarily faithful to Kafka's text in what he includes, in the order of the events, and even in the language itself. The major differences between the novel and a screenplay that is by necessity approximately one-third the length of the book lie in the screenwriter's choice of what detail or dialogue to retain and what to omit, and in the transformation of inner states to external scenes or images. Of such a process Klein notes that "where the narrative bulk proves too complex or unwieldy for cinematic legibility, the adapter must find some approach to editing the text for film. Ideally this reductive process produces minimal distortion of the source work" (6). Beyond this necessary reductive process, however, cinema relies on images, and the images the screenwriter chooses to repeat create motifs and emphases. I shall therefore discuss Pinter's selection and omission of details and the motifs created through repeated visual images which refer to eyes and living one's life in the eyes of others, to the depiction of a poisonous atmosphere which becomes increasingly pervasive, and therefore almost unnoticed, and to the repeated emphasis on K.'s assumption of superiority.

Welles begins the opening arrest scene with the warders turning the key into K.'s room. Pinter has K. awake and look out the window to see a woman watching him. Though there are many details which Pinter omits from this arrest scene, he also keeps one other "watching" scene and another in which K. shouts to the woman, now joined by two companions, to get away from her window. Thus Pinter establishes visually from the opening scene that it is not only the arrest, but the perception of the arrest that disturbs K. Indeed his anger in shouting at the "watchers" is stronger than any other emotion he demonstrates.[7]

This sense of K.'s need to maintain a feeling of superiority is further enhanced by an obviously interesting parallel with Pinter's play *The Birthday Party*. In both novel and screenplay K. is greeted at his office with a "Happy Birthday, Sir" (18) by his assistant and then given presents from other members of the staff. But in the following scene with Frau Grubach, when K. tries to determine the extent to which she has been disturbed by the events of his arrest, Pinter adds the detail that Frau Grubach has baked him a birthday cake. This emphasis would seem to suggest one level of seeing the film as a maturation process, either successful or failed.

In the scene of K.'s first interrogation, Pinter omits K.'s reflection that these people are easy to win over; therefore K.'s long speech which follows the outburst of applause after his remark that he may be late coming to the Court but at least he's come, seems more "playing to the audience" than the somewhat calculated strategy he adopts in the novel. In the dialogue, Pinter selects details which reinforce this view. "It is for these people I am speaking—not for myself," K. states (46).

Following his depiction of this initial interrogation by the court, Pinter creates five scenes to illustrate the following two sentences from the novel:

> During the next week K. waited day after day for a new summons, he would not believe that his refusal to be interrogated had been taken literally, and when no appointment was made by Saturday evening, he assumed that he was tacitly expected to report himself again at the same address and at the same time. (K 49)

In the first scene, the Anna who did not bring him his breakfast on the day of his arrest is shown dutifully doing just that. The scene seems to indicate that on the surface things have returned to normal. The second scene creates that same impression in the bank, with various men wishing K. good morning and shaking his hand. The third, however, shows him refusing to answer an important call from the Paris manager; the fourth, K. asking desperately at the office about any call "from anybody!" and the fifth his petulant questioning of Frau Grubach about any possible telephone message:

> FRAU GRUBACH: But Herr K. . . . the telephone hasn't rung at all today.
> K: How do you know? Weren't you out shopping this morning?
> FRAU GRUBACH: Yes. Yes . . .
> K: So how can you know it hasn't rung? How can you *know*? (53–54)

Though these scenes illustrate the text, they go beyond that in showing K. not waiting for the messages, but actively soliciting a new summons from the court. Thus this most extensive of Pinter's creation of scenes not actually in the text tends to support the view that at some level K. is indeed seeking this trial.

When K. returns of his own volition to seek the Court, only to find the rooms empty and the lawbooks full of obscene pictures, he is told by the woman who shows him the office that he has lovely eyes and that, in a phrase Pinter adds to Kafka's text, she "couldn't resist gazing at [him]" (59), thus tying her to the watching old woman in the first scene. She begins to lift her skirt and show K. her lovely stockings but stops because the student, Berthold, "is watching us" (60).

By carefully selecting the dialogue, Pinter makes this exchange between K. and the student a battle for possession. Thus he dramatizes visually certain thoughts that are present in K.'s mind: first, that "that supple, voluptuous warm body under the coarse, heavy, dark dress, belonged to K. and to K. alone" (K 56) and secondly, that K. considers himself defeated by the student because he is in a new element, one to which he continues to believe himself superior. "While he stayed quietly at home and went about his ordinary vocation he remained superior to all these people and could kick any of them out of his path" (K 58–59).

K. then wanders into the law offices where he meets the husband of the woman carried off by the student, a court usher. The usher bemoans the freedom the student takes with his wife and insists K. might do something about it "because you're an accused man. You've got nothing to lose" (65). As the scene continues, Pinter shows K. playing to a group of persons waiting on the court, presenting himself as someone who has also been summoned by the court, but one who is superior to others who are there. The trial in Pinter's script thus is truly an externalization of an attitude K. had clearly held before the trial had ever begun. Something in K. wants to be here, and while K. is aware of the danger, he is enjoying a battle he feels he can win at any time. As in many of Pinter's own plays, K. doesn't recognize what Pinter terms in his novel, *The Dwarfs,* his own "territorial limits."[8] He thinks that the rules which apply to his easy conquests in boarding house and bank will see him through here.

In the remainder of the scene in the court offices, Pinter selects details which emphasize the atmosphere of the court as opposed to the atmosphere outside. As K. suddenly wants to leave the court offices, complaining of the air, a girl offers to help the increasingly giddy K. when she is halted by a man who is described as the Court's Information Officer. In the screenplay, the man says, "I think the gentleman's disposition is due to the atmosphere in here" (71).

As K. nears the exit door, supported now by the information officer and the girl, he can no longer hear their voices, only a roaring sound like waves. Then as air from outside reaches K., the man's voice returns. Pinter visually dramatizes this world outside as "a sudden flash of light" (73). Kafka has all K.'s energies returning, and has him exit through the door, which the girl is holding open. Pinter has him falling out the door, sitting and gasping to take in air. He indicates a camera angle whereby the man and girl are looking down on him. Then Pinter evidently reverses the camera angle to K.'s point of view and the man and the girl suddenly look ill.

If Pinter's screenplay is moving at this point to a sense of two worlds, the poisonous one of the court and the one outside to which K. has been accustomed, that sense would have been blunted by fully dramatizing an eight-page chapter, "Fräulein Burstner's Friend."[9] Instead, without unduly interrupting the narrative flow, Pinter creates three brief scenes illustrating perfectly K.'s growing isolation and the attitudes of the others as uninvolved observers. The film then moves almost immediately to continue the dual perspective established at the conclusion of the scenes in the court offices, the spreading of the poisonous atmosphere into what K. had considered the safe domain of the offices where he works.

More and more, as K. learns that still another place is connected to the Court or another person belongs to the Court, there is the growing sense that the atmosphere, which once seemed localized and specific to K., is so omnipresent as to become the modus vivendi. What is everywhere cannot be confronted and is impervious to language and reason. Because Pinter, unlike Welles, has kept the screenplay on a matter-of-fact level, an audience is shocked, as is K., to find the two arresting warders being whipped savagely in a lumber room near K.'s office in the bank.

Whether this represents the actual whipping of the warders in K.'s mind or K.'s own desire for punishment, it is clear that at this point the subjective and objective worlds intersect as they do in Pinter's dramas, and that they play off against one another and interact across a line that is not discernible. The whipping is as real as the knife that kills K., if only in the sense that it is an inextricable link in the chain of events which bring K. to that end.

What the scene continues to show is K.'s almost comic belief, in the face of such evidence, that evil can be confronted logically. He still believes in the power of his language and his own ability to get the warders off and control the situation. K. pleads that the warders are blameless and that it's the organization that's at fault, when suddenly, as one of the men being beaten shrieks in pain, clerks from K.'s office come to find out what is the matter. Once again Pinter shows K. acting in the eyes of others. After K. has assured the clerks that it was only a dog howling in the yard, he tries to justify his own actions. In the novel Kafka writes:

> And K. would not have been stingy, he was really very anxious to get the warder off; since he had set himself to fight the whole corrupt administration of this Court, it was obviously his duty to intervene on this occasion. But at the moment when Franz began to shriek, any intervention became impossible. K. could not afford to let the dispatch clerks and possibly all sorts of other people arrive and surprise him in a scene with these creatures in the lumber room. No one could really demand such a sacrifice from him. If a sacrifice had been needed, it would almost have been simpler to take off his own clothes and offer himself to the Whipper as a substitute for the warders. (K 88)

Though except for the omissions I have indicated, novel and screenplay are essentially similar in this chapter, Pinter does introduce wording changes which emphasize another point which is almost comically presented here: that is the fracturing of the individual task from any larger sense of purpose or meaning in that individual's mind which allows the persecuting system to operate. Pinter changes, for example, the flogger's words in Kafka—"I am here to whip people, and whip them I shall" (K 86)—to—"It's my job to flog people I'm told to flog and that's what I'm going to do" (81).

The next chapter deals with K.'s uncle's attempt to help him by taking him to a lawyer. As the uncle begins to discuss K.'s arrest, Pinter includes the detail that the uncle is talking too loudly in front of other people, suggesting the "eyes" motif. The uncle takes K. to a lawyer, Dr. Huld, where instead of taking advantage of the opportunity of winning favor with the chief clerk, K. enters into an ill-conceived, amorous affair with Leni, the aging lawyer's nurse and mistress. The scene mirrors the irrational outside K. with the irrational within, and establishes another correlation between inner and outer worlds.

The words "The thought of his case never left him now" (K 113) occur at almost exactly the midpoint of the printed novel. The second half of the novel and the last one-third of the screenplay show K. returning to the lawyer, attending on a manufacturer, and then the Court painter, Titorelli, before dismissing the lawyer, hearing a long sermon by a priest and then going to his death. Each attempt at help from outside proves a maze, for each person to whom K. turns depends in some way on the system which has accused K. The lawyer talks in self-serving circles about a legal system "so secret that the officials themselves are out of touch, hamstrung, in despair, desperate for advice" (105), and so demonstrates not K.'s innocence but his own necessity. That sense of maze continues as Titorelli, who likewise depends on painting Court Judges as they wish to appear, explains the kinds of justice that would be available to K: actual acquittal, of which there are only vague rumors that in some golden past, in myth rather than reality, people were declared wholly innocent; ostensible acquittal; and indefinite postponement.

As K. then learns that with ostensible acquittal the records remain in circulation and that someday a judge will come across them and order an immediate rearrest, with the trial beginning again, and that his third choice of indefinite postponement consists only in preventing the trial from advancing beyonds its earliest stages, K. is shown as realizing that there is no hope from this area. Again Pinter emphasizes the stifling atmosphere in the painter's room, making two distinct references to this in the screenplay by having K. state that "it's unbearable" (118) and ask that a window be opened. When Titorelli explains that it can't be opened, K. takes off his jacket. Later, as Titorelli concludes his description of types of acquittal, Pinter has Titorelli ask if K.'s discomfort is due to the bad air, and then, as he leads K. through another door, we see K. holding a handkerchief pressed to his mouth as he finds that the painter's bedroom connects directly to the court offices. We see K. staggering down the corridor, thus linking the scene to the earlier one in the court offices. What has gone almost unnoticed in all the factual detail—and this is one sense of the banality of evil—is that "guilty" loses its meaning if, as Titorelli has stated, there is no such thing as innocence except in myth.

Determined now to dismiss his lawyer and tell his own story, K. is presented with a mirror image of what life in the maze would come to, of a man wholly poisoned. In an effort to dissuade K., Huld demonstrates his power by making a tradesman, Block, attend him in a slavish fashion before frustrating and dismissing him. First K. attempts to stop Block from humiliating himself; then he addresses him ironically as a dog: "Kneel down, why don't you? Crawl on all fours. Do what you want. Get back into your kennel. It won't bother me" (141). Block in turn accuses K. of missing the fact that he too is an accused man and so no better than he is. This exchange, with Pinter adding the lines, "Do what you want. Get back into your kennel," dramatizes K.'s reflection in the novel: "So the lawyer's methods, to which K. fortunately had not been long enough exposed, amounted to this: The client ceased to be a client and became the lawyer's dog" (K 193). Perhaps drained by this realization, K. never follows his intention of presenting his own story.

The dismissal of the lawyer is followed instead by K. being sent by the bank manager to show an Italian client the town cathedral. As the Italian fails to appear, K. becomes more anxious about the warning Leni had given him that they were hounding him and that he may have been summoned here by the court. As he is about to leave, he hears from the pulpit of the darkening church a priest's commanding voice call out his name. Warning K. that he is deluded about the Law, the priest tells the story of a man from the country denied admission to the Law by a doorkeeper who speaks of doors beyond his door, each with a doorkeeper stronger than he. The countryman spends the rest of his life waiting to be admitted, only to be told at the moment of his death that no one else could pass through the door because it was intended for him. In almost Talmudic fashion, the priest then offers the questioning K. a number of possible meanings of the story. Most critics consider that this parable comes closest to revealing the meaning of the novel. In terming it "the key moment of the novel," Malcolm Bradbury, for example, writes: "It is undoubtedly the mythic core of the book, and the closest it comes to a revelation, both for Joseph K. and the reader" (274). Certainly Welles's screenplay suggests such prominence by placing it at the very opening of the film and repeating parts of it in the normal sequence of the story. Pinter's screenplay, however, leaves open the possibility of such meaning or another circular maze of the type encountered with either Titorelli or the lawyer. While not including all the possible interpretations the priest offers in the novel, Pinter does have the priest reveal that "one opinion even has it that it is the doorkeeper who is deceived" (162), citing contradictions in the doorkeeper's story. The priest also reveals that his position as prison chaplain means that he too belongs to the Court.

Finally two men come to lead K. away. In the novel it is very unclear whether these two men are friendly, unfriendly, or merely indifferent. In the film script they seem more threatening. Pinter gives the direction that the men link arms with K. and adds the somewhat melodramatic direction: "They walk, passing from the light of the street lamp into shadow, into light and into shadow" (167). Before leaving his room with the men, K. sees in the window opposite babies playing in playpens and stretching their hands out between bars; in short, the normal life that K. now seems forever separated from or an image of a prison into which all are born. Pinter writes directly into the screenplay "K.'s POV" (166) to indicate that perspective. Pinter also includes a statement by K. which once more suggests that he is playing in the eyes of others. "I'm not going to leave this life like a raging idiot." Then Pinter places the words "Why should I? How can I put it?" before those of the novel: "I don't want people to say of me that at the beginning of my case I wanted it to finish and at the end of it I wanted it to start over again. . . . I don't want that to be said. And frankly, I'm very grateful that you two half-dumb imbeciles have been sent to escort me. I'm grateful that it's been left to me to tell myself all that needs to be said" (169).

Suddenly Fräulein Burstner appears, mounting a small flight of steps, and it is relatively clear that it is she, representative perhaps not only of herself but of others, whom K., with his concern with how he appears in the eyes of others, did not wish to seek his weakness. After Fräulein Burstner's appearance, Pinter shows K. abruptly propeling his two assailants over a bridge when a policeman appears ready to stop them (169). As the first man takes out a butcher knife and examines the edges, Pinter has K. watching the knife. As he lies there, K. sees on the top story of the house adjoining the quarry a window suddenly open, paralleling the window at the start of the film. A "human figure, faint and insubstantial at that distance and that height, leaned abruptly far forward and stretched both arms still farther" (K 228). In the novel Kafka has K. think:

> Who was it? A friend? A good man? . . . Was help at hand? Were there arguments in his favor which had been overlooked? . . . Where was the judge whom he had

never seen? Where was the high court, to which he had never penetrated? (K 228)

Certainly voice-over might have been justified at this one moment in the screenplay, just as Pinter used it at the conclusion of the screenplay for *The Handmaid's Tale,* but in this screenplay he completely eschews that device.

Then both Pinter and Kafka have K. raise his hands toward the figure and spread his fingers. In both the novel and the screenplay K. is seen still at the end seeking help outside himself, looking elsewhere for his salvation. What the extended passage in the novel accomplishes, however, is to suggest the utter dependence K. still has on the law seen as an external force, not as something of which he himself must be the judge. At this moment in both the novel and the screenplay, one of the men grasps K.'s throat and the second thrusts the knife into him. In both, K.'s last words are "Like a dog!" but the text of the novel emphasizes again even more than Pinter the external vision. "It was as if the shame of it must outlive him" (K 229).

If, however, we recall the scene with the tradesman Block in which K. felt superior to his fellow human kneeling before the lawyer, K.'s final words in Pinter's screenplay may well be K.'s recognition on an existential level of what he had socially and logically denied throughout the work: his oneness with a frail, often pathetic and broken humankind.

I am suggesting, then, that Pinter's screenplay does make a significant political statement. K.'s tools for dealing with his arrest and consequent trial are those of logic and reason, the inheritance of his Western tradition. The whole parable, "Before the Law," assumes that beyond the door there is another door and another, and implies that the journey through these is capable of yielding a preexistent meaning, whether discernible to human intellect or not. One such meaning is the notion of a radical evil that can be confronted and overcome by natural or supernatural forces. Discussing the banality of evil in an exchange of letters with Gershom Scholem, which followed the publication of *Eichmann in Jerusalem: A Report on the Banality of Evil,* Hannah Arendt wrote:

> It is indeed my opinion that evil is never "radical," that it is only extreme, and that it possesses neither depth nor any demonic dimension. It can overgrow and lay waste the entire world precisely because it spreads like a fungus on the surface. It is "thought defying," as I said, because thought tries to reach some depth, to go to the roots, and the moment it concerns itself with evil, it is frustrated because there is nothing. That is its "banality."[10]

In this impossibility of thought, formulas, or language to penetrate beyond surfaces, Pinter's play and Kafka's novel converge. Beyond surfaces there *is nothing* but the stories we tell about those surfaces. Pinter's plays have always been about competing stories and the struggle to make one or another prevail. That struggle implies that in the absence of the individual creation of such a mythos, one will be imposed. It is most significant then that in *The Trial* K.

never tells his story but looks instead for its meaning, as if meaning were something beyond his own telling. What he gets, as in Pinter's plays, is a plethora of self-serving stories not his own. The warders, judges, court attendants, lawyer, painter, priest—none of these is evil in any radical sense—each is simply "owned" by the Court because each relies on the Court for identity and being, and because none has created a story, a language, or meaning other than the official one. Pinter's screenplay may be seen on this level as a tragicomic version of *Mountain Language,* in which the growing realization of the pervasiveness of "officialese" ultimately deprives the individual of an authentic, personal, and responsible voice, of the need to create meaning. In the screenplay it is not the demonic force of an evil such as torture that accomplishes this, but the prevalent acceptance of a structure based on hierarchy and power, one in which K. himself is implicated. Thus on one level K. is guilty because he himself has based his relationships with others, particularly with women, on those very assumptions.

This difficulty of creating meaning is thus also intensified by the fracturing of self-serving individual from self-serving individual. Instead of unifying at some conscious or subconscious level, the official mythos represented by the Court becomes, as it does for a Titorielli or a Huld, a means to personal gain or survival. The mythos is to be used, "sold," just as Pinter would see political leaders today using myths of patriotism or the need for good to triumph as a means of fulfilling personal or official self-serving ends. What once may have been meaningful, the myth of the past to which Titorelli refers, is now, like the law in the novel, vulgarized and trivialized. At the same time it becomes impossible to confront these logically precisely because they retain the resonance of value of that which is self-evident in myth. Justice, law (secular or religious), and trial are self-evident archetypal values, as are patriotic courage or the triumph of good over evil. The political problem lies not with these but with the disjunction between their innate evocative power and the official, self-serving use to which they are put. If, therefore, one is not to live or die "like a dog," another story must be told to replace that of the vulgarized law. The individual must by such telling go through the door open to each person, even if, as for Kafka, the only story possible to tell is that of the inability to find meaning. The public, imposed, official, unauthentic myth of the trial is thus replaced by the authentic, personal detailing of the inner trial, and the mythos has at least the possibility of being authentically reborn. Unlike the Welles film, in which the viewer is clearly directed by the camera, Harold Pinter's relatively straightforward adaptation places this burden of "making meaning" on the viewer, just as the novel does on the reader.

Further political implications of the screenplay suggest the way by which our modern society is able to victimize the individual by fracturing job and individual gain, separating them from any larger meaning. Each of the court officials is doing that person's job, even explaining well what he or she does. It is the relation of that to the whole, to the effect of what one does on the whole fabric which is missing, and this is another way of suggesting the banality of evil. Through the repeated use of the image of a poisoning atmosphere, Pinter also shows the way in which the abnormal and destructive may eventually appear normal and thus banal. The bureaucracy and triviality of modern life do not so much confront the individual as radical evil would do, eventually rather wearing people down, gradually sapping their strength to oppose them.

At the same time as the film script suggests powerful and contemporary political meaning, individual complicity is not overlooked. Victim and victimizer, hero and villain are not easily distinguished, and so words like "law" and "justice" seem irrelevant. Through the images of eyes and looking, through dramatizing some of K.'s feelings of superiority to others, his treatment of them as objects, and his lack of concern with anything other than his own fate, Pinter's screenplay shows K. finally as a victim differing only in kind and degree but not in essence from those who destroy him. K. does not tell his story in part because before the trial had ever begun he had accepted and used the official "values" of the Court. And this is why it is symbolically fitting that he should go arm and arm with his executioners. Pinter indeed shows K. as a petty bureaucrat more intent on how he is perceived than on the reality of his situation, yet at the same time as one profoundly aware at some deep level of his own lack of soul, and so perhaps actively seeking even the punishment which seems to call him toward something which can only be sensed as other.

As the filming process moves beyond the script, directorial, casting, location and editing decisions will be made, and these will affect the final film. However, by not insisting as Welles did on an interpretation, Pinter has given the director and cast a screenplay which retains many of the multiple levels and essential ambiguity of Kafka's work.

Notes

1. I wish to acknowledge the invaluable research assistance of Honors Program Undergraduate Fellow Lawrence E. Letourneau in my writing of this paper.

2. Louis Marks, "Producing Pinter," keynote speech at *A Pinter Festival,* delivered 21 April 1991 (reprinted in this collection). Marks told of Pinter's intense reading at that age of Kafka's novels and short stories.

3. There are a number of translations of Kafka's novel. I use for purposes of quotation the "Definitive Edition," translated from the German by Willa and Edwin Muir, revised and with additional material translated by E. M. Butler (New York: Schocken Books, 1968). In a private conversation while he was working on the screenplay, Pinter told me he had read several translations. Since I quote from both the screenplay and the novel, I indicate a reference from the novel with a K before the page number.

4. Heinz Politzer makes such a case in chapter 6 of *Franz Kafka: Parable and Paradox.* Of K.'s raising his hands and spreading out his fingers at his death, for example, he writes: "Rejecting the light before him, K. may want to preserve his humanity in

an existential solitude, no longer persecuted by the court, but freed from it by his death. On the other hand, spread-out fingers are a sign of worship, even of blessing. Seen in this light, he may accept his judgment here, affirm it, and welcome death at the hands of the Court" (217). The strongest argument I have encountered for the law and all its representatives as essentially affirmative forces may be found in Pietro Citati's *Kafka,* pp. 127–61.

5. Pinter in conversation with the author, July 1989.

6. "A Report on the Banality of Evil" is the subtitle of Arendt's book, which will be discussed later in this essay. Referring to the year he wrote *The Birthday Party,* Pinter said in the Hern interview: "however, the distinction between then and now is that then, in 1957, the concentration camps were still an open wound which it was impossible to ignore, whereas now it's only too easy to ignore the horror of what's going on around us. There's too much of it" (9).

7. All references to and quotations from the screenplay are from the typescript dated 20 August 1989, which Harold Pinter graciously sent me.

8. I discuss this concept of going beyond territorial limits fully in "'To Lay Bare': Pinter, Shakespeare, and *The Dwarfs,*" published in *Harold Pinter: A Casebook,* edited by Lois Gordon.

9. There is indeed some dispute about Max Brod's placing the chapter here. Spano, for example, asserts that insofar as the fragmentary nature of the novel allows us to speak of its composition, comic scenes are followed by serious ones. His conclusion is that the "grotesquely amusing scenes in the tenement house should be followed by the chapter entitled *The Flogger,* demonstrating the archaic harshness of the mysterious Court, but Max Brod, the editor, put this chapter in the wrong place" (100).

10. Quoted in *Hannah Arendt: For the Love of the World* by Elizabeth Young-Bruehl, p. 369.

FOURTEEN

"I am powerful...and I am only the lowest doorkeeper": Power Play in Kafka's *The Trial* and Pinter's *Victoria Station*

John L. Kundert-Gibbs

From the beginning of his writing career, both Harold Pinter and many of his critics (including Cohn, Esslin, Gordon, Merritt, and others) have pointed out the playwright's indebtedness to Franz Kafka. Pinter's early drama, *The Birthday Party,* is in fact an avowed "remake" of *The Trial,* and has many "extraordinary parallels" with Kafka's work (Armstrong 1). During the sixties and seventies, though, Pinter's connection with Kafka's work grew to be less direct and observable. Pinter's development comes full circle, however, by the early eighties, when he writes the collection *Other Places.* In this trilogy of plays, Pinter returns in a more direct way to Kafka's work. This is particularly evident in the collection's short middle play, *Victoria Station,* where Pinter once again "rewrites" *The Trial,* this time in a more distilled, crystalized fashion; whereas in *The Birthday Party* Pinter attempted to reenact the scope of Kafka's work as a whole, in *Victoria Station* he works more closely with the priest's parable (found in the penultimate chapter of the novel). In an extremely minimalist way (even for Pinter), Controller and Driver represent forces which relate to each other in terms of a struggle for understanding as a means to power. Even disregarding our knowledge of his recent screenplay of *The Trial* (analyzed in Francis Gillen's essay), there is ample evidence in *Victoria Station* itself to show that Pinter is once again turning more explicitly to a work that has "been with" him since he first read it (Gordon 216).

Though *The Trial* is peopled with many characters, is more lengthy and makes use of a more or less standard narrative line throughout, it nonetheless has many parallels with the two-person, "surreal" *Victoria Station.*[1] One way to see more clearly (perhaps merely by similarity of scale) the intimate relationship between *Victoria Station* and *The Trial* is to look at the parable which the preacher presents to K. in the city cathedral as a study-in-miniature of

Kafka's novel as a whole. This parable, which appears in "the writings which preface the Law" (213), is effectively a two-person drama about a doorkeeper who guards the entrance to the Law and a supplicant who "begs for admittance." In it, the supplicant, with whom K. readily identifies, "parts with all he has, however valuable, in the hope of bribing the doorkeeper" (214) to let him into the "Law" (213). No matter how long he waits or what he tries, however, the doorkeeper will not relent and let him in. At one point, the doorkeeper tells the supplicant that he can slip by if he desires, but that he, the doorkeeper, is only the lowest of many such people who "stand at every door. . . . and the sight of the third man is already more than I can stand" (213). The supplicant, too frightened to do more than try to sneak a "peek" into the building of the Law, waits "for days and years" (213) until he nears death. Finally, as he approaches the end of his life, a question which he has never put to the doorkeeper before dawns on him: he asks why, if all want admittance to the Law, no one else has ever shown up at this door during all his years of waiting. The doorkeeper stoops near the now nearly deaf man's ear and bellows loudly, "No one but you could gain admittance through this door, since this door was intended for you. I am now going to shut it" (214–5).

On this horrifyingly blunt and pathetic note the parable ends and we, the readers, along with K. and the priest, are forced to try to interpret what seems at first like a tale of the doorkeeper's outright abuse of power.[2] As we consider the parable more closely, however, we realize that, while the tale *is* one of fundamental horror and waste, it is not nearly as clear who is to blame for this as we may have at first assumed. For one thing, if, as the priest points out, the doorkeeper has been keeping the door to the Law open for many years just for this particular man, then he is really "subordinated to the man" (218), so that the one "in power" (or the one who controls the situation) is actually the supplicant and not the doorkeeper. Many other of the priest's arguments also point out that the doorkeeper was only doing his duty, and even being "nice" to the man during his tenure.

While poking fun at the excesses of the scholastic method of arriving at the truth through investigation of others' interpretations, the priest's contentions do serve to point out very nicely that one cannot take this parable at face value—in fact, there is no face value at which to take it. As the priest points out, "the right perception of any matter and a misunderstanding of the same matter do not wholly exclude each other" (216). Just as with the novel as a whole, we cannot make any all-encompassing statements about what the parable is pointing out: (modern) indeterminacy lies at the very heart of the parable; "[i]n this fundamental ambiguity lies Kafka's secret" (Camus 147). We can, however, see from the priest's conversation with K. that, whoever is "in control," the parable is concerned with a power struggle of sorts between the two men. That this struggle is one which exists on many levels at once only makes it more fundamental to the tale and consequently makes the tale resonate more deeply, giving it mythical overtones.

In *Victoria Station,* a struggle for control takes place in a similarly absurd environment. Here, as Driver and Controller go through their comical 'routine' of trying to figure out where Driver is located, where he should go, and how he can find Victoria Station, we become aware that underneath (and sometimes on the surface of) this Laurel-and-Hardyesque banter there is a real contest of wills going on between the two for something which is not immediately evident. Possible catalysts for this struggle appear as the play develops—the sleeping woman P.O.B.—or passenger on board—Driver has in his car, the fact that Driver has a family, even that Driver is in a mobile "Ford Cortina"—yet these reasons do not fully explain the deadly serious and threatening nature of the "play" in which the two engage. (Driver's woman, seemingly the most obvious reason for Controller's jealousy, is not revealed until late in the play, well after many threats and pleas have been exchanged.) What is evident, however, is that the two are using and abusing what power, or control, they have over one another.

When the play commences, Controller, like the supplicant in the parable (and K. in *The Trial*)[3] assumes that he understands and therefore has control over the situation—he orders his "son" to pick up a gentleman at Victoria Station (46-47). It quickly becomes evident, however, that this "Controller" is in fact not in a position to order Driver around: Driver's obtuseness (whether intentional or not) forces Controller to plead with, cajole, and even attempt to bribe Driver with talk of a good tip. Just as the supplicant is proved wrong in his assumption that the Law (and those who serve it) is a tool for his use, Controller has made the mistake of assuming that his drivers will simply obey him because of his position.[4] As Controller finally confesses, "I lead a restricted life. I haven't got a choke and a gear lever in front of me" (50). He needs Driver in order to fulfill his "function" as much as the supplicant needs the doorkeeper to interpret the (unexpectedly) incomprehensible Law for him.

But the power situation is not as simple or static as even this may appear: once Controller determines that Driver number 274 cannot complete the job, he begins looking for other drivers. The dynamics of the situation now flip, as Driver is now the one who begs Controller not to "leave me" (53). Controller's victory is short-lived, however, as he soon finds that no other drivers will answer his summons—he is trapped in a world peopled only by himself and Driver, a world which is very similar to the room which Kullus and the author fight over in Pinter's early short story, "The Examination" (a title which itself pays homage to Kafka's *Der Prozess*). Just as in Pinter's early short story, the two characters in the play trade an eagerly desired control back and forth several times during the course of the play, paralleling K.'s fortunes with the representatives of the Court and the parable's supplicant's struggle with the doorkeeper in *The Trial*.

What these individuals do when they are alternatively in subordinate and superior positions (as all are potentially in both positions at some point) reveals even more about the deep links between Kafka and Pinter. In *The Trial*'s parable, the supplicant, with whom K. identifies (215), serves through his actions and attitudes as a kind of double for K., allowing us to witness in miniature the range of K.'s reactions to the representative of an inscrutable, powerful, yet at the same time subservient force. In an almost exact parallel with K.'s initial reaction to his confrontation with the Law, the supplicant assumes that the Law "should be accessible to every man and at all times" (213). He is thus confused both by the doorkeeper's refusal to let him in to the courts of the Law and by the doorkeeper's leniency toward him when he says that the supplicant can "slip by" him and into the outer halls if he likes (thereby breaking the law). On the one hand, the doorkeeper is proclaiming his right or power to disallow entrance; on the other, he makes it clear that he could not resist the man's insistence to get in if he wanted to do so intensely enough. The doorkeeper is at the same time a part of the high and mighty law and one of the lowest of the low servants. Once their complicated relationship is presented, the supplicant and doorkeeper become locked in a years-long struggle to see who has the final right to shape the other's destiny, and in this bloodless chess game the characters' very inaction is what shapes their fate. As they wait out the years together, the man loses all perspective or sense of scale about his quest, finally thinking that the fleas on the doorkeeper's coat collar will plead for him with the doorkeeper, whom he comes to think is the only obstacle between himself and the Law, and the doorkeeper is unable to move from his place and only able to entertain himself by asking innocuous questions of his companion.

In the body of *The Trial* we see this same standoff, or battle of feints, take place between K. and several other characters, yet here whoever has the upper hand at the moment is more likely overtly to abuse his power than are the two characters in the parable. When K. feels that he is in a better position than his fellow, he feels no compunction about snubbing the other (or others) and even outrightly using them for his own purposes, yet when he discovers that the other is in an advantageous position, he grovels before him, complains to himself how unfair it is that they are treating him poorly (just as the supplicant does), and at the same time accuses them of maliciousness when they are doing what he would do if given the opportunity.

An example of his hypocrisy may be seen in K.'s dealings with the assistant manager. At first, when K. feels he has the upper hand with the assistant manager, he makes it quite clear that he will usurp the other's position without a qualm on his way to becoming manager of the bank. When the trial distracts K., however, and the assistant manager "fights back" by taking K.'s clients into his office, K. considers this counter-maneuver both malicious and unfair (as he is unable to defend himself since the court case is taking up all his time and energy), though it is evident that if he had seen the same evidence of weakness on the assistant manager's part, he would have done no less to assure his rise. What this conflict all comes down to for K. is made very explicit in one of the unfinished chapters of the novel. In it, K. decides to confront the assistant manager. As he makes this decision, however, he realizes that "it could surely profit him nothing to keep on opposing the Assistant Manager in all his weakness, thus increasing the latter's sense of power. . . . But K. could not have altered his conduct had he wished to do so . . . " (252). K. is consciously fighting a losing battle with forces he is unable to comprehend, much less defeat.[5]

Why then does he go ahead and confront the assistant manager (with disastrous results) when he knows that he is in no position to come out the winner? According to Bassoff, one possible answer to this question is that K. sees those above him in the power structure (or his perception of it) as role models, yet these models stand in the way of K.'s achieving their status; e.g., there cannot be two assistant managers at the bank. As Bassoff states, using René Girard's psychological theory of the model-as-obstacle, K. searches "to find a model of strength and authority to emulate. To be worthy of emulation, however, the model must vanquish the disciple, whose subsequent hatred is also longing" (Bassoff 301). Thus, when K. attacks the assistant manager, he does so *in order to fail*, for this leaves the assistant manager in a position of strength and makes him worthy of emulation. That this also generates antipathy toward the assistant manager is obvious from K.'s comments about him. Other examples of this kind of relationship abound in the novel, as K. constantly oscillates between denigrating those whom he is able to defeat (like Huld the lawyer) and groveling before those who appear to be invincible. However, the purest example of this Girardian model-obstacle in *The Trial* is probably the doorkeeper in the parable. The doorkeeper exactly fits this loved-hated object (in the eyes of the supplicant): he is one "who both points the way to transcendence and guards the way" (Bassoff 306).

In *Victoria Station,* the stark nature of the play makes this love-hate, model-obstacle relationship even more apparent than in the bulk of Kafka's work. The actions which Driver and Controller take when they are in subordinate and superior positions show very clearly their need to control each other, yet at the same time, their animosity toward the other person if they are able to gain this control. One may most easily see this complex of feelings in Controller who, once he realizes that he has gained the upper hand in their "battle" by calling for other drivers, proceeds to threaten to annihilate his unworthy double: "I'm going to tie you up bollock naked to a butcher's table and I'm going to flog you to death all the way to Crystal Palace" (54). When Controller is forced into a position in which he must admit his dependence on Driver, however, he becomes jealous of and angry with Driver for having what he (Controller) wants: a "steering wheel," "four wheels," "a gear lever," and "a jack in the boot" (50). Controller shows his jealousy when he complains that he leads "a restricted life," and his anger at his advantaged counterpart erupts when he says that, given the "jack in the boot" that Driver has, he would "stick it right up your arse" (50). Thus anger and longing (a longing with distinct homosexual overtones) run together in Controller's feeling toward Driver when Driver is and has what Controller wants. But when Controller temporarily defeats Driver, making him admit *his* loneliness and need—when Controller forces him to say "Don't leave me"—Controller has no pity or sympathy toward Driver, who is no longer worthy of his desire.

Driver too reacts to the play of power between the two, though in a much more subtle way than Controller. He parallels the Law's doorkeeper in *The Trial*'s parable inasmuch as Driver is officially subservient to Controller, but at the same time he represents something inscrutable to him. As Burkman states, "through his quiet, naive questions and his lack of concern for what interests Controller, Driver has captured him. His [Driver's] are the secrets and his is the power" (Burkman, "The Multiple Levels of Action" 26). Controller, the obvious figure of control or power, is quickly reduced by Driver's stubborn, inscrutable obtuseness to a position of subordination—in point of fact, he is fairly easily knocked down from his position of superiority.

As Driver usurps Controller's position, his passive-aggressive stance ceases being merely comical (as it at first appears), becoming potentially threatening (potentially because Driver is almost never more than a potential character). He changes his claimed activity from "I'm just cruising about" to I'm sitting "by the side of a park," and he asserts he does not know where Victoria Station is (whether he really does know or not is not the major issue here), then even claiming that he does not know where the park he is near is located. These contradictions and claims could be construed as supreme ignorance on the part of Driver, but his later actions suggest otherwise: when Controller decides to ask some other driver to pick up the job, Driver suddenly becomes actively defensive (in fact, active period) for the first time, telling Controller that the other drivers will "lead you into blind alleys by the dozen" and that he's "the only one you can trust" (54). Then, as Controller in turn abuses his position of power, telling Driver that he will flog him to death, Driver suddenly recalls where he is located—a park beside the Crystal Palace—and additionally (after Controller does not respond to this first revelation) that he has a wife and daughter, both "probably asleep." (Cf. Deborah and Rose R. in *A Kind of Alaska* and *Awakenings*, respectively.)

As soon, however, as Controller once again becomes interested in what Driver is saying, Driver slips back into his comical yet maddening air of density:

CONTROLLER: Oh, you've got a little daughter?
Pause
DRIVER: Yes, I think that's what she is.

Though he is answering questions more directly than at first, Driver is already retreating from his directly confessional stance of the previous lines. As the play proceeds, Driver continues to waver between confessing something about himself or his P.O.B. and being obtuse, depending on his power position relative to Controller.

An ambivalent, oscillating relationship between oppressor and victim is thus set up in the deep structure of both Kafka's and Pinter's works, a relationship that links the main characters in a battle with no evident resolution, save the supplicant's (and K.'s) death in *The Trial*. Is death then an indication of what will occur in *Victoria Station?* Is Controller going to find Driver at the end of the play in order to "destroy [him] bone by bone" (58)? Or is he perhaps going to meet Driver as a means of reconciliation? Pinter leaves us with many more questions than does Kafka about the end result of what he presents to us. If Pinter is rewriting *The Trial,* then he is leaving out the novel's final chapter.

By not making clear whether Controller and Driver are going to kill each other or join each other in friendship (or something in between), Pinter sustains a more ambiguous attitude toward the eventual outcome of the power struggle than does Kafka. Whereas K. dies "like a dog!" (229), Controller's threats of murder and destruction are not as necessarily negative. *Victoria Station* fits the model of "Death and the Double" in Pinter which Burkman proposed in her article on *A Slight Ache, No Man's Land,* and *Old Times.* As she states, "for Pinter death is both an enemy and a friend." For the playwright, "confrontation with the double is in each case a confrontation with an enemy in so far as that double threatens death. . . . By threatening death, however, each of Pinter's doubles offers the possibility of new life" (Burkman, "Death and the Double"141). While K. dies thinking only that "the shame of it must outlive him" (229), the confrontation with death in *Victoria Station* brings with it both the possibility of total destruction ("You'll end up looking like a pipe cleaner") and of a rebirth of the two characters, "just the two of us." Pinter is reworking Kafka's basic power struggle, but with the possibility at least that *his* supplicant and the doorkeeper can be united in some sense beyond, or perhaps through, death.

If we understand the doorkeeper and the Driver (Controller) as retainers of a higher power—the Law and Victorian Time (culture), respectively—we can see even more clearly how Pinter both follows and goes beyond Kafka's lead. The underlying conflict and quest of the parable in *The Trial* involves the supplicant's desire to enter into the mysteries of the Law, which the doorkeeper represents (to a greater and greater extent as the supplicant waits for admittance). The two characters in this parable represent two opposing conceptions of the world: the supplicant, the "normal," rational view of the world; the doorkeeper, the mysterious world which is here called the Law.

The understanding/power relationship presented in Kafka's work is further complicated in Pinter, however, as the playwright refuses even to fully identify each of his characters with a single worldview—both, to some extent, represent the Victorian frame of reference—reductively, a nineteenth-century conception of the universe that understands colonialist England as the center of an ordered world—which is no longer workable in the (modern) world of the play. Neither of the characters represents the whole of this mind-set, however, but both are partially "stuck" in this mode of thought. Whereas Controller assumes a world wherein Victoria Station is the center of the known world (and therefore represents Victorian cultural norms), Driver appears to live in the Victorian time period (his car is parked under Crystal Palace). Thus, while the ambiguity of their relative hierarchical positions and quests closely follows Kafka's in *The Trial,* they have more of an opportunity for (re)unification than do Kafka's characters: they are, in some senses, two halves of a self, or rather pieces of a whole worldview.

Whether or not these characters will find rebirth or reunification instead of, or beyond death, there is (as we have begun to discover) inextricably intertwined with and giving impetus to the power struggle in the two works, a need or quest that the characters seem bound to fulfill. The supplicant's suitably mythic quest is to "enter into the mystery of the Law," while both Driver and Controller have a less blatant, but just as archetypal need to join another—to lose their separateness. In the parable, we see how, as the man waits "days and years," he finally begins to see at least the "radiance that streams inextinguishably from the door of the Law" (214), and it is only then that he is finally able to ask the profound question that allows him to discover on his death-bed that this door to the Law had always been solely for him. Though he has given up his life and dignity in the pursuit of this piece of knowledge, the man is at last allowed one moment of partial entry into the mystery of the Law—a moment which, of course, proves the futility of his long and dogged quest, but one which does finally connect him with that inscrutable radiance.

In *Victoria Station* the situation is again complicated further than in the parable because the characters not only represent pieces of the same (and different) worldviews, but both of them are on a quest at the same time. On a first reading, we would tend to associate Driver with the supplicant, as Controller represents "the office," or authority. As we have found, however, Driver is in the driver's seat and Controller needs him in order to fulfill his "function." Controller is also the one who comes to Driver by calling him up on the radio, mirroring the supplicant's journey to the Law.

Just as with the supplicant and the doorkeeper, what Controller expects of his Driver and what he gets are completely different. Both supplicant and Controller expect to find the Law or Driver, respectively, playing a subservient role toward them, yet they are both confronted with forces that, while polite, are nonetheless obscure and impenetrable. Both supplicant and Controller are then forced to go back and question the very foundations of their assumptions about the forces they are confronting and about themselves. Neither of them is readily willing to lay aside his 'old' assumptions and assume the role of beggar, so both put up a fight. Eventually, however, they realize their true dependence on the "other" and even that what they seek is not to use them for their purposes, as they first supposed, but to seek a communion with them—to enter into the mysteries of the Law, or to (re)unite with Driver (or Controller) who inhabits another time or place.

That Controller has at least partially entered into these mysteries is evident from the end of the play when he says, "Don't move. Stay exactly where you are. I'll be right with you" (62). Whether he is going to destroy or befriend Driver, Controller feels capable of entering the time zone of Driver: he doesn't need Driver to move from his park beside a no longer existent Crystal Palace; he is confident that he can find that place in time.

Driver is also involved in a quest for union with something he cannot fully understand: he tells Controller that he has a wife and what he thinks is a daughter, that he has fallen in love with the girl in his back seat whom he is going to "keep," and that he has no knowledge of the whereabouts of Victoria Station. That Driver is unable to understand our everyday physical world is evident from this: he doesn't know whether he has a daughter, a son, or— what? He sees the girl in the back of his taxi as an object to "keep." And he is unable to get around in the geographical world of Victoria Station.

In an additional complication, at one point, Driver says in humorous exasperation, "well, I honestly don't know what I've been doing all these years" (53), indicating that he is also unable to function in the time frame of the world where there is such a thing as the "10:22 from Boulogne." Driver's line of reasoning connects him with Deborah in the companion play, *A Kind of Alaska,* who parallels Driver's above statement in her questions to Hornby: "What have I done? What have I been doing? Where have I been?" (17). Deborah connects place, movement (or action), and (implicit) meaning in these and following questions to her doctor, indicating her quest is one for identity through knowledge of place and time—or frame of reference (Dukore 168-69). As Burkman has recently put it, "Pinter's characters in these dramas [*Other Places*] are . . . displaced, suspended outside of the norms of realistic time and space," making "possible [the] integration of self" (Burkman, "Displacement of Time and Space" 116). The three "acts" in *Other Places* are then a connected "exploration of the quest for self in the modern world" ("Displacement of Time and Space" 110), and the parallel between Deborah's and Driver's questions is an indication of the unified themes which underlie Pinter's work in this collection.

Once we have made an internal connection between these plays, we can see the extent to which Oliver Sacks's *Awakenings* informs *Victoria Station* as well as *A Kind of Alaska.* When Driver claims he is parked "underneath Crystal Palace," a structure which burned down in 1936, the possibility of his being another *encephalitis lethargica* patient,[6] awake in his own "utterly foreign" world (35), must be entertained. In describing the bizarre actions of one of his patients, Aaron E., Sacks states:

> he may use a frame-of-reference (or coordinate-system, or way of judging space-time) which departs from "the normal" in an ever-increasing and accelerating way; and . . . he may be so enclosed within his own (contracting) frame-of-reference, that he is unable to perceive the contracting scale in his own movements. (342)

Just as Deborah is unable to establish (at least for most of the play) her whereabouts either in space ("I want to go home") or time ("Where have I been?"), Driver is initially unable to find Victoria Station—he is unable to fit into the so-called normal world's frame of reference.

As opposed to the apparently realistic setting and action of *A Kind of Alaska* and Sacks's extreme confidence in the primacy of "normality" in *Awakenings,* in *Victoria Station* Driver's frame of reference is not disadvantaged. As soon as the play begins, we realize we are in a "Beckettian," or better yet Kafka-esque world where the convention of "realism" has been thrown out of the dramatic equation. The first question of *Victoria Station,* and the question that gives the play its whole structure and motivation—"Where are you?"—is profoundly urgent, as the "Where" (as we discover) is not just one of place, but also of time, and ultimately of reality. Thus the person who controls the "where," or the frame of reference, or the reality, controls Controller and Driver's relationship: the one who knows where he "is" has the power.

In Kafka's work as well, knowledge of place and time (or lack thereof) plays an important role in the power struggles between the characters.[7] K. is constantly forced to attend meetings in bizarre attic rooms which change size from vast to small and cramped and back to vast again. When he visits the church where he is told the parable, he is also outside the "normal" conventions of space—the church is impenetrably vast and gloomy—and time— K. "had been punctual" (204), yet the man he was to meet does not appear. And it is precisely in these situations where K. loses his dignity, self control— even his power to breathe. When he enters "the Court's" mysterious frame of reference, he enters a world where he loses knowledge and power (and identity) at the same time. In the church, K. desperately thinks that what he needs is "not . . . some influential manipulation of the case, but . . . a circumvention of it, a breaking away from it altogether, a mode of living completely outside the jurisdiction of the Court" (212)—he wants to return to the "normal" world where he had knowledge and power—where he was in control. Instead, we see that K. is punished "like a dog" for his inability to adapt to this "other" time-frame. K. (paralleling the supplicant in the parable) has made the wrong choice when facing an inscrutable, implacable opponent and is therefore (in "just" and "inevitable" (84) fashion) stripped of all knowledge and power.

In *Victoria Station,* I believe another resolution is reached. In contrast to *The Trial,* and as stated above, in the play both parties are trying to understand the other's reality. That Driver does need and is trying to understand the mysteries of the secular world is evidenced by lines like, "I honestly don't know what I've been doing all these years" (53) and "Here. Waiting. What do you want me to do?" (55). And Controller, isolated in his "office" (which word he uses to identify himself), facing the "loneliness of man in modern mass society" (Mengel, "Yes! In the Sea of Life" 161), needs "a holiday in sunny Barbados" (59).[8]

Driver and Controller are on seemingly absurd quests, each to find (at least a piece of) another kind of reality—a "kind of Alaska," and both Driver's and Controller's quests are in some senses fulfilled. When Controller says that he is going to meet Driver by the park, Driver asks "but what about this man coming off the train at Victoria Station—the 10:22 from Boulogne?" (61). He is finally able to use time and place as "we" understand it. That this may cost him his life seems like an acceptable risk, as he ends the play by reassuring Controller that "I'll be here" (62). At the same time, Controller discovers the ability to move (or at least the idea of his own movement), to leave his static, mundane post and strike out in search of the displaced driver, evidence that he is confident that he can make the transition into Driver's frame of reference.[9] Unlike K., Controller and Driver do not end up trying to get "outside" of the other's "jurisdiction," or frame of reference, but to get "inside"—to enter into the "mysteries" of the other's reality. Whether, like the supplicant (and therefore doorkeeper) in the parable, they will fail, or will succeed is unclear, but they have begun the first "move" toward success.

In both *The Trial* and *Victoria Station,* the characters' quest for power over one another is moderated and/or enhanced by a quest for intimacy with that same other. When the parable, the novel, and the play commence, the "seeker" feels that he understands, or will be able to understand, what he is up against and therefore that he has power over it. But what these "protagonists" find is, "to try to understand is to fail from the beginning" (Harter 154). The desire/ quest to make the other fit within one's *Weltanschauung* in order to gain the upper hand and thereby use and abuse him is doomed to failure in both Kafka's and Pinter's world. The only hope—the only way out of this rational trap—is the possibility of a mystical union with that other. But this union, in order to come to fruition, imperils the life or identity of the individual who seeks it. The real power in *The Trial* and *Victoria Station,* the power to join the participants into a whole, is wielded by death: the death of our old-fashioned (Victorian) monistic understanding of reality. A power that is grounded on the belief that others share one's frame of reference, or view of reality, is shown in both of these works to be unreasonable—even impossible—given the multiplicity of realities which exist in the modern world. K. dies because he cannot understand this, and Driver and Controller may die in attempting to merge their different realities, but the death of an egocentric understanding of reality is necessary before modern man can solve his isolation—before people can stop talking past one another—by realizing that true power is empathy: the power to understand and share another's vision of the world.

Notes

1. Cohn has recently stated about Pinter's early play that "*The Room* [is] . . . a diminished version of Kafka's *Castle*" (Cohn 15), an observation which I feel can aptly be applied to *Victoria Station* and *The Trial* respectively.

2. This act of "forced" interpretation parallels what the reader is compelled to do while reading *The Trial,* as well as *The Castle* and Kafka's other works.

3. In the linear organization of an analytical paper, it is very difficult to deal with all the possibilities presented by ambiguous works such as *The Trial* and *Victoria Station.* For example, one can easily propose the "opposite" situation that Controller parallels the doorkeeper, and Driver the supplicant: The doorkeeper is the one in the position of offical command, and the supplicant should take orders from him. In such a scenario, the supplicant's inability to comprehend the simplest of rules (from the doorkeeper's

point of view) forces the doorkeeper to stay at his post for years and years, while he attends to the supplicant's unfathomable questions and irritating demands.

4. Or, as per the note above, the opposite (or rather a complementary) case can be made: Just as the doorkeeper, the apparently powerful figure in *The Trial*'s parable, is in some senses the supplicant's "'bondsman,'" so also Controller is in a situation where he needs Driver in order to fulfill *his* orders.

5. This works both in terms of his external battles with those around him (e.g., the Law), and, by implication, an internal struggle with a part of himself he does not understand and "could not have altered."

6. The argument here is not that he is *literally* a sleeping sickness patient, but that he inhabits that type of space-time which identifies so many of Sacks's patients. As his patient, Francis D. put it, "'*my* space, *our* space, is nothing like *your* space'" (Sacks 343).

7. In a rather terrifying coincidence, *The Trial* was written during the height of the *encephalitis lethargica* epidemic in Europe. Whether one could ever make a connection between this epidemic and Kafka's writings is, though very tantalizing, highly doubtful.

8. This need for a holiday, as well as the "blue Caribbean" water imagery provides yet another striking parallel between this play and *A Kind of Alaska*.

9. Once again, whether this visit implies violence or reconciliation is unclear, but the fact that Controller makes this move is what is important and relevant here.

V. Pinter and Film

FIFTEEN

Art Objects as Metaphors in the Filmscripts of Harold Pinter

Steven H. Gale

While Harold Pinter's artistic achievements have been connected primarily with his work in the theatre, since his first scripted film, *The Servant,* appeared in 1962, he has been building a reputation as a master screenwriter as well. In the thirty years since then he has authored nineteen additional film scripts, has had numerous cinematic successes, in terms of both popular acceptance and critical acclaim, and has won several prestigious awards for his screenplays.[1] Besides being entered in major festivals, films made from Pinter's filmscripts have been listed among the year's ten best consistently, and he received the Berlin Film Festival Silver Bear and an Edinburgh Festival Certificate of Merit for *The Caretaker* in 1963, the British Screenwriters Guild Award and the New York Film Critics Best Writing Award for *The Servant* in 1964, the British Film Academy Award for *The Pumpkin Eater* in 1965, the Cannes Film Festival Special Jury Prize and a National Board of Review Award for *Accident* in 1967, the Cannes Film Festival Golden Palm for Best Film and the British Academy Award for *The Go-Between* in 1971, and a National Board of Review Best English-Language Film Award for *The Last Tycoon* in 1975. His more recent films, *The French Lieutenant's Woman, Betrayal, Turtle Diary,* and *The Handmaid's Tale,* also have received high praise. Indeed, critics such as Martin Esslin, John Russell Taylor, and Andrew Sarris claim that Pinter's distinctive style and unmistakable writing ability have been responsible for the best work done by several of his directors. Sarris, for example, in commenting on the extent of Pinter's filmic accomplishments, states in his examination of *The American Cinema* that "*The Servant* and *Accident* have done more for [Joseph] Losey's general reputation than all his [20] other pictures put together," and "Michael Anderson's career [13 previous films] is so undistinguished until *The Quiller Memorandum* that two conclusions are unavoidable, one, that Harold Pinter was the true *auteur* of *The Quiller Memorandum,* and two, Pinter found in Anderson an ideal *metteur en scene* for his (Pinter's) very visual conceits"

(96, 252).[2] There are a number of elements in Pinter's filmscripts that contribute to this kind of success in a field in which the director is generally the recognized superstar. Several of the elements are minor or subtle in nature, yet have a cumulative, holistic effect that is vital in the writer's workmanship.

One element, so far unremarked upon by scholars, is that *objets d'art,* particularly paintings, figure prominently in Pinter's films. In *Harold Pinter* Taylor concludes that *The Servant* and *Accident* assume "the character of Pinter creations" (Taylor, *Harold Pinter* 20); in part this effect certainly is due to Pinter's inclusion of art objects in his screen adaptations of the novels.

At times the art objects incorporated into the motion pictures made from his film scripts operate in a fairly traditional manner, as plot devices for instance. An example of Pinter's use of an art work for this purpose occurs in *The Quiller Memorandum* when Quiller has been taken prisoner by the neo-Nazi group headed by Oktober, the Max von Sydow character, and a truth serum is administered. Quiller focuses on *"an oil painting of a nude blonde, leaning across a chair, on the far wall"* (165). As seen in the movie, the canvas certainly does not appear to have any special artistic or symbolic qualities, and the sole purpose for its presence appears to be to give Quiller an object to center his attention on during his interrogation so that he can avoid giving up any vital information. The importance of the object, however, is that Pinter specifically calls for it in his script yet gives it no special significance beyond its use in the development of the plot. Interestingly, in the novel the painting in Oktober's base is carefully delineated; the symbolism is literally spelled out.[3] This difference between the function of the painting in the novel and in the film is a result of Pinter's removing the narrator and ironically thereby diminishing or expunging the symbolic element.

Other conventional uses of artworks include merely setting the time and locale of the event; sometimes the objects function as simple characterizing devices. The decor of a character's habitat conveys a considerable sense of the person, whether reflected in frameless Calder posters in *The Pumpkin Eater* or gilt-framed etchings of eighteenth-century hunting scenes in *Accident.* These two uses, setting and characterization, are evident early in *The Servant* when the social context of the friction between Tony's fiancé, Susan, and his manservant, Barrett, is manifest as she examines the decor. The servant proudly notes that the "simple and classic" is always best. The woman, looking at a large, dark, Rubenesque oil painting of a naked woman surrounded by cherubs and bearded men, observes that rather than classic the canvas is "prehistoric." Immediately the audience is aware of the class differences between Susan and Barrett, and there is also a realization that the two have not hit it off.

There is a more important utilization of art objects in Pinter's films, however. This has to do with the thematic relationship between the plot and the objects. In the film version of *The Servant,* for instance, Pinter masterfully transforms Robin Maugham's novelette about a former army officer's degradation at the hands of his newly hired servant into a study of dominance that reveals as much about the servant's psychology as it does about the master's. The penultimate scene in the film begins with the camera panning down from a painting of an eighteenth-century battle. Given the military history of Tony and Barrett, the film's two main characters, the portrayal of a heroic, flag-carrying officer leading a charge serves as an ironic comment on what has been happening in Tony's house. The final sequence also begins with the camera panning from a painting over the mantel. The painting in this case is of a partially clad woman; a love song is heard over. Since Tony's destruction is manifest by his debauchery, as demonstrated later in the scene, the painting functions concurrently as an illustration of his disintegrating personality and as a foreshadowing device.

Another example of the kind of usage that links art and theme can be found in *The Pumpkin Eater*. Clearly, the creation of the mise-en-scene is enhanced by the use of artifacts, but thematic resonances abide in the art pieces too. The opening sequence, in which Jo Armitage's current mental state is demonstrated, shows the contemporary, clean, neat interior of her home matched by her severe hairstyle, austerely tailored clothing, and coldly blank demeanor. A Romanesque bust on a pedestal, a statuette on an end table, a glass figurine, a modern white marble head on another pedestal, a porcelain tea set, an Indian or African head, and other figurines along with paintings done in a darkly modern, almost Picassoesque style, are revealed as the camera tracks through the room. This setting contrasts markedly with that of the flashback scene in the barn when Jo first meets Jake and instead or art objects she is surrounded by boisterous, swirling children. The barn is barren of works of art, while Jo's hair is unbound and free; she is dressed casually in a loose sweater, and her face glows warmly. The addition of *objets d'art* later in her life may reflect Mrs. Armitage's improving financial situation, yet the presence of so many objects suggests that she has replaced her children with cold, modern plastic, and the uneven and catholic nature of the collection implies that her personality is unsettled and decidedly not centered in the way that it was in the flashback scene. How else can the substitution of a sail-less windmill for the novel's tower in *The Pumpkin Eater* be explained, for example, except as a symbolic representation of Jo's lack of functionality, especially after her hysterectomy.

Finally, one of Pinter's most interesting utilizations of art objects is more subtly metaphorical in nature. In fact, at times the objects form a kind of subtext. For example, the Buddha figurine in *The Caretaker* becomes a metaphor in both the stage play and the film version. Actually, this is the first notable appearance of an art object in Pinter's writing, and the mysterious and conspicuous Buddha statue that Mick smashes (much as society has crushed Aston) is both more and less than a religious artifact in the play. The object has no apparent religious function, but it is the figurine of a sensitive man. In the play the statue *seems* to have no significance other than its mere existence. Like the stove, it has no obvious connection, it is absurd—unless it represents the uselessness of religion and/or the meaninglessness of symbols.

At the same time, the drama is about exclusion rather than inclusion and the Buddha, like Davies, does not belong in the dark, compressed, junky world that Aston inhabits. On the screen the statue is more conspicuously omnipresent than it is on stage. Bright, light, and pearly white, it is seen in the background in many shots. It may represent Aston's past, when he saw what others could not. Mick gets so emotional at the end of the movie that he goes too far and breaks the object ("Look, ummm," he says, as he stands in the doorway about to leave, the hesitation indicating that he feels badly about his action, though he never completes his apology, [84]), but breaking it also demonstrates that Aston can break/has broken from his past—the possibility of the break having been implied by his bringing Davies home in the first place. There is also an indication that he can move on in his life, since the Buddha, having been smashed into smithereens, cannot be brought back and Aston will not go back either. Similarly, while the object cannot be put back together (Aston is engrossed with repairing things), conversely the man can be. Possibly involved, too, is an implication that Mick can move on without Aston if he must. The destruction of the statue thus takes on the suggestion of a signal between the two brothers, a physical representation of Mick's statement that the Davies affair is closed. Aston's lack of reaction seems to be a concurrence. What each man does is aimed at fulfilling his own personal needs. And, the multiplicity of possibilities contained in the Buddha invests the figurine with a rich metaphoric stature.

Another of Pinter's films that clearly demonstrates this type of usage is *The French Lieutenant's Woman,* one of the screenwriter's cinematic masterpieces. In the source, John Fowles's novel, when Charles finds Sarah at the second "end" of the story, she is living in the house of an artist (presumably Aubrey Beardsley). The protagonist comments on the paintings that he sees in a studio and Sarah states that she is the painter's amanuensis. Pinter makes a significant alteration in transferring this incident to the screen: he makes Sarah the artist who has painted the works about which Charles remarks. The importance of this change lies in its relationship to earlier incidents in the screenplay that are not included in the original. The first time that Anna is seen in the Victorian movie plot as Sarah, she is drawing a dark umber picture of her late employer. The camera shows us the anguished face of *"an old woman on her death bed."* The shot is specified in Pinter's script (9). After Sarah has joined Mrs. Poulteney's service, there is another shot of her sketching. In this instance the script calls for *"a self portrait"* (47). Again the face pictured in the drawings in one filled with pain and despair. In contrast, the paintings that Charles discovers at the conclusion of the film are very different in both style and subject matter. According to the script, Charles "looks at the drawings. They are of children." "These are yours?" he asks. When Sarah replies, "Yes," he responds, "You have found your gift" (100). In the movie the paintings are light and bright. One is a figure of a woman wearing a pastel yellow apron or jumper. By making Sarah the artist and presenting the dark, close-up, agonized faces in contrast to the sprightly, full figures, Pinter creates an artistically symbolic representation of the psychological change that Sarah has undergone. The recognition in modern psychology literature of the correlation between a psychotic artist's deteriorating state of mind and the artist's work is found in a number of case studies such as the famous painter of pictures of cats whose works moved dramatically from the representational to the geometrically abstract. Pinter has reversed the normal sequence by presenting the drawings performed by Sarah in her abnormal state first and in her cured state later.

Perhaps Pinter's filmscript that most strikingly incorporates art for metaphoric purposes is *Accident.* The story of a married Oxford philosophy don, Stephen, and two of his pupils, Anna and William, who are involved in a relationship, is derived from Nicolas Mosley's novel, *Accident.* Stephen soon becomes involved in a contest with William over Anna's affections. Much of the art work in *Accident* is utilized conventionally by the filmmakers and is what might be expected in the home and office of an Oxford don. Stephen's home is adorned with a Persian throw rug in the hallway and a landscape painting on the wall of his study. In other rooms there are pictures of street scenes, small golden sitting dog statuettes on the living room mantel, along with a clutter of knickknacks, small photos, and other figurines, a dark, Rembrandt-like oil portrait in the bedroom, and a framed landscape and colored prints in the dining room. As in *The Pumpkin Eater,* the varied collection of artifacts suggests a catholicity in the home's inhabitants' artistic taste and a fondness for items with which the possessors have personal connections, though in the case of the don's family there is more homogeneity and a sense of settled comfort—the decorations primarily seem to be eighteenth- to early twentieth-century British in origin and subject matter. In *The Pumpkin Eater* the artifacts were a jumble of everything from classical Greek or Roman to contemporary African and seemed to have been chosen to reflect the film director husband's world travels rather than to complement the personalities of the husband and wife, albeit this may well have been the unintended result.

In a couple of instances artwork is used for a humorously ironic effect. Observations on the nature of the aristocracy occur occasionally in the novel *Accident,* as in Stephen's monologue: "I was rather fascinated by aristocrats at this time," Stephen admits (Mosley 23), and later he comments on Anna and on William's family. Because Pinter abandoned the device of a narrator, yet evidently felt that the aristocracy subtheme was important, he retains it by putting it into the dialogue in several scenes. In fact, there is an expansion of the implications of Stephen's thoughts when they are taken out of the first-person narrator's narration and embedded in the character's dialogue. When William and Stephen talk in the don's room at the college, Stephen observes that "Aristocrats were made to be . . . Killed."[4] Although not called for in the script, in the film there is a pan of the gargoyles on the roof of the building while the voices are heard over. The statues, frozen in their humorous grotesquery, thus appear to be equated with the aristocracy being spoken about— ancient, hideous beings, stiff and unfeeling while paradoxically expressing emotion, above and separate from humankind. Since historically many of the visages are of former popular dons or scouts (dormitory servants), there is a further ironic undercutting of the role of the aristocracy. At the opposite end of the scale from the subtle humor based on aristocratic elements is the wonderfully evocative shot taken from the outside through a rain-streaked window of a scene in a restaurant at 19 Mossop Street where Stephen and Francesca are seen eating. When the two enter the restaurant they pass a painting of a large, naked Adam and Eve (with an apple). Since it may have been the sin of fornication that resulted in the acquiring of knowledge of sexuality which is represented by the Biblical apple, the backdrop is appropriate. The shot of the couple dining is humorously enhanced by the poster that hangs on the opposite wall. It reads, "Have your Meals Here and Keep the Wife as a Pet." There is no dialogue to detract from the debasing message that is ironically diminished further by the fact that Stephen and Frances are not husband and wife, that in fact Stephen's wife is allotted pethood status because she is not there but at home about to have a child. The sign is not called for in the script, but the shot through the window must have been intended by Pinter, for the dialogue is indicated as being voice-overs (*Accident* 258).

The most interesting usage of art in this film, however, is important specifically because of its symbolic focus. There is a fascinating scene in Stephen's room at Oxford when Anna is first seen through the window. When novelist Mosley's Stephen sees Anna for the first time, he is alone in his office at the college; she is squatting down by the white goat in the courtyard (14). Pinter quickly sets the triangle theme by introducing William into the scene: "WILLIAM *and* STEPHEN *are sitting by the open window. The window looks down to a quadrangle. On the grass a white goat is tethered. The scene is framed between them, below. . . . From the same viewpoint,* ANNA *appears in the quadrangle. She stops and talks to the goat"* (229, 230). Unobtrusively in the background in the film, though frequently centered in the frame, there is a statuette of a satyr. When Anna is observed, she is petting a goat in the middle of the college quadrangle but, barely out of focus in the foreground, the statuette is visible, standing between Stephen and William. Because of the film's sexual theme, the attempted seduction of Anna by Stephen while William unknowingly assists, the combination of satyr statue, goat, and supposedly innocent female at the center of the triangle created by the two competing males who lean out of the window to watch her is symbolically appropriate, and the statuette serves metaphorically to capture the film's thematic essence. Unlike Pinter's earlier use of art objects, however, in this case the artwork itself is never focused upon—it is only with repetition and in retrospect that it gains significance, along with several other art objects employed similarly. The iconography is subtle and achieves its effect through accumulation; the collective preponderance of the related items thereby provides a substructure for the film.

Another instance of art objects serving as metaphors is found in one of the most famous sequences in the motion picture, the rugby scrum in the corridor of Lord Codrington's country house. Stephen describes the scene in the novel:

"a long stone corridor with high windows and cream paneling. There were family portraits on a wall—men in full armour and wigs, fleshy faces like women, a few recent ones dry as matchsticks. . . . There was a green baize door at one end and at the other an archway like a cloister. . . . Above us were the portraits of plumes and horses and shining metal. . . . Beyond me gothic vaulting like a church" (Mosley 89). Pinter's stage directions are similar: "A large stone corridor. High windows. A green baize door at one end. An archway to the main body of the house at the other. Large family portraits on the walls" (Pinter, *Accident* 269). In the film the corridor, shot at Syon House,[5] contains marble columns and has a domed ceiling decorated with five rows of painted octagonal designs. Heraldic crests are embossed on the wall on either side of the doorways. There are embroidered chairs and marble urns and on a table sit several large silver bowls. The floor is tiled with a black and white checkerboard interlaced with a geometric design. But instead of family portraits, the hall is lined with marble busts and statues on pedestals, statues of draped male and female Greek or Roman patricians. At the opposite ends of the corridor are a larger than life-size copy of the restored *Apollo Belvedere* and a life-size copy of *The Dying Gaul*. Art historian Robin Middleton has described the niche in which *Apollo Belvedere* stands as being architecturally "large, soft, [almost] intimate" and the niche of *The Dying Gaul* as "hard and strong, elevated,"[6] with the dynamic pattern of the ceiling and floor leading from the *Apollo* to the *Gaul*. Into this gladiatorial arena come the combatants.

Pinter has been interested in sports throughout his life, and there are numerous sporting incidents and references in his works.[7] In this case, the event takes on an added significance because of the art objects in the setting that metaphorically underscore the movie's thematic content. If something is seen on the screen, it is there because someone chose to put it there for a particular purpose. Just as the triangular shot of Stephen and William looking out the window at Anna with the satyr statue positioned between them was no accident, the use of this setting and the camera angles aligning the characters with the statues (low angles from in front, the statues towering above and behind the two men) were designed to express a symbolic content.

The rugby game degenerates into a brawl between the players. During the action, Stephen and William grapple and Stephen purposely knees his pupil in the face. The mock combat between the two males occurs under the statues of *Apollo Belvedere* and the *Dying Gaul*, the presence of which suggests the division between the classical and the pagan, the intellectual and the emotional. The *Apollo Belvedere* is one of the best-known, and some art critics say the most notorious, Roman copies of a Greek statue (Janson, 117). Embodying the lyrical, harmonious qualities of Praxitelean beauty, the *Apollo Belvedere* was probably sculpted in the late fourth century B.C. There is a sense of cerebral, Platonic removal from feelings in the aloof blank stare of the demi-god-like figure. Copies of the marble statue became especially popular at the time of the Greek Revival in the eighteenth and nineteenth centuries because it was seen as the perfect example of the admired Greek spirit.

The artistic style of the *Dying Gaul* is more realistic than that of the posed, idealized *Apollo Belvedere*. The life-size Roman copy, done in marble, was modeled after a bronze original cast between 220 and 230 B.C. in Pergamum, a city in northwestern Asia Minor, to celebrate the Greek leader Attalus I's defeat of the Celtic Gauls. The partially supine figure with its clearly delineated musculature and non-Greek but very human facial features conveys a more solid, animalistic quality than does the *Apollo Belvedere*. The pathos of the fallen warrior's exhausted struggle to rise comes through because of the dignity resident in his demeanor and the configuration of his body.

An interesting juxtaposition occurs when the rugby scene is followed by another sporting event, the comparatively civilized cricket match on a carefully manicured field at Oxford. Although the match takes place much later in Mosley's novel, Pinter moves it to this point in the film and simultaneously incorporates here some of the events that occur elsewhere in the original. Not only does the restructuring compress and omit some unnecessary action, but by immediately moving out of doors away from the ancient, cold marble Pinter makes this event seem much less confined. In the civilized, ordered milieu of the hall the pagan aspect of the game is emphasized by the contrast, just as the civilized, ordered elements of the cricket match are underscored by its taking place in a natural locale. In contrast to the statues the green grass and trees and bright sun provide an open, healthy setting in which occurrences are seemingly more normal and social—Anna announces that she is going to marry William.

While Pinter claims that he has "nothing to do with the use of art objects in any film. That's entirely to do with the director and designer" (personal letter), his denial sounds similar to his comments about the presence of symbolism in his works, and there is plenty of evidence that he is deeply involved in the entire filmmaking process, even after the script has been finished. "I have absolute and contractual artistic control over my scripts and act as a consultant to the director in both pre and post production work," he says, though he admits that "my post production activity is variable" (personal letter). Normally, Pinter is on the set during shooting and works closely with the director and sometimes the author of the source novel as well—a practice referred to in interviews with John Fowles and others.[8] Losey distinguishes between "two kinds of writers who work on films. . . . One who is very personal and contributive, like Pinter . . . and others . . . who never make the same creative contributions that a man like Pinter does" (Leahy 14). Pinter insists on exactitude in his plays; this is not the case in the movies. Where he demands that actors refrain from engaging in uncalled-for "business" on stage and wants the dialogue exactly as it is written in the script,[9] the difference between his filmscripts and the finished motion picture varies considerably in relative terms (not only are shots, even scenes, inserted or deleted, but even the words are changed throughout, though admittedly usually only in insignificant ways).

The real world existence of the room at Syon House may be fortuitous, but a conscious, agreed upon choice was made to use it in the film. Further choices were made in the camera angles used in the sequence and in positioning the characters so that the artistic contents of the room assume a metaphorical quality in reflecting the movie's themes. Pinter's involvement in the collaborative aspect of film making is extremely important and cannot be ignored.

The significance of art objects in relation to the thematic content of the film version of *Accident* is clear. The use of plastic art objects in a nonplastic medium in order to explore the movie's theme gives added scope to both the theme and the film. By incorporating material from another medium, Pinter reveals not just how the film makers may reflect, emphasize, or express the theme of the film, but also something about the nature of the media themselves and how they can be used for symbolic reinforcement and to create metaphorical dimensions. The artist's conscious recognition of this is demonstrated by Anna's removing a carving from the wall of her room as she leaves to return to her homeland. No mention of the carved decoration is made in either the novel or the filmscript, yet clearly in the minds of the film makers it was important to include this piece of art as an object that Anna consciously feels defines her and which she cannot leave behind.

Pinter's traditional use of art objects as plot devices, for establishing the time and locale of events, and for simple characterization is obvious, effective, and cinematically appropriate. His utilization of these objects as metaphors, however, is subtle and one of the major elements in his writing that elevates his filmscripts to a rare stature, for it sets up resonances and endows his work with depths present only in the screenplays of his most accomplished contemporaries.

Notes

1. Of these twenty-one filmscripts, four are adaptations of his own dramas (*Betrayal, The Birthday Party, The Caretaker* [released in the United States as *The Guest*], and *The Homecoming*—several of his other plays, *The Basement, The Collection, The Dumb Waiter, The Lover, Mountain Language, Old Times, One for the Road,* and *The Room,* have been televised)—one is from another dramatist's play (Simon Gray's *Butley*), and sixteen are cinematic translations of novels (some based on books given him by director Joseph Losey). The novels adapted are: Nicholas Mosley's *Accident,* Adam Hall's *The Berlin Memorandum* (released as *The Quiller Memorandum*), John Fowles's *The French Lieutenant's Woman,* L. P. Hartley's *The Go-Between,* Margaret Atwood's *The Handmaid's Tale,* Aidan Higgins's *Langrishe, Go Down,* F. Scott Fitzgerald's *The Last Tycoon,* Penelope Mortimer's *The Pumpkin Eater,* Marcel Proust's *A la recherche du temps perdu* (*Remembrance of Things Past,* published but never filmed), Kazuo Ishiguro's *The Remains of Day* (written in 1990 but not yet filmed), Fred Uhlman's *Reunion,* Robin Maugham's *The Servant,* Franz Kafka's *The Trial,* Russell Hoban's *Turtle Diary,* Ian McEwan's *The Comfort of Strangers,* Joseph Conrad's *Victory* (published but not filmed).

Pinter has also written several television adaptations, including Elizabeth Bowen's *The Heat of the Day.*

2. See also Esslin, *The Theatre of the Absurd* (New York: Doubleday/Anchor, 1969, rev. ed.), p. 255.

3.

> Her skin was the shade and texture of a wax rose, quite flawless, and her hair fell across her naked shoulder in blond rivulets. Her regard was innocent, the eyes wide and frankly gazing, too young to have learned that you must sometimes glance away. She leaned across the white chair without coquettishness, insouciant, her small breasts barbed with nipples of carmine, her thighs heavy with pubic hair. . . . It was no good thinking in terms of taste. She was there for raping. They might just as well have hung a whore on the wall. There was no signature, but the painter had been a German, a true blue Prussian-born hypocritical bloody Aryan. You portray the face as symbolizing purity—like the flawless skin, the innocent gaze, the little-girl look—and then you go to town on the tits and pussy, symbolizing carnality till it moans. Result: you have a picture you can give to your own mother-in-law for hanging in the needle-room, and she'll always think you've come to admire her petit point. Hypocrisy. Schizophrenia. They've always been like it. (Hall, *The Quiller Memorandum,* p. 93)

4. In the printed script of *Accident,* p. 237, Pinter uses "Slaughtered" instead of "Killed." Possibly the original word was considered too loaded, suggesting a conscious, ritualistic sacrifice rather than simply a death with no value judgment appended.

5. Designed by eighteenth-century architect Robert Adam, the house, which is presently the home of the Eleventh Duke of Northumberland, is located about midway between London and Heathrow Airport. The room has been used as a set in other movies, too, most recently in *King Ralph* (1991).

6. Lurcy Professor in the department of art history and archeology at Columbia University, Middleton gives a brief tour of Syon House in the "Age of Reason, Age of Passion," segment of the 1989 PBS *Art of the Western World* series.

7. Pinter was athletic in his youth; he set a track record in school, for instance. His affection for cricket has been noted many times (see *Butter's Going Up,* for instance) and there are sporting games in *Tea Party* and *The Basement,* as well as references to boxing (*The Homecoming*), squash (*Betrayal*), and cricket (the character's names in *No Man's Land*), to mention just a few examples of how this interest is included in his writing.

8. See also Fowles, "Foreword" to *The French Lieutenant's Woman: A Screenplay* by Pinter (Boston: Little, Brown, 1981), pp. ix ff.

9. Pinter has expressed this demand a number of times, as confirmed by both director Carey Perloff and producer Louis Marks in their keynote remarks at *A Pinter Festival,* Columbus, Ohio, 20 April and 21 April, 1991, respectively.

Pinter and Bowen:
The Heat of the Day

Phyllis R. Randall

Every time Harold Pinter adapts a novel for movies or television, we have a chance to examine his artistry at work, for we can see how he adapts to the medium, altering the structure, changing the dialogue, shifting the emphasis. Though different editions enable us to see some revisions in his own plays (for example, *The Birthday Party;* see Carpenter 96–97), when he adapts from someone else's work, we have evidence of precisely what is cut away or altered to make the new version. Certainly that is true with Pinter's adaptation of the Elizabeth Bowen novel *The Heat of the Day* for a two-hour television drama, broadcast in the United States on PBS, 31 October 1990. It is that recent television drama that I wish to examine, emphasizing those alterations that reveal Pinter's revision of the original.

It is easy to understand the attraction of Bowen's work for Pinter. In an interview after the broadcast, he acknowledged the "strong impact" the novel had had on him when he read it at nineteen. He liked its "convoluted" and "self-conscious style," terms that apply equally well to Pinter's style. The 1949 novel, moreover, is about betrayal, one of Pinter's most frequent themes. The most obvious betrayal is that of Robert Kelway, who, working in the War Office in London during World War II, is giving secrets to the enemy. The plot of the novel, however, concerns another kind of betrayal: the espionage agent, Harrison, is onto Robert Kelway, and in the course of tracking him down for several months has come to know all about Stella Rodney, since she and Robert are lovers. From afar, Harrison becomes enamoured of Stella, and when his information about Robert's activities reaches a certainty point, he offers to avoid reporting what he knows in exchange for Stella's favors, both social and sexual. Now the betrayal extends to all three protagonists: Robert, who is actively giving secrets to the enemy; Harrison, who offers to cover up that betrayal if Stella, in turn, is willing to betray both her trust in and loyalty toward Robert.

But Bowen's style and the theme of betrayal were not all that attracted Pinter. In the interview following the broadcast, Pinter specifically called attention to

Bowen's language, like "glass you can't see through." That language of clarity with obfuscation is cut from much the same cloth as Pinter's own. Indeed, the dialogue in the novel is so much like Pinter's that sometimes it is hard to tell the two apart: "So you remembered me though you never met me?" (B 199) sounds like a precursor to Anna's line in *Old Times*: "There are things I remember which may never have happened but as I recall them so they take place" (28). Or compare this exchange between Harrison and Stella with the style of Goldberg and McCann's interrogation of Stanley in *The Birthday Party*: "Most people don't know the half—in fact no one does. Certainly not you." "What don't I know?" "What I know." "You want to me to ask what that is?" "Better not, I think. Better just take the hint" (B 30).[1]

Moreover, Bowen, like Pinter, is enamored of silence as communication. When Robert and Stella meet after Stella knows that what Harrison has been telling her about Robert must be true, Bowen writes, "Now, no other vocabulary, least of all that of silence, at once offered itself" (180). So Stella chats about this and that until at last she asks Robert directly if he is spying. He denies it, and, though hurt and angry, pushes for marriage in order to protect her from such influences as Harrison. Stella, relieved to hear his denial after living for months with the fear that Harrison must be right, thinks that they should keep their usual relationship until both are more at an equilibrium. Robert asks directly, "Do you love me?" Bowen writes, "Eloquently she answered nothing whatever, not even looking up" (192).

With such a sympathetic, almost empathetic, source from which to adapt, it is little wonder that Pinter's dialogue in his adaptation (and even a stage direction) comes mostly verbatim from the novel. Certainly Pinter needed to insert bridges of his own dialogue to begin new scenes, and certainly he had to condense dialogue, so that a line is taken here and there from a scene in Bowen's novel and put together in Pinter's play, but more often than not, the dialogue in this Pinter play comes directly from the Bowen novel. It is instructive, therefore, to look at specific changes.

First, Pinter, to fulfill his own dictum that revising for a visual medium requires both condensation and a visual focus (Ciment 21), had to find each. To focus on the trilogy of characters (and to condense to two hours), he deleted entirely the subplot.[2] To find a visual point of view, Pinter turned to a technique he has used in a number of movie adaptations, a series of silent images. His teleplay begins with the scene of a man, back to camera, opening an envelope, looking at the pictures therein of Robert, some with Stella, and lingering over those with Stella, finally taking one of her alone and pinning it to the wall. In that one brief scene Pinter introduces us directly and visually to Robert and Stella, and indirectly to the mystery man over whose shoulder we are looking. Moreover, the obsession of this mystery man with Stella is also established, as well as the official nature of his business, since the scene is set in an office-like room. Thereafter, Pinter uses this inventive adaptation many times as scenes of the play are frozen by the click of a camera from the moving color picture to a black and white photograph, a recurring visual reminder that this story is a spy case.

Pinter wholly invents the scene immediately following this silent opening. In it Francis Morris, a cousin of Stella's late husband, comes to visit his wife in a rest home. While he is still talking with the owner/operator of the home, however, he suffers an apparent heart attack and dies on the spot. Bowen alludes to this incident in her novel, and the scene of Morris's funeral is fully developed (chapter 4). So Pinter invents this scene, places it as his first scene with dialogue, and reorders others to put the plot in chronological sequence. But why did Pinter decide to open the teleplay with this scene, which focuses on minor characters who play no role directly in either story, plot, or theme?

Certainly its cheerful, homey set and the broad daylight contrast strikingly with the lamplit looking-at-photographs scene immediately preceding it. Certainly the scene adds to the mystery, not only of new characters, but of intent: Why is this man coming to see his wife, why is his wife sequestered in this place rather than at home? I suspect, however, that the reason has more to do with Pinter's establishing a pervasive idea in Bowen's novel, namely, that havens of peace and rest were hard to find in England in World War II, that the conditions of the war had affected, indeed distorted, every aspect of the daily lives of those living in it. Bowen includes two scenes away from that war-damaged milieu, one between Stella's son and Morris's wife in this very rest home and another in Ireland, where Stella goes to check on the estate Morris left to her son. Ireland (Bowen's native land) was neutral during the war, and the idyll that Stella could have enjoyed there, the respite from the cares of war-torn London, is clouded by her wrestling with her doubts and fears about Robert's loyalty to his country. Pinter includes both the idyllic possibilities and the inner turmoil in a long segment, mostly silent, in Ireland. The only complete respite from the war that he shows, then, is in this rest home, a trope for the madhouse as the only refuge of normalcy when the world is engaged in war.

More surprising, perhaps, than Pinter's expository bridges or his invented opening scenes are his alterations to make the dialogue clearer. A number of times Pinter adds dialogue, or slightly changes the original, to be more explicit than Bowen. For example, when Harrison confronts Stella with Robert's treachery, Bowen writes, "We've traced a leak—shortly, the gist of the stuff he handles is getting through to the enemy" (32–33). Pinter's dialogue is more direct since he adds, "He's working for the enemy. Do you see?" (20), to which Stella responds, "Yes, I see." Such directness is not what we expect in Pinter, and it occurs often enough in his adaptation to be notable. Sometimes the directness is needed to shock the contemporary audience, more jaded than Bowen's. When Harrison makes his infamous proposal to Stella and asks if she understands what he wants, Bowen has Stella respond, "Perfectly. I'm to form a disagreeable association in order that a man be left free to go on selling his country" (34). Pinter alters that to "Perfectly. I'm to sleep with you in order that a man be left free to go on selling his country" (21).

Another kind of change Pinter makes is adding a few lines—rarely more than two—of circular repetitions. Since they fit in so inconspicuously with Bowen's own repetitions, they are further evidence that the two writers are indeed similar. For instance, when Stella meets Harrison at Morris's funeral, she asks him, "What do you do?" Harrison responds as if the question is difficult to comprehend. "What do I do?" "Yes." "Government work" (P 10–11). Both the circular repetition and the noncommittal answer are typical of Pinter's plays as well.

Indeed, Bowen explicitly refers in her dialogue to that kind of circumlocution. Harrison points out to Stella her peculiarity in conversation: "when you begin 'you mean,' you remind me of a girl I met in the park. I could say, for instance, 'How blue the sky is,' whereupon she'd say, 'You mean, the sky's blue?'" (B 30).

Pinter deletes that clear reference to his and Bowen's trademark repetitions, but goes on adding them throughout his adaptation. One last example. In the first scene of the novel (Pinter's fifth scene in his strictly chronological version), Harrison is listening to a concert in Regent's Park while he waits for the time to have his first visit with Stella at her flat. In the park he is encountered by Louie, a working-class girl from the country. Annoyed at her conversational attempts, Harrison finally rises to get away from her, but she follows, announcing that she's going home. She asks, "Are you?" "Am I what?" "Going home?" When he chastises her for approaching strangers, Louie repeats:

> LOUIE: . . . I'm going home.
> HARRISON: Well, which way do you live?
> LOUIE: Oh, I can go any way really.
> HARRISON: All right. I go this way. You go that way.
> LOUIE: Yes, that's right. Wait a minute.
> HARRISON: What?
> LOUIE: I don't know your name.
> HARRISON: No. You don't. (P 16, B 18–19)

Four of these lines are Bowen's (very slightly altered). Pinter's four additional lines shift the emphasis of the scene from Harrison's suspicion of Louie to his barely masked belligerence toward her. That emphasis provides a neater, more pointed contrast to the following scene with Stella, where we see the belligerence barely masked directed toward Harrison, and we see Harrison, like Louie, squelched, indeed shaking—literally, as he tries to light Stella's cigarette.

The dialogue, then, though mostly Bowen's, includes seamless Pinter additions for transitions, for exposition, for clarity, and, especially through repetitions, for emphasis. When it comes to recurring linguistic motifs, Pinter retains only one from Bowen, playacting. Bowen introduces the idea of acting early in the novel. When Harrison makes his proposition to Stella, he suggests that it would take "some tiptop acting" (P 22, B 35) for Robert to behave normally if he knew that an agent was on to him, and then plants the first seed of doubt, that "if a man were able to act being in love, he'd be enough of an actor to get away with anything." (In the telecast, unfortunately, ominous music is heard, decidedly not a subtle Pinter—or Bowen—touch.) That idea comes out again when Stella finally asks Robert directly if he has been spying.

"No, of course not! . . . What do you take me for? . . . What do I take you for? How well you've acted with me for the last two months" (P 66, B 183).

But another Bowen metaphor Pinter omits entirely—game playing. When Robert finally confesses all to Stella, he says that he could not have confided in her earlier because spying "was quite a game." To which she responds, "Which you loved" (B 261). The omission is rather surprising, given how frequently Pinter uses the game motif in other adaptations (see Klein 185–91). Yet omitting it incurs no loss, since the acting motif serves many functions— it comments on the artifice of the play before us, it distances the perspective from our time in the nineties to a time fifty years before (both reminders of Pinter's adaptation of *The French Lieutenant's Woman*), and it emphasizes the theatre-of-war idea, where each person acts his or her part, whether abroad or at the home front. These first two functions, of course, accrue only to Pinter, creating a subtext not found in the original novel.

His additional subtext, however, does not diminish his goal in adapting from one medium to another, which is to remain true to the essence of the original (Ciment 20). Certainly he is faithful to the themes. Bowen is exploring the layers of betrayal in a world gone mad with war. She makes much of the setting in wartime London, and many of her descriptive passages concern the strangeness of the times, the abnormality of life. Each of the trio, for example, is in a sense homeless: Stella lives in a furnished flat, Harrison has one or two places to stay but no home, and Robert's home is a mausoleum of his past—Stella notes that his room seems "empty" (P 38, B 112). That abnormal normality contrasts with what Stella finds on her trip to Ireland. Not at war, people in Ireland can have bacon and eggs, can have lights on at night without blackout curtains, and can live without constant attention to the war effort. In London the abnormal life has become so normal that when Stella and Robert visit his family at Holme Dene, his mother can say, and truly believe it, that the war is having a dreadful effect on them in the country while life is normal in London. In the country they haven't enough tea (as she makes clear to Stella at tea) or butter (Stella and Robert have not brought their butter coupons with them). It is as if she believes rationing does not extend to London! At the very end, when Robert, who has confessed all to Stella, now trapped in Stella's apartment, decides to exit through the skylight and across the roofs, Stella wonders if they ever would have fallen in love in normal times. In the teleplay, all that remains of her wondering is Robert's noting that they have never gone dancing, a normal activity in courtship but precluded because of the knee injury he suffered in the escape from Dunkirk in his soldiering days.

In that convoluted world Bowen and Pinter show the many betrayals layered in degrees of mistrust and deception, secrecy and lies. Robert not only is selling out his country, he lies to Stella about it. For months Stella keeps secret her suspicions about Robert, and even after she receives Robert's assurances that he is not spying, she continues to see Harrison occasionally, for the doubts refuse to go away. Finally, in a dramatic scene in both versions, she agrees to Harrison's terms, but does so in a restaurant setting where they unexpectedly come across Louie, who remembers Harrison from their meeting in Regent's Park. Her presence triggers an ugly response in Harrison—perhaps because she reminds him that he is forcing Stella into intimacy, a situation he himself could not endure with Louie in the park when she tried to strike up a conversation with him—and he sends them both away.

Harrison is, in effect, betraying what he admires about Stella by forcing her into this position. He is decidedly not playing a fair game in love or war, and must confront his own deeply flawed character. Stella, moreover, agrees that they are alike, telling him that he has "made a spy out of me" (P 46, B 132).

In the play as in the novel, the root of Robert's disaffection for England, and, consequently, the Allied cause, is his mother. Her comments about tea and butter while Stella sits as her guest at her tea table are indicative of the self-centeredness of this monstrous character. When Robert brings Stella to Holme Dene, he assures her (as Teddy assures Ruth in *The Homecoming*) that "They're harmless. Honestly" (P 29). Robert knows that she will need protection. After introductions, his mother does not acknowledge Stella's presence nor invite her to sit. When Stella mentions her son in the army, Mrs. Kelway changes the subject. When Robert decides to take Stella for a walk, his mother says they cannot since tea will be served. When he proposes a look at the house, she protests that the "better" rooms are shut up. No wonder that Robert must say something as he leads Stella up to his top-floor room: "Don't think you're making a bad impression. I assure you you're making no impression at all" (P 37, B 110).

To Mrs. Kelway, Stella does not exist, as, it seems from Robert's report, her own husband did not. Certainly to her son she represents all that is wrong with England. Indeed, in the novel, in their last meeting, Robert tells Stella that he thinks his mother knew he was about to be caught and so got him down to her country home again so that the arrest could take place there, not with her in London. In dialogue that Pinter did not retain (though he retained all the negatives from the tea scene), Robert says "My mother had been waiting for this [his downfall]; she wished it! It would be they who had got me into this trap. . . . It never suited them that I should be a man" (B 269).

Robert's embrace of the "wrong side" in the war may also have intrigued Pinter. Recently Pinter has become more openly political, both personally and artistically, as *The Hothouse* (written in 1958 but not published until 1980), *Mountain Language, One for the Road, The Handmaid's Tale,* and *Reunion* attest. (See Prentice, "Love and Survival" 35, Hern, and Sakellaridou 3–4, 211, for commentary on Pinter's political bent.) Certainly in his revision of Bowen's novel Pinter seems acutely conscious of the intertwining of the personal with the political, political not only at the interpersonal level, which has always interested him, but also at the international level, in the clash of ideologies.

The reasons for Robert's betrayal of his country Pinter leaves intact from Bowen, and they are all bound up in his manhood. The defeat at Dunkirk was the defeat of idealism, and those who were left were "scum" (P 93, B 263), including Robert. But Dunkirk was inevitable because all his race, his class, was "born wounded" (P 93, B 263). Turning his back on that bred his father out of him; "It gave me a new heredity. I was living" (P 93, B 264). The German idea could give a shape to society, so he felt like a man again. He admits that the Axis is, in Stella's words, "horrible, unthinkable, grotesque." Robert's response is that "In birth anything is grotesque" (P 94, B 264–65).

His treason, then, stems from his desire for order, for structure, for, in a contemporary political phrase, the patriarchal system restored. Its wrongheadedness (from our perspective—and Stella's) is mitigated, however, because of his own particular circumstances, his own particular weak father, monstrous mother, and silly sister, a character retained by Pinter, presumably because her vacuity, in spite of her seemingly endless activity in the war effort (so busy she rarely takes off her hat), contrasts sharply with the quiet strength of Stella.

It is the character Stella and the love story that Pinter focuses on in his adaptation, remaining true to Bowen—and to Pinter's own long-time interest in love, particularly love triangles. And in that story Pinter makes a major deletion from the novel. Bowen tells us that Stella's first marriage ended in a divorce when her husband, wounded in World War I, told her he preferred the kindness of his nurse to Stella's own ministrations. Since he was shattered mentally and physically and since Stella was young, pretty, and lively, virtually the whole family assumed that she had sued for divorce, deserting her wounded husband, and so treated her accordingly. With her self-esteem shattered by his betrayal of her affections, Stella found it more soothing to let the family believe that she was at fault than to tell them the truth. In Pinter's adaptation, when the family at Morris's funeral treats Stella with coldness, the implication is that it is because they have just learned that her son is to inherit Morris's estate. Not so in the novel. The family treats her coldly because they still hold Stella responsible for the divorce and even for her ex-husband's death, which occurred shortly thereafter, before he could marry his nurse. That twist in the novel, of course, intensifies the likeness of Stella and Harrison, for at the end she holds him responsible for the death of Robert. Though Robert may indeed have jumped to his own death, he felt forced because of Harrison to take matters into his own hands.

Because he omits this bit of history about Stella, Pinter loses a chance to show this less open side of Stella's character, and the audience loses a more complete understanding of Stella's relationships with the two men. The relationship between Stella and Harrison is as distorted as war-torn London. Harrison's obsession with Stella appears fanatical, almost sinister (the telecast uses ominous music frequently at Harrison's appearance). Yet Stella cannot dismiss either him or his accusation against Robert. In one of the most compelling scenes of both novel and teleplay, their cat-and-mouse relationship reaches a climax that results in a scene very like a love scene. When Stella arrives back at her flat after the visit to Holme Dene, Harrison is waiting. Tired, she relaxes in slippers while he fetches her a glass of milk. Her thoughts turn, unexpectedly, to her ex-husband, her son Rodney's father, and she recognizes that that marriage was a "false start," that her husband was "corrupted before death by undoings and denials of love" (B 113). In their ensuing conversation, which is where Pinter picks up the scene, Harrison remarks that they are getting to know one another. "We're not so unlike—underneath" (P 46, B 132). To that, Stella snaps, "You're right. We're horribly alike. You've succeeded in making a spy of me." Stunned at this rebuff, Harrison steps outside to a balcony, and Stella, chagrined at her outburst, follows. Together they breathe the night air, Stella, in amends for her retort, asking where Harrison stays, keeps his razor. Finally, quiet together, Stella invites him to "Breathe it [the air] . . . for as long as you like." "Stay with me. You breathe too," Harrison pleads (P 48, B 135). Pinter adds a line for him, "I can feel you breathing" (P 48). It is as close to a love scene as these two characters will have.[3] Pinter captures the essence of that intimacy, certainly, but without Stella's ruminations about her own failed marriage and her own less-than-honest handling of it (she has never told her son the truth), the source of the attraction remains unknowable. Pinter's version adds mystery, the unknow-ableness of each of us, while Bowen's version, because it clarifies just why and how these two characters are alike, deepens our sense of their understanding of their own personal flaws, adding poignancy to the scene.

The primary love story, of course, belongs to Robert and Stella. Pinter highlights that love by additional dialogue. When Stella goes off to Ireland, Robert asks and Stella assures him that she will "keep loving" him (P 49). When she returns, having wrestled with her demons of doubt, Robert asks, "Do you love me?" "Why?" she responds (P 60–61, B 175). Later, in the same scene, after she tells Robert of Harrison's charges, Robert accuses her of acting on the assumption that the charge was true. Stella protests in Bowen, "I love you" (183), but in Pinter, "I . . . loved you" (67), an ambiguous change of tense. In both writers, Robert's response is, "No. It's the appearance of love you keep up so beautifully" (P 67, B 184).

Despite their many betrayals of trust, their love remains. In their last meet-ing, having confessed all, Robert asserts that "There's been you and me in everything I've done" (P 92, B 261). Stella lashes out: "I have *not* been in what you've done. The more I understand it the more I hate it. I hate it" (P 94, B 266). Just as Harrison, in the earlier love scene, stung by Stella's ac-cusation, abruptly left to go to the balcony, now Stella abruptly leaves the bedroom, going to the living room. Picking up Robert's picture, she silently calls his name. At that very moment, Robert appears at the door asking if she had just called him, and they fall into each other's arms. Their love, which can survive betrayals of every sort, can speak through doors, through silence.[4] But the paradox of this love triangle is how it splits between personal and political: in intimacy Stella and Robert are as one but in ideology they are worlds apart; in intimacy, Harrison and Stella are still worlds apart, but in ideology they are as one.

After Robert's fall from the roof (whether intentional or not is left ambiguous in both Bowen and Pinter), the empathy between Harrison and Stella brings them together again, several years later. During an air raid (it is now 1944 during the blitz), Harrison finds Stella in her new flat, sitting out the bombs rather than going to a shelter. They catch up on news—he was not fired over the Robert affair, she is engaged to be married—and Stella asks him why he turned her down the night she finally said she would accede to his request. In Bowen, Harrison's response is "[T]hat was not what I wanted" (309); in Pinter, "It wasn't going to work out" (102)—more contemporary, perhaps, but less precise than Bowen's idiom.

In this last scene, however, Pinter adds highly effective dialogue that gives his adaptation his own particular focus. In the novel Harrison says, "I didn't come back all this way only to say goodbye—did I?" (310), to which Stella responds, "You don't think there is any virtue in a goodbye? I do. I've wanted to be able to say goodbye to you; till this could be possible you've haunted me." In Pinter's adaptation, Stella's lines underscore the unlikely love triangle: "But now we can say goodbye, can't we? We're not what we were. We're no longer two of three. We're apart. . . . [W]e had to meet to say goodbye. Don't you understand . . . Harrison?" (102–103).

The use of his name for the first time in their relationship reminds her that she does not know his Christian name. He assures her she will not like it: Robert. In his teleplay, Pinter inserts a *Pause* (a long one in the acted version on PBS). In Bowen, Stella pauses and then invites him to stay, including staying the night, if it will help him finish his thoughts. And they go on with other inconsequential dialogue. Pinter cuts all that dialogue and ends the scene, as Bowen does, with a reference to the raid that periodically has shaken the room. Stella suggests it might be over. In the novel, Harrison asks, ". . . would you rather I stayed till the All Clear?" (311). Pinter ends more dramatically but just as quietly. Immediately after a long pause, Stella says, "Listen. I think it's over. Don't you? I think the raid's over." Harrison responds, "I'll stay till the All Clear" (103). They sit in silence for a time, and the All Clear sounds. Pinter's stage direction says, *They do not move* (103).

That silent ending (with its stage direction right out of Beckett) underscores that this story is about love, a deep love between two who betray each other and lose, and a firm attachment between two who bargain to betray and also lose. But in a world at war, everything is flawed, including love.[5] The alterations Pinter makes at the very end, underscoring Harrison's and Stella's need for resolution of their story, their need for companionship, their compatibility, all point up this firm attachment, akin to love, between Stella and Harrison. Stella agrees that "there must have been something between us—if there had not been something, how should we both, tonight, know that it isn't there any more?" (B 309). Their silent sharing of the night's torment and calm recalls their earlier love scene where they shared the calm of breathing the same air after the torment of acknowledging their deep character flaws.

Volker Strunk has written of Pinter's deep distrust of "the levity, the rashness and ease with which love and friendship are devalued" (211). With his adaptation of Bowen's novel, Pinter explores again themes that have interested him from the beginning—love, friendship, the triangle, the betrayal of love—but with a difference. As he had in *A Kind of Alaska,* Pinter "mollifies his pessimistic world vision of history" (Sakellaridou, *Pinter's Female Portraits* 210). Unlike Bowen, who ends with Louie returning to her parents' bombed-out home in the country, where she lifts up her son to watch the swans fly west, emphasizing hope, Pinter emphasizes endurance. Unlike Bowen, who writes from the perspective immediately after World War II, Pinter adapts from a perspective forty-odd years later, a perspective that includes a cold war, the Korean war, the Suez crisis, various Middle East wars, Vietnam, the Falklands, Grenada, countless revolutions in Africa and South America, and all the while the economic recovery of the countries that created the war while Britain itself declined. From such a perspective, faith in humanity and hope for the future are badly damaged. What Pinter leaves us with, post faith, post hope, is a quiet suggestion of charity. It may suffice.

Notes

1. To show the extensive use of Bowen's dialogue, I will use double documentation: P(inter) with page, B(owen) with page. The texts referred to are listed in Works Cited.

2. The subplot concerns Louie, a country girl in London, her vulnerability and "innocent" betrayal of her husband—she becomes pregnant while he is overseas. Pinter retains the character for two scenes, but eliminates the subplot entirely in order to focus on the major trio of characters.

3. That association of breath and love must have struck a responsive chord in Pinter. Whether Bowen's novel directly influenced Pinter is impossible to say, but surely it entered his subconscious; Pinter has said that "you're bound to absorb and digest other writing" (quoted in Hinchcliffe 33). At any rate, in the *Times Literary Supplement* of 2 Feb. 1990, Pinter published a love poem, which he dedicated to "A," entitled "It Is Here" that brings breathing and love together again. "What sound was that?/ . . . /What was that sound that came in on the dark?/ . . . /It was the breath we took when first we met./Listen. It is here" (113).

4. In the telecast, in a gesture right out of *Now Voyager,* another story of doomed love, Robert lights two cigarettes at once and hands Stella one, just as Paul Henreid does for Bette Davis.

5. Interestingly, both men are also physically flawed, Robert with his limp and Harrison with a squinty eye that does not work in coordination with the other, a trope for his skewed vision of love.

VI. Alaskan Perspectives

SEVENTEEN

Portrait of Deborah:
A Kind of Alaska

Moonyoung C. Ham

Harold Pinter's *A Kind of Alaska* (1982) is the dramatization of a case history of a postencephalitic female patient which is included in Oliver Sacks's *Awakenings* (1973).[1] Hélène Cixous's *Portrait of Dora* (1976) is a dramatized version of Freud's Dora case, a case history of a female hysteric.[2] Dramatizations of case histories,[3] both plays demonstrate a correlation between theatre and psychoanalysis and their relation to the workings of a gender politics. In fact, Cixous wrote *Portrait of Dora* as groundwork for a feminist project to create a woman's theatre by simultaneously deconstructing Freud's psychoanalysis and a paradigm of traditional theatre, a project that assumes their connection. Pinter also exposes the workings of gender politics in *A Kind of Alaska.* Thus both plays provide us with a space where we can talk about the relationship among psychoanalysis, feminism, and theatre.

Both Freud's and Sacks's case histories are concerned with theatrical terms and relationships. Watching the patients placed under their care and control, Freud and Sacks keep the patients under their power in order to master the knowledge of the mysterious diseases. Their case histories offer theatrical representations of the bodies of female patients as spectacles for the mastering male analytic gaze. Because of the gift of "somatic compliances,"[4] the hysteric and postencephalitic patients make their bodies spectacular by suddenly bursting out of fixed states into violent movements or frenzies. Freud and Sacks as analysts want to use the theatricalizing bodies as merely objects for their analysis. In this theatricalizing process, however, they happen to collide with their patients' own desires which disrupt their representations. Thus Freud blames his analysand, Dora, for her own theatrical desire to make herself spectacular and to be watched by an audience: "she *acted* an essential part of her recollections and phantasies instead of reproducing it in the treatment" (141; his emphasis). So Freud represses Dora's disruptive desire in favor of the representation of "an intelligible, consistent, and unbroken case history" (32). Sacks also disregards Rose's theatrical desire as a side effect of L-DOPA, which makes a gap in the theatrical sequence of his case history.[5]

The paradigm of the theatre constructed from the relationship between an analyst (audience) and a patient (spectacle) in Freud's and Sacks's case histories is that of the dominant theatre in patriarchal society. It is the paradigm of a traditional theatre which is criticized and deconstructed by such feminist theorists as Hélène Cixous, Luce Irigaray, and Teresa de Lauretis. The theatre is based on the binary structure that classifies and fixes differences and boundaries between spectator and spectacle, subject and object, and man and woman and so raises "some" to positions of power and relegates "others" to subordinate positions, according to male fantasies. Thus, as Hélène Cixous comments, the theatre which "is built according to the dictates of male fantasy" (546) has exploited and victimized woman as an object, as a spectacle offered to a male gaze to satisfy a desire for mastery. In such a theatre, woman is not alive, but frozen, fixed, and immobilized in the frame of the proper gender position—the position of analysand, victim, the opposite of the male analyst's position: that is, the position Deborah occupies in A Kind of Alaska and Dora occupies in Portrait of Dora. Based on this analysis of theatre, feminists have tried to create a new theatre in which living women can enjoy themselves by playing the roles of subject and object, spectator and spectacle all at once, free of the oppositional frame imposed by male fantasy.

In the theatre which exploits sexual differences, a family romance scenario usually unfolds. This family romance scenario provides Freud and Sacks with a presuppositional model for interpreting the case histories. That is, according to the family romance scenario, they read Dora and Rose as daughters realizing their identities under the influence of strong father figures. The daughter's mother, the father's wife, is "nothing" in this scenario and so is excluded from the scene. The daughter also will soon be married off or traded to another father figure as a sacrifice or an object of exchange between the father figures. Thus Freud interprets the symptoms of hysteric Dora as the expressions of repressed sexual desire for her father and for another father figure, Herr K, according to the family romance scenario, rather than as those of her own female sexuality and subjectivity. Dr. Sacks also uses a pattern of the family romance scenario in his analysis and is more conscious of it by directly taking a part in the scenario. He awakens Rose with the injection of L-DOPA; that is, he becomes her Prince Charming—a stronger father figure—who can awaken the Sleeping Beauty from her long and deep sleep with his kiss and who can disenchant a witch's magic (a sort of feminine power) with a stronger male power, so restoring male mastery over the female. Sacks even associates the relationship between himself and Rose with that between James Joyce and his mad daughter (79). Thus he desires that she come to identify herself within the family romance scenario, feeling very anxious about her absorption in "a private, inaccessible world of her own" which disrupts such a scenario.

The representations in the case histories of family romance scenarios make something beyond the scope of the male gaze invisible. That is, the male analysts are blind to something. Thus they can only selectively read or misread the signs of the female bodies of hysteric and postencephalitic patients, and so they fail in their treatments. Freud acknowledges his failure and his blindness in a late footnote to his main text (142n). And Dr. Sacks also acknowledges his inability to read the symptoms of Rose R in an epilogue added in 1982: "and then she fell back, for ever, into her own secret realm: whether it was darkness, lightning-lit, nothingness, or dream—*what* it was I never really penetrated or understood" (290; his emphasis).[6] In this way, both analysts inadvertently hide the holes in their analyses of the patients by marginalizing them, although they know and admit their failures. Cixous and Pinter, the playwrights, however, displace these "holes" from the margins and relocate them in the center to reveal and stress them in their theatrical versions.

In the main texts, although both analysts acknowledge their failures in the margins, they ascribe the causes of their failures to the analysands and their transferences. According to Freud, he failed in the analysis because Dora transferred her revengeful feelings about her father and Herr K to Freud himself, cutting off the analysis as a revenge before he got to a complete case history. Thus he regrets that he could not succeed in mastering her transference in good time. Sacks also detects Rose's transference to him in her treatment with L-DOPA, and so he interprets Rose's sexual approach to him as the transference of her repressed sexual desire. But he thinks that Rose's true, "normal" self is suspended or imprisoned by her false, bewitched self, and so he regards the transference as just a working of her false, charmed self. Thus Rose should be restored to the true self by getting rid of "an insatiable urge" for "dirty things"—i.e. by destroying the transference through the processes of "tribulation" and "accommodation." But, regretfully, she relapses into reticence and a fixed position again. Neither male analyst can interpret the patient's expression of female sexuality because of his blind fantasy; they even misread it as the patient's emotional transference which should be frustrated in the processes of analyses.

The true reason for the failure of both male analysts is, in fact, their countertransferences. Sensing this in the theatrical versions, Cixous and Pinter emphasize Freud's and Hornby's countertransferences in their relationships with Dora and Deborah. Cixous's Freud himself inadvertently shows his countertransference in his treatment of Dora at the moment when Dora abruptly cuts off Freud's analysis: "Freud: I'd like to hear from me. (This slip of the tongue is not necessarily noticeable.) Write to me" (32). And just before cutting off the analysis, Dora defiantly disapproves of Freud's male fantasy about her transference in her relationship with Freud: "You could make me laugh. But I don't want to hurt you. Because, you, doctor, I could never have loved" (31). Thus, Dora frustrates Freud's male fantasy according to which he desires to represent the portrait of Dora. In this way, in the theatrical version, psychoanalysis is deconstructed by placing the analyst's countertransference instead of the patient's transference in the center, that is, shifting the positions between the analyst and the analysand. And at the same time, the paradigm of traditional theatre is also deconstructed by liberating the victim, the woman, from a subordinate and fixed position, that is, by shifting the roles of subject and object. By doing so, Cixous shows the portrait of Dora, Freud's analysand, as the "newly born woman" in theatre.

Like Cixous, Pinter places the doctor's countertransference in the center in *A Kind of Alaska.* Dr. Hornby in Pinter's play reveals his countertransference from his first speech: "Hornby: Do you know me? (*Silence.*) Do you recognize me? (*Silence.*) Can you hear me?" (5). As Dora disavows her transference and resists Freud's countertransference in their relationship, Deborah also does so by disregarding Hornby's presence and by not looking at him from the moment of her awakening. Although he makes her erupt into life again, he is really absent in the process of her awakening as a "newly born woman" through the struggle of her escape from the position of victim. That is, he cannot be an audience in her theatre in which "something is happening." But he still insists: ". . . (*Pause*) You see, you have been nowhere, absent, indifferent. It is we who have suffered" (34). He even insists on his right to demand the countertransference in their relationship as a privileged audience and identifies her suffering as his own suffering. He has regarded her merely as a mirror reflecting himself. By keeping her under his gaze, he can confirm and uphold his own male identity; hence he has lived with her and has never let her go. But she defiantly declares: "You've had your way with me. You made me touch you. You stripped me. I cried . . . but . . . it was my lust made me cry. You are a devil. My lust was my own. I kept it by me . . ." (12). In this way Hornby's countertransference is rejected by Deborah, as she awakens from her long sleep during which she has journeyed from the position of victim to the position of a living woman.

In *A Kind of Alaska,* Pinter also unfolds Freud's family romance scenario. The relationship between Deborah and Hornby is more complex than that of Dora and Freud because Hornby is not only a doctor, but also a member of the family; he is her sister Pauline's husband and a substitute for her father, who has become blind. He awakens her by the injection of the miracle drug, makes her alive again, and so takes the role of powerful father figure, who can destroy or redeem her. Another female figure, Pauline, is placed in the role of sacrifice and also accomplice in keeping alive the family romance relationship between Deborah and Hornby. Pauline is "nothing" to Hornby as his wife. As Dora finds herself an object of exchange between the two father figures, her father and Herr K, for the solution of their entangled sexual relationships, Deborah also finds herself offered as an object to another father figure, Hornby, after her awakening: "Deborah: My father? My mother? (*Pause*) Did they bring me to you as a sacrifice? Did they sacrifice me to you?" (12). Deborah knows well her position in the family romance. Her father was placed in the center of her world, and her mother was excluded from her world. Hence, her mother has been already dead before Deborah's awakening. Deborah loved her father, but her father had a mistress, like Dora's father; that is, the object of his desire was elsewhere. Since her father exchanged the object of his desire, Deborah felt that she was also placed in the position of an object which could be exchanged for the family economy—as the means to satisfy the family head's desire. At last, Deborah comes to realize that she has been forced to be a "part of the White Slave Traffic" (14), a victim in the patriarchal system which is based on the family romance.

Thus both Dora and Deborah realize that they are victims in the patriarchal family romance. In this sense, their hysterical reactions can be regarded as defiant manifestations of female sexuality which can disrupt patriarchal social and sexual economies. From this realization the women's awakenings begin. Deborah's immobilization in a fixed position becomes the beginning of her awakening. The vase of flowers which blocks her gaze at her father absorbs her gaze into itself and suddenly deviates her gaze into "her own secret realm," just as in oculogyric crises (attacks of forced deviation of the gaze) suffered by Rose in the case history. In oculogyric crises, Rose can think of just one thing, the object of her gaze, but suddenly she is led into "an absolute torrent of thoughts" rushing through her mind. But Sacks cannot interpret the torrent as an expression of her female sexuality or he consciously evades interpreting it. Actually it is not Rose but himself who is frightened by her experience during the crises. Although he transfers the fear to Rose, in fact he (not Rose) "could or would not specify the nature of these intrusive thoughts." Thus, only in a note, and also in another analyst's terms (Jelliffe's) he tries to admit that the thoughts are of "an inadmissible nature, either sexual or hostile" (81–82n), because, according to the family romance, he cannot admit that she can be a subject of desire, free of the position of an object, and that she also has her own sexuality. Thus Deborah's freezing functions as a lure for her to lead her gaze into "her own secret realm." And she experiences her awakening as a woman, which is happening within her self, her body, somewhere in the realm Hornby cannot "penetrate," i.e., in the space lost to his gaze.

In a sense, Hornby is also a victim in the system that is based on the family romance. In fact, he knows that Deborah has not remained static "in a kind of Alaska" and that she has been on the move in her adventure "into quite remote . . . utterly foreign . . . territories" (35). He actually cannot follow her in her struggle for awakening. In a sense, Hornby has no eyesight to see through her movement in her secret realm; he is like Deborah's father who becomes blind. But Hornby is obsessed with the male fantasy that he should watch her and chart her itinerary, keeping her within his view in order to keep her under his mastery.

In spite of his misgivings, Hornby awakens his "Sleeping Beauty" with the injection of L-DOPA, expecting a spectacle of a "normal" and charming beauty who has been imprisoned or suspended by the disease, as Sacks does in the case history. The disease of postencephalitis is a mystery; its source remains unknown, and its protean symptoms cannot be scientifically formulated according to patterns. Although L-DOPA is a miracle drug, its injection after the time gap of almost a half century cannot restore the former self of the patient just like a time machine. L-DOPA can only restore the ability to use language (a product of male-dominated culture) and to move the body. Thus, with the injection, the patient desires to talk about her struggle and adventure to someone, like Rose in the case history and Deborah in Pinter's play. In other words, after awakening, they feel theatrical desires—to make themselves spectacular and to search for an audience in theatre.

The awakening by L-DOPA, thus, is closely related to the problem of theatre, and only the success of theatre can cure the patient. In dealing with the case history, however, Sacks treats Rose's theatrical desire as one of the side-effects of L-DOPA, not as the beginning of the real cure. He expresses his anxiety about the fact that he cannot be an audience in Rose's theatre, which is "a private, inaccessible world of her own" (79). Her talking is cryptic to him, and so he cannot listen to her. Realizing that the doctor cannot be an audience in her theatre, she substitutes a tape recorder for the audience, playing with it in her room alone, recording her "innumerable songs of an astonishing lewdness." Sacks, however, diagnoses the activity as "forced reminiscence," or "incontinent nostalgia," not as her enactment of sexuality and narcissistic desire,[7] free of the gender frame imposed on her through her adventure. Falling back into "her own secret realm," a sort of internalized theatre where she herself is the only audience to an enactment of her sexuality and femininity, Rose turns away to search for her audience in herself. By introverting her theatrical desire, she becomes a spectator who sees herself see herself. And she experiences "the mirror stage" in the internalized theatre.[8]

In the theatrical version, from what Deborah tries to say after awakening, we can guess that she has experienced a kind of mirror stage. Dora's second dream in the theatrical version also can be interpreted as an allusion to the mirror stage (Willis 287–301), where, as a spectator before the image of the Madonna, Dora finds her own image behind it, enjoying the visual pleasure: voyeuristic and narcissistic all at once, through a sequence of substituting stills (the Sistine Madonna, substitution for the Madonna, and Frau K., Dora behind the Madonna, seen through a mirror). Here Dora's mirror stage is more complicated because she (the subject) sees "not only the image of her own bodily integrity, but her separation both from the mother and *from the image*" (301; my emphasis). That is, Dora experiences "a gap," "a space between," which Clément and Cixous refer to as the separation.[9] In this narrow space between, she enacts her impassioned desire for femininity.

Deborah's trance-like state in a "vast series of halls" and her report of dancing in narrow spaces suggest the same mirror stage as Dora has experienced in her second dream and a following scene. Deborah is imprisoned in halls with "enormous interior windows masquerading as walls. The windows are mirrors," and so mirror reflects mirror. Just like Rose's nightmares about her imprisonment in a castle which has a shape of herself, Deborah is imprisoned by masquerading reflected images of herself in the mirror. Thus she can see herself seeing her masquerading images in the mirror in the opposite mirror. During this stage, she can hear the sound of dripping water from a faucet, the sound functioning as a reminder of her own sexuality beyond the scope of gaze.[10] In this sense, her dance in narrow spaces can be explained as an impassioned dance of her sexual desire. She feels as if she is dancing with someone dancing on her feet, but sometimes she feels light and free in an open space, and so she can freely enact an impassioned dance of desire. Through her mirror stage, Deborah at last awakens as a newly born woman.

Dora and Deborah, in the theatrical versions, at last become "newly born women" in theatre who are no longer placed in the subordinate position of victim, spectacle, object. By resisting the analyst's countertransferences and by experiencing their mirror stages they are free of the frame of the proper gender position imposed in the family romance scenario. And they can enjoy themselves by playing the roles of subject and object all at once, experiencing "a space between" where they simultaneously enjoy voyeuristic and narcissistic pleasures.

In the last scene of *Portrait of Dora,* Dora defiantly cuts off Freud's analysis and frustrates him, but in Pinter's last scene, Deborah's attitude toward Hornby is ambivalent. It seems that Deborah contradictorily tries to accept her gender position reimposed by Hornby. Here we cannot be sure whether Pinter is suggesting that as she returns to a man's world, it is inevitable for her to accept a subordinate gender position again (to be "accommodated" to a "normal" lady, an object of desire through the process of "tribulation," just as Sacks desires), or if he is suggesting that her gesture to accept it implies an ironical attitude toward the incorrigibly stubborn father figure. Certainly Deborah's final speech to Hornby after a silence, "Thank you," conveys a cynical tone that reverberates for a long time after the curtain falls. And Deborah still remains a mystery to Hornby, just as Dora frustrates Freud's male fantasy and remains an unmasterable woman to him.

In this way, Pinter awakens a woman fixed in a gender frame, but he also shows how a father figure tries to reimpose the frame back on "the newly born woman." In simultaneously deconstructing psychoanalysis and a paradigm of a traditional theatre, he reveals the workings of a gender politics. And we can inscribe *Portrait of Dora* as a "newly born woman" in theatre on Pinter's portrait of Deborah. Thus, in two theatrical versions of the histories, we confirm again that the problems of psychoanalysis, theatre, and feminism are inseparably linked to each other.

Notes

1. According to Sacks's explanation in *Awakenings,* an unbelievable and mysterious epidemic suddenly appeared in several European cities in the winter of 1916–1917 and soon spread over the rest of the world. The disease, whose signs are protean (delirium, mania, trances, coma, sleep, insomnia, restlessness, and states of Parkinsonism, etc.) was called "a Hydra with a thousand heads" by the physician Constantin von Economo and at last identified as encephalitis lethargica, or sleeping sickness, by the physician himself. In 1927 the epidemic suddenly disappeared as it had arrived, leaving almost

two million casualties and three million surviving patients. Some of the survivors had recovered their original aliveness, but the majority developed severe "postencephalitic syndromes." The worst patients sank into singular states of "sleep"—into immobilized and speechless states, although they retained "the higher faculties"—the power to remember, to compare, to dissect, and to testify. At last in 1967 with the development of the "miracle drug," "L-DOPA," some survivors were awakened into life again. Nevertheless the disease still remains a mystery and is almost excluded from our memory, which has a tendency to evade reality that is beyond our mastery. Sacks includes twenty case histories of the survivors (thirteen female and seven male patients) in the book. Pinter himself has not identified which case history he has dramatized, but Sacks mentions in his epilogue that Pinter's *A Kind of Alaska* originated from the case history of Rose R. Although there are some allusions to various symptoms shown by other female patients in portraying Deborah in the theatrical version, it is probable that the model for Deborah is Rose.

2. Freud wrote the case history and planned to publish it in 1901, but he withdrew it and published it in 1905, with the title "Fragment of an Analysis of a Case of Hysteria."

3. As Sacks remarks, the symptoms of postencephalitic disease show great affinities to neurotic and Parkinsonian symptoms. The symptoms of female patients after awakenings are especially similar to the symptoms of hysterics described by Freud in his analyses of cases of hysteria.

4. By referring to the analysis of Jelliffe, a neurologist and psychoanalyst, and using Freud's term, Sacks indicates that postencephalitic patients show, like hysterics, "an extraordinary ability to 'absorb' intense feeling and to express it in indirect psychological terms." That is, "they were gifted—or cursed—with a pathologically extravagant expressive facility or (in Freud's term) 'somatic compliance.'" See Sacks 18.

5. Sacks presents his case history in a sequence of "awakening," "tribulation," and "accommodation," which parallels the linear sequence of a traditional drama.

6. In the footnote to this admission, Sacks remarks that Pinter can penetrate and understand "her own secret realm" as "*A Kind of Alaska.*"

7. Sacks interprets Robert O's absorption as a narcissistic one, but he cannot do so for Rose because he cannot admit the existence of female subjectivity.

8. In Lacanian theory, "the mirror stage," is a stage in the chronological development of the infant in which the infant emerges as an individual separated from the mother. In using the term "the mirror stage," I want to focus on the infant's desire for its own subjectivity as a separate individual which can be found in Dora and Deborah in the dramas. Lacan also calls the stage a drama in "The Mirror Stage as Formative of the Function of the I": "The mirror stage is a drama whose internal impetus lunges forward from insufficiency to anticipation—and which, for the subject captivated by the lure of spatial identification, machinates the succession of fantasies which go from an image of the body in bits and pieces to a form which we call orthopedic of its totality—and to the armor finally assumed of an alienating identity, which will mark with its rigid structure his entire mental development" (*Ecrits: A Selection* 4). Here we can see the problem of the mirror stage is closely related to that of the dramatic representation. As Jane Gallop also said in *The Father's Seduction*, the infant is "fixed, constrained in a representation which the infant believes to be the Other's, the mother's, image of her" (121). Thus the infant's desire to be free of rigid representation and to enter into another representation in the mirror stage is the same one that the female protagonists in the dramas experience.

9. Cixous and Clément compare the "gap," the "space between" which the child experiences in the mirror stage to the space where separation is experienced as pleasure, in a positive sense (166).

10. In the case history, Rose interprets another female patient's frequent water drinking from the faucet of the water fountain as her expression of her repressed sexuality: "Stop sucking that spout, Margaret, we all know what you really want to suck!" (Sacks 87).

EIGHTEEN

Deborah's Homecoming in
A Kind of Alaska:
An Afterword

Katherine H. Burkman

Why honor Pinter? What is it about this playwright that brought over 250 scholars and artists together from around the world to celebrate his sixtieth birthday and his drama? There is, of course, his unflinching honesty and his perceptiveness about the human condition, his uncanny ear for how we talk, so that hearing Pinter enables us to hear ourselves, his use of subtext and silence to reveal what is hidden under what we say and what we don't, and the political passion that informs his work. But what I think is perhaps most important about Pinter is his courage as he charts our efforts to come home.

In his 1982 one-act drama, *A Kind of Alaska,* Pinter has taken up the question of coming home that was the subject of his 1965 play, *The Home-coming.* Deborah, who has just been awakened by Dr. Hornby from twenty-nine years spent in a comatose state (she fell asleep when she was sixteen and is now being awakened at forty-five), speaks with her doctor and her sister Pauline for some time, and then she says, "I want to go home." By all realistic standards she is home. Hornby informs her that he has lifted her onto this bed when she went into her deep sleep, when she, so to speak, stopped, an event that occurred in the dining room when she was surrounded by her family, and that he has, despite marrying her sister some years later, preferred to live with her. What, then, does Deborah mean when she says that she wants to go home?

Some clues to answering this question lie both in the play and in Pinter's former drama, in which Teddy, who has left his home in England to teach philosophy at an American university, brings his wife of several years "home" to meet the family. But it is Ruth who finds a home with Teddy's family, not the philosopher, who prefers to return to America and his life away from his origins. The absurdity of both Deborah's seemingly incoherent desire to go home when she is already there and of Teddy's leaving his wife in his former home while he returns to his American exile has been a deep part of Pinter's work from the start. His very first play, *The Room,* was about displacement from home, and Deborah's question, "What room is this?" (11), along with her desire to go home, reveals the persistence of homelessness as Pinter's concern[1] and is at the heart of his explorations of the absurd.

Critics, who had been baffled by some of Pinter's depictions of the absurd, responded to *A Kind of Alaska* with some relief—it was, after all, based on fact, a case history from Oliver Sacks's *Awakenings,* a book in which he had detailed the case histories of twenty patients suffering the aftereffects of a 1916–1917 epidemic of *encephalitis lethargica,* a sleeping sickness. Sacks had treated these patients in the 1960s with what at first seemed like a miracle drug, L-DOPA, and he had successfully awakened many of his one hundred patients. His book, however, explored the failures as well as the successes of the drug, as many of his patients were unable to sustain the waking state, suffering from the drug's severe side effects, among which were terrible tics and paranoia.

Although based on fact, Pinter's play is finally no less enigmatic than any of his former ones. All one needs to do is to compare the recent Robert De Niro film's treatment of Sacks's *Awakenings,* in which the male patient Leonard is the central concern, with Pinter's treatment of Deborah to see how differently life's absurdities are treated. The Doctor Sacks character in the film (brilliantly portrayed by Robin Williams) is a withdrawn person who is "awakened" by the patients he awakens while they slip back into their various forms of withdrawn sleep. Pinter's Hornby, however, continues to struggle, caught up in a desperate triangle that Pinter explores both in terms of the homelessness of the three characters and their attempt to come home.

The journey imagery of such attempts gives the play its name and its ambience. In an effort to explain to Deborah where she has been for twenty-nine years, Hornby suggests that her mind has been on a journey. "Your mind has not been damaged," he explains. "It was merely suspended, it took up a temporary habitation . . . in a kind of Alaska. But it was not entirely static, was it? You ventured into quite remote . . . utterly foreign . . . territories. You kept on the move. And I charted your itinerary. Or did my best to do so. I have never let you go" (34–35).

This sleeping beauty, then, has not been static in her homelessness but has "kept on the move." Her own description of the experience is that she "danced in very narrow spaces. Kept stubbing my toes and bumping my head. Like Alice" (24). And like Alice all was not negative, as sometimes "the space opened and became light," and Deborah herself became light and found she could dance "till dawn" (26).

While Hornby accuses Deborah of not listening to the version of reality that he and Pauline give her, she accuses them of not listening to her, offering from her Alaskan perspective a critique of their condition. "No-one hears what I say. No-one is listening to me" (6), she says. "I can't get to sleep. The dog keeps turning about. I think he's dreaming. He wakes me up, but not himself up" (7). Since it is Hornby who has injected Deborah and awakened her, her lines suggest that he, like the dog, is "not himself up."

Indeed, Suzanne Costello, who played Pauline in the drama, asked me when she first read the play, "What kind of man is this Hornby, wanting to live with a dead woman?" and Stuart Pimsler, who played Hornby, was very put off by him, finding him, and correctly so I think, intrusive. When we asked a student audience of the play why Hornby does choose to live with Deborah rather than with her sister, whom he has married, one student suggested that it was because he fell in love with Deborah's helplessness. Deborah asks him if he is her Prince Charming, and as such he probably finds her helplessness desirable because he can fantasize the awakening of a sleeping beauty totally under his control. As Ann Hall suggests, the play offers a critique of a patriarchal society in which the Sleeping Beauty cannot have a happy ending because she speaks out. "Deborah," Hall writes, "describes the place of the feminine in patriarchal or phallocentric thought—confined, other, silent, and even a bit tortured" (11).

To be fair to Hornby, however, and to think of him as well as Pauline as doubles or alter egos of Deborah, he has attempted to chart her voyage, perhaps to awaken himself (recall the sleeping dog who wakens Deborah) from his own kind of Alaska. Indeed, choreographer Stuart Pimsler has spoken about the dance/drama, *Pausing in the Avalanche,* that he and his company created as an outgrowth of their work with the play, as being about the three characters as aspects of a single being seeking to integrate, to find wholeness, another way of talking about a homecoming. As in some versions of The Sleeping Beauty fairy tale in which everyone falls asleep with the princess, Pauline's and Hornby's lives have been suspended—Pauline calls herself a widow and Hornby has been keeping watch rather than living with his wife. It is they, Hornby insists, who have suffered.

The crisis, then, involves all three characters, who form a family faced with a general need for a homecoming. This family constellation becomes clearer in terms of the myth of Demeter and Persephone, which has been compared to The Sleeping Beauty fairy tale.[2] In that myth, Persephone has been picking flowers when Hades, Lord of the Underworld, molests her and takes her off to be the queen of his domain. Demeter, who causes winter to come because of her grief over her lost daughter, only permits the return of spring when she has recovered Persephone, who nevertheless must return each year for a time to her husband. Suzanne Costello has noted that Deborah was moving a vase of flowers when she made her descent. She was moving it, one recalls as well, to better see her father. Because Zeus gave Persephone to his brother, for whom he acts as a double, the myth suggests an incestuous theme that also permeates the play. One may view Pauline as grieving sister/mother, Hornby as seductive father, and Deborah as daughter. Coming home in these terms means in some way working through the adolescent Oedipal crisis that was befalling Deborah when the disease overtook her.

Scenes from *Pimsler Honors Pinter: A Kind of
Alaska* and *Pausing in the Avalanche,* as per-
formed by Stuart Pimsler Dance & Theater
(Stuart Pimsler, Suzanne Costello, Janet Slifka,
Tim Talty, Janet Parrott, Loraine Jeffery, and
Romy Noltimier. Photos by Brad Feinknopf.

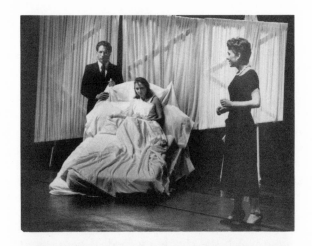

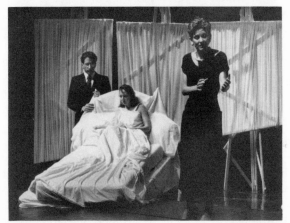

For though a reasonable interpretation of Deborah's desire to go home is her desire to return to the sixteen-year-old who "stopped," not to face the death of her mother, the blindness of her father, her own aged self that she cannot fail to see reflected in her sister, whom she accuses of aging overnight, everything she says in the play suggests that home was a place of tension and conflict from which she may have fled into disease. "Sisters," she complains, "are diabolical. Brothers are worse. One day I prayed I would see no-one ever again, none of them ever again" (18). Apparently there were pressures to settle down into family expectations, to suppress her emerging sexuality. She agrees at one point to settle down with Jack and meet all those expectations, but she complains that her mother isn't coming in to tuck her in and "to warn me about not going too far with boys" (20). She then rages at her sister, whom she says has suggested that her father has a mistress (21).

If Deborah's desire to go home is not to return to her sixteen-year-old surroundings, from which she clearly escaped, is her desire to go back into a kind of Alaska? Yet another audience member at a postproduction discussion pointed out that Rose R., the patient on whom the play is based, did return to her withdrawn, Alaskan condition. Another student, Maureen Voight, has suggested that Deborah's desire to go home may be the more Freudian/Rankian one of returning to the womb, of seeking death, the final stasis. Certainly the play is filled with birth trauma: Deborah looks forward to a birthday in which presents will be hers to keep, she strives to dance, and she dreams of swimming as well.

Here, *The Homecoming* offers its clues. In that play as in this, the unity of the home is in a shambles—the men are fragments, and they in turn seek to fragment Ruth, to see her as they had seen their now dead mother Jessie as either wife, mother, or whore, but never as a human being who integrates sexuality and warmth. Since Jessie's death, the house itself has been changed— a wall has been knocked out, leaving an arch and an emptiness. Here, too, the men are just as needy as Ruth, not offering her sexuality (I reject all readings of Ruth as a nymphomaniac revelling in her sexual duties) since they are as impotent as Teddy; they have "rocks," but they are "frozen, stiff" as Lenny suggests, "in the fridge" (77). Here Teddy has the Hornby role, preferring to watch life rather than to live it, insisting that he will "observe" and not be caught up in living. And Ruth, like her biblical counterpart, is the one who offers new life and finds it with her new family.

Because Deborah is a descendent of Ruth's, with her own biblical heritage as "the Old Testament prophetess who helped deliver her people from captivity" (Zeifman, "A Rose"), and because Hornby has stayed with her (not returned to the desert aridity of America, Pinter's verdict on us perhaps), the case for Hornby is more hopeful than it is for Teddy. Pinter has infused him with some of Dr. Sacks's own yearnings, his own fascination with mapping the course of the disease as an exploration and not just an escape from life. Critical of the dry, inhumane way neurologists tend to write about disease, Sacks writes, "And yet it [the disease] is the most enchanting of subjects, as dramatic, and tragic, and comic as any. My own feelings when I first saw the effects of L-DOPA, were of amazement and wonder and almost of awe. Each passing day increased my amazement, disclosing new phenomena, novelties, strangenesses, whole worlds of being whose possibility I had never dreamt of—I felt like a slum child suddenly transplanted to Africa or Peru" (207). Continuing to talk about this landscape that has haunted him since his first encounter with his postencephalitic patients in 1966, Sacks writes:

> It is a very mixed landscape, partly familiar, partly uncanny, with sunlit uplands, bottomless chasms, volcanoes, geysers, meadows, marshes; something like Yellowstone—archaic, prehuman, almost prehistoric, with a sense of vast forces simmering all round one. Freud once spoke of neurosis as akin to a prehistoric, Jurassic landscape, and this image is still truer of post-encephalitic disease, which seems to conduct one to the dark heart of being. (231)

Seeking a home in this play, as in all of Pinter's dramas, is seeking a whole self, what Sacks talks about in terms of the disease as a transcendence of "I" over "it," person over mechanism. The patient whom Pinter based his play on, Rose R., did not make it—"She is a Sleeping Beauty," Sacks writes, "whose 'awakening' was unbearable to her, and who will never be awoken again" (87). Yet I agree with Stuart Pimsler that Pinter has based his play on the entire book, not on one case history, and it is a book about courage and transcendence, as comic as it is tragic. When Deborah accepts a combination of the lies and truths that they tell her at play's end, and thanks them, I believe it is her way of going on to receive her presents at her birthday, which she wishes to keep, her way of achieving presence, and Pinter's way of celebrating life at the dark heart of being.

Notes

1. Martin Esslin, who coined the term "the theatre of the absurd" and opened the way for our understanding of such absurdist playwrights as Beckett, Pinter, Ionesco, Genet, and others, began his definition with Albert Camus's efforts to define the absurd hero. Camus spoke of our contemporary condition as "an irremediable exile" in which we are "deprived of memories of a lost homeland as much as . . . hope of a promised land to come." He goes on to say, "This divorce between man and his life, the actor and his setting, truly constitutes the feeling of absurdity" (Esslin, *The Theatre of the Absurd* 5).
2. John Taylor and Lisa Tyler both gave papers at the meeting that made this connection.

Works Cited

Alighieri, Dante. *The Divine Comedy: Inferno 1*. Trans. Charles S. Singleton. Princeton: Bolligen Series, 80, Princeton University Press, 1970.
———. *The Divine Comedy: Inferno 2*. Trans. Charles S. Singleton. Princeton: Bolligen Series, 80, Princeton University Press, 1970.
Arendt, Hannah. *Eichmann in Jerusalem: A Report on the Banality of Evil*. Revised and Enlarged Edition. New York: Viking Press, 1965.
Armstrong, Raymond. "The Influence of Franz Kafka upon the Theatre of Harold Pinter— with Specific Reference to the Struggle between Father and Son." *DAI* 51 (1988): 02A. University of Ulster, Northern Ireland.
Auslander, Philip. "Toward a Concept of the Political in Postmodern Theatre." *Theatre Journal* 39.1 (1987): 20–34.
Baranczak, Stanislaw. "All the President's Plays." *New Republic* 23 (July 1990): 27–32.
Barthes, Roland. *The Pleasure of the Text*. Trans. Richard Miller. New York: Hill and Wang, 1975.
———. *S/Z*. Trans. Richard Miller. New York: Hill and Wang, 1974.
Bassoff, Bruce. "The Model as Obstacle: Kafka's *The Trial*." *To Honor René Girard: Stanford French and Italian Studies* 34. Ed. Alphonse Juilland. Saratoga, CA: ANMA Libri, 1986.
Baudrillard, Jean. "Ecstasy of Communication." *Postmodern Culture*. Ed. Hal Foster. London: Pluto Press, 1985.
———. *Les Stratégies Fatales*. Paris: Bernard Grasset, 1983.
Beaufort, John. Review of *Mountain Language* by Harold Pinter. *The Christian Science Monitor* 18 Dec. 1989: 12.
Beckett, Samuel. *Endgame*. New York: Grove Press, 1958.
———. "Krapp's Last Tape." *The Collected Shorter Plays of Samuel Beckett*. New York: Grove, 1984.
———. *Waiting for Godot. The Complete Works of Samuel Beckett*. New York: Grove, 1954, 1970.
Benjamin, Walter. "The Work of Art in the Age of Its Mechanical Reproduction." *Illuminations*. Trans. Harry Zohn. London: Fontana, 1970.
Bensky, Lawrence M. "The Art of the Theater III: Harold Pinter: An Interview." *Paris Review* 10 (Fall 1966): 12–37.
———. "Harold Pinter: An Interview." *Writers at Work: The Paris Review Interviews, Third Series*. Ed. George Plimpton. 1967. Rpt. in *Pinter: A Collection of Critical Essays*. Ed. Arthur Ganz. Englewood Cliffs, NJ: Prentice, 1972. 19–33.
Bishop, Tom. "The Temptation of Silence." *As No Other Dare Fail, For Samuel Beckett on His 80th Birthday*. London: John Calder, 1986. 24–29.
Blackwell, Vera. "Havel's *Private View*." *Cross Currents: A Yearbook of Central European Culture* 3 (1984): 107–19.
Blau, Herbert. *The Audience*. Baltimore: Johns Hopkins University Press, 1990.
———. *The Eye of Prey: Subversions of the Postmodern*. Bloomington: Indiana University Press, 1987.
Bloom, Harold, Ed. *Franz Kafka's The Trial*. New York: Chelsea House, 1987.
Boling, Becky. "From Pin-Ups to Striptease in Gambaro's *El Despojamiento*." *Latin American Theatre Review* (Spring 1987): 59–65.
Bowen, Elizabeth. *The Heat of the Day*. London: Cape, 1949.
Bradbury, Malcolm. "Franz Kafka." *The Modern World: Ten Great Writers*. New York and London: Penguin, 1988.
Brecht, Bertolt. "Im Dickicht der Städte [In the Jungle of Cities]." *Erste Stücke*. Berlin: Suhrkamp Verlag, 1957. 207–318.

Broumas, Olga. "Artemis." *Beginning with O.* New Haven: Yale University Press, 1977. 23–24.

Brown, John Russell. "Beckett and the Art of the Nonplus." *Beckett at 80/Beckett in Context.* Ed. Enoch Brater. New York: Oxford University Press, 1986. 25–45.

———. "Mr. Pinter's Shakespeare." *Critical Quarterly* 5 (1963): 251–65.

Bull, John. *New British Political Dramatists.* New York: Grove, 1983.

Burkman, Katherine H. "Death and the Double in Three Plays by Harold Pinter." *Harold Pinter: You Never Heard Such Silence.* Ed. Alan Bold. Totowa, NJ: Barnes & Noble, 1984. 131–145.

———. "Displacement in Time and Space: Harold Pinter's *Other Places.*" *Harold Pinter: A Casebook.* Ed. Lois Gordon. New York: Garland, 1990. 109–118.

———. *The Dramatic World of Harold Pinter: Its Basis in Ritual.* Columbus: The Ohio State University Press, 1971.

———. "The Multiple Levels of Action in Harold Pinter's *Victoria Station.*" *The Pinter Review* 1. 1 (1987): 22–30.

Camus, Albert. "Hope and the Absurd in the Work of Franz Kafka." *Kafka: A Collection of Critical Essays.* Ed. Ronald Gray. Englewood Cliffs, NJ: Prentice-Hall, 1962.

Carpenter, Charles A. "'What Have I Seen, the Scum or the Essence?': Symbolic Fallout in Pinter's *The Birthday Party.*" *Harold Pinter: You Never Heard Such Silence.* Ed. Alan Bold. Totowa, NJ: Barnes & Noble, 1984. 93–112.

Chase, Donald. "The Pinter Principle." *American Film* 15 (Oct. 1990): 16.

Chekhov, Anton. *The Best Plays of Chekhov.* Trans. Stark Young. New York: Modern Library, 1956.

Ciment, Michel. "Visually Speaking: Harold Pinter Interviewed." *Film Commentary* 25.3 (1989): 20–22.

Citati, Pietro. *Kafka.* Translated from the Italian by Raymond Rosenthal. Minerva Paperback Edition. London: Mandarin Paperbacks, 1991.

Cixous, Hélène. "Aller à la Mer." Trans. Barbara Kerslake. *Modern Drama* 27 (1984): 546–48.

———. *Portrait of Dora.* Trans. Sarah Burd. *Diacritics* (Spring 1983): 2–32.

Cixous, Hélène, and Catherine Clément. *The Newly Born Woman.* Trans. Betsy Wing. Minneapolis: University of Minnesota Press, 1988.

Cocteau, Jean. "*Preface to the Wedding at the Eiffel Tower.* 1922." *Modern French Drama.* Ed. Michael Benedikt and George E. Wellwarth. New York: E. P. Dutton, 1966.

Cohn, Ruby. "Growing (Up?) with *Godot.*" *Beckett at 80/Beckett in Context.* Ed. Enoch Brater. New York: Oxford University Press, 1986: 3–24.

Connor, Steven. *Postmodern Culture.* Oxford: Basil Blackwell, 1989.

Croyden, Margaret. "Pinter's Hideous Comedy." *A Casebook on Harold Pinter's* The Homecoming. Ed. John Lahr. New York: Grove, 1971. 45–56.

Cypess, Sandra Messenger. "Physical Imagery in the Works of Griselda Gambaro." *Modern Drama* 8 (1975): 357–64.

Dawidowicz, Lucy. *The War against the Jews 1933–1945.* New York: Bantam, 1976.

Day, Barbara. "Czech Theatre from the National Revival to the Present Day." *New Theatre Quarterly* 2.7 (1986): 250–74.

Debord, Guy. *Society of the Spectacle.* Paris: Buchet-Chastel, 1971.

Dukore, Bernard. "Alaskan Perspectives." *Harold Pinter: You Never Heard Such Silence.* Ed. Alan Bold. Totowa, NJ: Barnes & Noble, 1984. 166–177.

Duras, Marguerite. *L'Amante anglaise.* Paris: Cahiers du Théâtre national populaire, 1968.

———. *L'Amante anglaise.* Paris: Gallimard, 1967.

———. *Les Viaducs de la Seine-et-Oise.* Paris: Gallimard, 1959.

Echague, Selva. "Griselda Gambaro: Escribir me justifica." *Clarin* (3 Feb. 1972): 12–13.

Elliott, Susan Merritt. "Fantasy behind Play: A Study of Emotional Responses to Harold Pinter's *The Birthday Party, The Caretaker,* and *The Homecoming."* Diss. Indiana University, 1973.

Esslin, Martin. "Epic Theatre, the Absurd, and the Future." *Reflections: Essays on Modern Theatre.* New York: Doubleday, 1969.

———. "Language and Silence." *Pinter: A Collection of Critical Essays.* Ed. Arthur Ganz. Englewood Cliffs, NJ: Prentice-Hall, 1972. 34–59.

———. *Pinter: The Playwright.* First published in 1970 as *The Peopled Wound: The Work [Plays] of Harold Pinter.* 4th ed. London and New York: Methuen, 1982. Corrected repr., 1984.

———. *The Theatre of the Absurd.* Rev. ed. New York: Doubleday/Anchor, 1969.

Freud, Sigmund. "Fragment of an Analysis of a Case of Hysteria." *Dora: An Analysis of a Case of Hysteria.* Trans. Philip Rieff. New York: Macmillan, 1963.

Fried, Michael. *Absorption and Theatricality: Painting and the Beholder in the Age of Diderot.* Chicago: University of Chicago Press, 1980.

———. "Art and Objecthood." *Minimal Art: A Critical Anthology.* Ed. Gregory Battcock. New York: Dutton, 1968.

Gale, Steven H. *Butter's Going Up: A Critical Analysis of Harold Pinter's Work.* Durham, NC: Duke University Press, 1977.

Gallop, Jane. *The Father's Seduction: Feminism and Psychoanalysis.* Ithaca: Cornell University Press, 1982.

Gambaro, Griselda. *El Campo.* Trans. William Oliver. *Voices of Change in the Spanish-American Theatre.* Ed. William Oliver. Austin: University of Texas Press, 1971. 47–103.

———. "Teatro de vanguardia en la Argentina de hoy." *Universidad* 81 (1970): 301–31.

Garbus, Martin. "'Godot Is Here.'" *Nation* 29 Jan. 1990: 124.

Gillen, Francis. "'To Lay Bare': Pinter, Shakespeare, and *The Dwarfs."* *Harold Pinter: A Casebook.* Ed. Lois Gordon. New York: Garland, 1990. 189–99.

Goetz-Stankiewicz, Marketa. "Variations of Temptation—Václav Havel's Politics of Language." *Modern Drama* 33 (1990): 93–105.

Gordon, Lois. Introduction to *Harold Pinter: A Casebook.* Ed. Lois Gordon. New York: Garland, 1990. ix–xxviii.

Green, Penelope. "Weighing Anchors." *New York Times Magazine.* 28 April 1991: 56.

Gross, Miriam. "Pinter on Pinter." *The Observer* 5 Oct. 1980. Rpt. in *Critical Essays on Harold Pinter.* Ed. Steven H. Gale. Boston: Hall, 1990. 37–44.

Gussow, Mel. "Pinter's Plays Following Him out of Enigma and into Politics." *New York Times* 6 Dec. 1988: C17.

Hall, Adam. *The Berlin Memorandum.* London: Collins, 1965. Rpt. as *The Quiller Memorandum.* New York: Simon and Schuster, 1965.

Hall, Ann Christine. "'A Kind of Alaska': The Representation of Women in the Plays of Eugene O'Neill, Harold Pinter, and Sam Shepard." Diss. The Ohio State University, 1988. Ann Arbor: UMI, 1989. 8820302. *DAI* 49.8 (Feb. 1989): 2214-A.

Harter, Deborah. "The Artist on Trial: Kafka and Josefine, 'Die Sängerin.'" *Deutsche Vierteljahrs Schrift für Literaturwissenschaft und Geistesgeschichte* 61 (1987): 151–62.

Havel, Václav. *Audience.* 1976. *Sorry . . .* 7–35. *The Vaněk Plays* 1–26.

———. *Disturbing the Peace: A Conversation with Karel Hvíala.* Trans. Paul Wilson. New York: Knopf, 1990.

———. *The Garden Party.* 1963. Trans. and adapted by Vera Blackwell. London: Cape, 1969.

———. *The Increased Difficulty of Concentration: A Play in Two Acts.* 1968. Trans. Vera Blackwell. New York: French, 1976.

———. *Largo Desolato.* English version by Tom Stoppard. New York: Grove, 1987.

———. *Letters to Olga.* Intro. Paul Wilson. New York: Holt, 1989.

———. "Light on a Landscape." *The Vaněk Plays* 237–39.

——. *The Memorandum.* 1965. Trans. Vera Blackwell. Intro. Tom Stoppard. New York: Grove Weidenfeld, 1980.

——. *Mistake.* 1983. Trans. George Theiner. *Index on Censorship* 13.1 (Feb. 1984): 13–15. [Incl. "'Many Thanks to Our Swedish Friends': Václav Havel's Message for the Stockholm Première of His Latest Play" (15).]

——. *The Mountain Hotel.* 1976. [Also entitled *A Hotel in the Hills (Horsky Hotel).*]

——. "On Kafka." *New York Review of Books* 27 Sept. 1990: 19.

——. *The Power of the Powerless: Citizens against the State in Central-Eastern Europe.* Armonk, NY: Sharpe, 1985.

——. *Private View.* 1976. *Sorry . . .* 37–64. Also translated as *Unveiling, The Vaněk Plays* 27–49.

——. *Protest.* 1978. Trans. Vera Blackwell. *The Vaněk Plays* 51–75.

——. *Sorry . . . : Two Plays:* Audience *and* Private View. Trans. and adapted by Vera Blackwell. London: Eyre Methuen (in association with BBC-TV), 1978.

——. "Stories and Totalitarianism." *Index on Censorship* 17.3 (1988): 14–21.

——. *Temptation.* Trans. Marie Winn. New York: Grove, 1989.

——. *Václav Havel: Living in Truth.* Ed. Jan Vladislav. London and Boston: Faber, 1987.

Hays, Michael. "Declassified Documents." *boundary 2* (Summer 1990): 102–27.

Henley, William Ernest. *Echoes* (Poem IX). *Poems.* London: Macmillan, 1926.

Hern, Nick. "A Play and Its Politics." Printed with *One for the Road* by Harold Pinter. London: Methuen, 1985. 7–23.

Hernadi, Paul. "Doing, Making, Meaning: Toward a Theory of Verbal Practice." *PMLA* 103.5 (1988): 749–58.

Hinchcliffe, Arnold. *Harold Pinter.* Boston: Twayne, 1967.

Holzapfel, Tamara. "Griselda Gambaro's Theatre of the Absurd." *Latin American Theatre Review* 4.1 (1970): 5–11.

Jameson, Frederic. *The Political Unconsciousness: Narrative as a Socially Symbolic Act.* Ithaca: Cornell University Press, 1981.

Janson, H. W. *History of Art: A Survey of the Major Visual Arts from the Dawn of History to the Present Day.* New York: Abrams, 1962.

Kafka, Franz. *The Diaries of Franz Kafka, 1910–1913.* Trans. Joseph Kresh. New York: Schocken, 1949.

——. *The Trial.* Trans. Willa and Edwin Muir. Revised and with additional material translated by E. M. Butler. New York: Schocken, 1937, 1968, 1984.

Kane, Leslie. "The Weasel under the Cocktail Cabinet: Rite and Ritual in Pinter's Plays." *Pinter Review* 2 (1988): 19–32.

Kennedy, Douglas. "Breaking the Silence." *New Stateman and Society* 28 Oct. 1988: 38–39.

Kirkpatrick, Melanie. Rev. of *Mountain Language,* by Harold Pinter. *The Wall Street Journal* 29 Nov. 1989: A14.

Klein, Joanne. *Making Pictures: The Pinter Screenplays.* Columbus: Ohio State University Press, 1985.

Knowles, Ronald. "Harold Pinter, Citizen." *The Pinter Review: Annual Essays 1989.* Tampa: University of Tampa, 1989. 24–33.

Krauss, Rosalind. *Passages in Modern Sculpture.* Cambridge: MIT Press, 1981.

Lacan, Jacques. "Alienation." *Four Fundamental Concepts of Psycho-Analysis.* Ed. Jacques Alain Miller. Trans. Alan Sheridan. 1978. Reprint. New York: Norton, 1981. 203–15.

——. *Ecrits: A Selection.* Trans. Alan Sheridan. New York: Norton, 1977.

Lahr, John. "Introduction." *A Casebook on Harold Pinter's* The Homecoming. Ed. John Lahr. New York: Grove, 1971. xi–xix.

Langer, Lawrence L. *Holocaust Testimonies: The Ruins of Memory.* New Haven: Yale University Press, 1991.

Laughlin, Karen L. "The Language of Cruelty: Dialogue Strategies and the Spectator in Gambaro's *El desatino* and Pinter's *The Birthday Party.*" *Latin American Theatre Review* (Fall 1986): 11–20.

Leahy, James. *The Cinema of Joseph Losey.* International Film Guide Series. London: A. Zwemmer, 1967; New York: A. S. Barnes, 1967.

Levi, Primo. *Survival in Auschwitz.* New York: Macmillan, Collier Books, 1961.

Lifton, Robert Jay. *The Nazi Doctors: Medical Killing and the Psychology of Genocide.* New York: Basic, 1986.

Lutterbie, John. "Subjects of Silence." *Theatre Journal* 40.4 (1988): 468–81.

Maugham, Robin (Sir Robert). *The Servant.* London: Falcon, 1948; NewYork: Harcourt, Brace, 1949.

Mayer, Hans. *Outsiders: A Study in Life and Letters.* Trans. Denis M. Sweet. Fwd. Ihab Hassan. Cambridge, MA, and London: MIT Press, 1982.

McMillan, Dougald, and Martha Fehsenfeld. *Beckett in the Theater.* London: Calder, 1988.

Mengel, Ewald. "Pinter's Politics of Violence." Paper presented at the session on "Pinter and Politics" at *A Pinter Festival,* 19 Apr. 1991.

———. "'Yes! In the Sea of Life Enisled': Harold Pinter's *Other Places.*" *Harold Pinter: A Casebook.* Ed. Lois Gordon. New York: Garland, 1990. 161–88.

Merritt, Susan Hollis. "Pinter and Politics." *Harold Pinter: A Casebook.* Ed. Lois Gordon. New York: Garland, 1990. 129–60.

———. *Pinter in Play: Critical Strategies and the Plays of Harold Pinter.* Durham and London: Duke University Press, 1990.

Mosley, Nicolas. *Accident.* London: Hodder and Stoughton, 1965; rpt. Elmwood Park, IL: Dalkey Archive Press, 1985.

Müller-Hill, Benno. *Murderous Science: Elimination by Scientific Selection of Jews, Gypsies, and Others, Germany 1933–1945.* Trans. George R. Fraser. Oxford: Oxford University Press, 1988.

Nelson, Hugh. "*The Homecoming:* Kith and Kin." *Modern British Dramatists: A Collection of Critical Essays.* Ed. John Russell Brown. Englewood Cliffs, NJ: Prentice, 1968. 145–63.

Pavis, Patrice. "The Classical Heritage of Modern Drama." *Modern Drama* 29 (1986): 1–22.

Pawel, Ernst. *The Nightmare of Reason: A Life of Franz Kafka.* New York: Farrar, Straus, Giroux, 1984.

Pinter, Harold. *Accident. Five screenplays.* London: Methuen, 1971; New York: Grove, 1973. 217–84.

———. *Betrayal. Complete Works: 4.* New York: Grove Weidenfeld, 1981, 1990. 155–268.

———. *Betrayal.* Directed by David Jones. Starring Ben Kingsley, Jeremy Irons, and Patricia Hodge, 1983.

———. *The Birthday Party. Complete Works: 1.* New York: Grove Weidenfeld, 1976, 1990. 17–97.

———. *The Caretaker. Complete Works: 2.* New York: Grove Weidenfeld, 1977, 1990. 13–87.

———. *The Collection. Complete Works: 2.* New York: Grove Weidenfeld, 1977, 1990. 119–57.

———. *The Comfort of Strangers and Other Screenplays.* London and Boston: Faber, 1990.

———. *Complete Works: 1.* New York: Grove Weidenfeld, 1976, 1990.

———. *Complete Works: 2.* New York: Grove Weidenfeld, 1977, 1990.

———. *Complete Works: 3.* New York: Grove Weidenfeld, 1978, 1990.

———. *Complete Works: 4.* New York: Grove Weidenfeld, 1981, 1990.

———. *The Dumb Waiter. Complete Works: 1.* New York: Grove Weidenfeld, 1976, 1990. 127–65.

———. *The Dwarfs* [play]. *Complete Works: 2.* New York: Grove Weidenfeld, 1977, 1990. 89–117.

———. *The Dwarfs: A Novel.* New York: Grove Weidenfeld, 1990.

———. *The Examination. Complete Works: 1.* New York: Grove Weidenfeld, 1976, 1990. 251–56.

———. *The French Lieutenant's Woman. The French Lieutenant's Woman and Other Screenplays.* London: Methuen, 1982. 1–104.

———. *The Heat of the Day.* London: Faber, 1989.

———. *The Homecoming. Complete Works: 3.* New York: Grove Weidenfeld, 1978, 1990. 19–98.

———. *The Hothouse.* 1958. New York: Grove, 1980.

———. "It Is Here." *Times Literary Supplement* 2 Feb. 1990: 113.

———. *A Kind of Alaska. Other Places: A Kind of Alaska, Victoria Station, Family Voices.* New York: Grove, 1983. 5–40.

———. *Landscape and Silence.* New York: Grove, 1970.

———. *Landscape. Complete Works: 3.* New York: Grove Weidenfeld, 1978, 1990. 173–98.

———. "Language and Lies." *Index on Censorship* 17.6 (1988): 2.

———. Letter to the author dated 5 Jan. 1991.

———. *Mac.* London: Pendragon, 1968.

———. *Mountain Language.* New York: Grove, 1988.

———. *No Man's Land. Complete Works: 4.* New York: Grove Weidenfeld, 1981, 1990. 73–153.

———. "Oh, Superman." Talk broadcast on *Opinion.* BBC 4. 31 May 1990.

———. *Old Times. Complete Works: 4.* New York: Grove Weidenfeld, 1981, 1990. 1–71.

———. *One for the Road.* Published with "A Play and Its Politics: A Conversation between Harold Pinter and Nicholas Hern." New York: Grove, 1986.

———. *Party Time.* A Staged Reading. Dir. John Clum (with notes from the playwright). Stadium Theatre, The Ohio State University. Columbus, Ohio, 20 Apr. 1991.

———. *Precisely. Harper's* (May 1985): 37.

———. *The Room. Complete Works: 1.* New York: Grove Weidenfeld, 1976, 1990. 99–126.

———. *Silence. Complete Works: 3.* New York: Grove Weidenfeld, 1978, 1990. 199–219.

———. *A Slight Ache. Complete Works: 1.* New York: Grove Weidenfeld, 1976, 1990. 168–200.

———. Talk presented at the University of East Anglia. East Anglia, Eng., 29 Oct. 1981.

———. *The Trial.* Unpublished screenplay. Typescript dated 29 August 1989.

———. "The U.S. Elephant Must Be Stopped." *London Guardian* 5 Dec. 1987: 10, col. 4.

———. *Victoria Station. Other Places: A Kind of Alaska, Victoria Station, Family Voices.* New York: Grove, 1983. 41–62.

———. "Writing for the Theatre." *Complete Works: 1.* New York: Grove Weidenfeld, 1976, 1990. 9–16.

A Pinter Festival: An International Meeting. The Ohio State University. Columbus, OH, 19–21 Apr. 1991.

Pittel, Christine. "How One Tiny Theatre Snared Harold Pinter." *New York Times* 8 Jan. 1989: 17, 40.

Polan, Dana. "Above All Else to Make You See." *Postmodernism and Politics.* Ed. Jonathan Arac. Minneapolis: University of Minnesota Press, 1986: 55–69.

Politzer, Heinz. *Franz Kafka: Parable and Paradox.* Revised, expanded edition. Ithaca: Cornell University Press, 1966.

Prentice, Penelope. "Ambiguity, Identity and the Violent Struggle for Dominance in Harold Pinter's *The Birthday Party.*" *The Pinter Review: Annual Essays 1989.*Tampa: University of Tampa, 1989. 9–23.

——. "Love and Survival: The Quintessence of Harold Pinter's Plays." *Cithara* 27.2 (May 1988): 30–39.

Pryce-Jones, David. Rev. of *Mountain Language,* by Harold Pinter. *Times Literary Supplement* 4 Nov. 1988: 1228.

Pugh, Marshall. "Trying to Pin Down Pinter." London *Daily Mail* 7 March 1964: 8.

Rabillard, Sheila. "Destabilizing Plot, Displacing the Status of Narrative: Local Order in the Plays of Pinter and Shepard." *Theatre Journal* 43.1 (1991): 41–58.

Rayner, Alice. "Harold Pinter: Narrative and Presence." *Theatre Journal* 40.4 (Dec. 1988): 482–97.

Rich, Frank. Rev. of *Mountain Language,* by Harold Pinter. *New York Times* 15 Dec. 1988: B4.

Sacks, Oliver. *Awakenings.* New York: Harper Collins, 1973, 1990.

St. John Butler, Lance. *Samuel Beckett and the Meaning of Being.* London: Macmillan, 1984.

Sakellaridou, Elizabeth. "Audience Control: British Political Theatre and the Pinter Method." Paper presented at the session "Pinter and Politics" at *A Pinter Festival,* 19 Apr. 1991.

——. *Pinter's Female Portraits: A Study of Female Characters in the Plays of Harold Pinter.* London: Macmillan; Towota, NJ: Barnes, 1988.

——. "The Rhetoric of Evasion as Political Discourse: Some Preliminaries on Pinter's Political Language." *The Pinter Review: Annual Essays 1989.* Tampa: University of Tampa, 1989. 43–47.

Salem, Daniel. "L'Étranger dans *A Slight Ache* de Pinter." *L'Étranger dans la littérature et la Pensée Anglaises.* Centre Aixois de Recherches Anglaises 9. *Actes du Colloque, Aix-en-Provence 11–12 Mars 1988.* Aix-en-Provence (Cedex): Université de Provence, 1989. 279–90.

Sarris, Andrew. *The American Cinema: Directors and Directions, 1929–1968.* New York: Dutton, 1968.

Schiff, Stephen. "Havel's Choice." *Vanity Fair* Aug. 1991: 124–28, 156–63.

Schürmann, Robert. *Heidegger on Being and Acting: From Principles to Anarchy.* Bloomington: Indiana University Press, 1987.

Shakespeare, William. *The Complete Works.* Ed. G. B. Harrison. New York: Harcroft, 1968.

Shinkarev, Leonid. "Metamorphosis in Prague." *World Press Review* 37 (May 1990): 36, 38.

Spann, Meno. *Franz Kafka.* Boston: Twayne, 1976.

Speirs, Logan. Rev. of *Mountain Language* by Harold Pinter. *English Studies* (Feb. 1990): 113.

States, Bert O. *Great Reckonings in Little Rooms.* Berkeley: University of California Press, 1985.

Strindberg, August, "Author's Foreword." *Six Plays by Strindberg.* Trans. Elizabeth Sprigge. Garden City: Doubleday, 1956. 61–73.

Strunk, Volker. *Harold Pinter: Towards a Poetics of His Plays.* New York: Lang, 1989.

Taylor, Diana. "Theatre and Terrorism." *Theatre Journal* 42.2. (May 1990): 165–82.

Taylor, John Russell. *Anger and After: A Guide to New British Drama.* London: Methuen, 1969. Rev. ed.

——. *Harold Pinter.* Longmans' Writers and Their Work Series, No. 212. London: Longmans Green, 1969.

———. "Pinter's Game of Happy Families." *A Casebook on Harold Pinter's* The Homecoming. Ed. John Lahr. New York: Grove, 1971. 57–65.

Thompson, David T. *Pinter: The Player's Playwright.* London: Macmillan, 1985.

Uhlman, Fred. *Reunion.* 1971. Intro. Arthur Koestler. London: Collins, 1971. New York: Farrar, Straus and Giroux, 1977.

The Vaněk Plays: Four Authors, One Character. Ed. Marketa Goetz-Stankiewicz. Vancouver: University of British Columbia Press, 1987.

Welles, Orson. *The Trial:* a film by Orson Welles. English translation and description of action by Nicholas Fry. New York: Simon and Schuster, 1970.

Whitelaw, Billie. "From Billie Whitelaw." *As No Other Dare Fail . . . For Samuel Beckett on His 80th Birthday.* London: Calder, 1986: 81–85.

Williams, Raymond. *Marxism and Literature.* Oxford: Oxford University Press, 1977.

Willis, Sharon. "Hélène Cixous's *Portrait de Dora:* The Unseen and the Un-scene." *Theatre Journal* 37.3 (Oct. 1985): 287–301.

Winn, Marie. "The Czechs' Defiant Playwright." *New York Times Magazine* 25 Oct. 1987: 78–82, 94, 100.

Wyschogrod, Edith. *Spirit in Ashes: Hegel, Heidegger and Man-Made Mass Death.* New Haven: Yale University Press, 1985.

Young-Bruehl, Elizabeth. *Hannah Arendt: For the Love of the World.* New Haven and London: Yale University Press, 1982.

Zeifman, Hersh. "Ghost Trio: Pinter's *Family Voices.*" *Modern Drama* 27 (1984): 486–93.

———. "A Rose by any other name: Pinter and Shakespeare." Paper presented at *A Pinter Festival,* Columbus, OH, 19–21 Apr. 1991.

Contributors

ALICE N. BENSTON, Chair of the Department of Theater and Film Studies and Associate Dean of the Graduate School of Arts and Sciences at Emory University, has published widely on dramatic literature in such journals as *Shakespeare Quarterly, Genre, Modern Drama, Style,* and *Sub-Stance.* She was coeditor of "Essays in European Literature for Walter A. Strauss," a special issue of *Studies in Contemporary Literature,* 1990.

KATHERINE H. BURKMAN, Professor of English at The Ohio State University, has written widely on modern drama. Among her books are *The Dramatic World of Harold Pinter: Its Basis in Ritual* and *The Arrival of Godot: Ritual Patterns in Modern Drama.* She is also the editor of *Myth and Ritual in the Plays of Samuel Beckett* and *Simon Gray: A Casebook* and the coordinator of *A Pinter Festival: An International Meeting* (1991); she is currently writing a book entitled *Myth, Murder, and Modern Drama.*

JEANNE COLLERAN teaches modern and contemporary drama and fiction at John Carroll University. She has published articles on Athol Fugard, Simon Gray, Nadine Gordimer, and J. M. Coetzee and is currently at work on a book about contemporary political theatre.

JON ERICKSON is a performance artist and Assistant Professor of English at The Ohio State University. His essays on performance and culture (including painting, conceptual art, and poetry) have been published in *Journal of Dramatic Theory and Criticism, Theatre Journal, Discourse, boundary 2,* and *Psychiatry and the Humanities.*

MARTIN ESSLIN is Professor Emeritus at Stanford University. As Head of Radio Drama for the BBC, he frequently worked with Pinter. Among his many publications are the now classical discussion of absurdist drama, *The Theatre of the Absurd,* as well as *Pinter: The Playwright, Brecht: The Man and His Work,* and most recently, *The Field of Drama: How the Signs of Drama Create Meaning on Stage and Screen.*

MARTHA FEHSENFELD is an actress and scholar who has done extensive work on Samuel Beckett, on whom she has published articles in *Modern Drama* and *Theatre Journal.* She is coauthor of *Beckett in the Theatre* (John Calder Publishers) and is the designated editor for *The Letters of Samuel Beckett* for Grove Press.

STEVEN H. GALE holds the University Endowed Chair in the Humanities at Kentucky State University. Among Professor Gale's many books are *Butter's Going Up: A Critical Analysis of Harold Pinter's Work, Harold Pinter: An Annotated Bibliography, Harold Pinter: Critical Approaches,* and *Harold Pinter: Critical Essays.* President of the Harold Pinter Society and coeditor of *The Pinter Review: Annual Essays,* Professor Gale is currently working on a monograph on Pinter's filmscripts.

FRANCIS GILLEN is Dana Foundation Professor of Literature at the University of Tampa and Director of the University Honors Program. The author of numerous essays on

Pinter, Anthony Shaffer, Tennessee Williams, Tom Stoppard, and Arthur Miller, he has also published on several modern novelists. He is coeditor of *The Pinter Review: Annual Essays.*

MOONYOUNG C. HAM is a Ph.D. candidate in English at the University of Delaware. She has published articles on the drama of W. B. Yeats, J. M. Synge, and Harold Pinter, and she is currently writing a dissertation on the subject "Doubling Women in the works of Harold Pinter, Hélène Cixous, Simon Gray, Caryl Churchill, Jean Genet, and Marguerite Duras."

JOHN L. KUNDERT-GIBBS was assistant coordinator of "A Pinter Festival" and is presently working on his dissertation in drama at Ohio State University. He recently gave a presentation at the International Beckett Symposium and is author of several plays, two of which, *A Date for the Nineties* and *9-1-1: A Still Life,* have been produced at Ohio State University.

ROSETTE C. LAMONT teaches French at the Graduate Center of the City University of New York and at Queens College. She has edited and contributed to *Ionesco: A Collection of Critical Essays* and *The Two Faces of Ionesco* and has written many articles on modern French drama. She was elected to the rank of Officier in the French Order of Arts and Letters, and her book, *Ionesco's Imperatives: The Politics of Culture,* has recently been published by the University of Michigan Press.

LOUIS MARKS has a degree in history from Balliol College, Oxford University and a D.Phil. degree from Oxford. He currently works as a writer and producer in film and television with the BBC. His first contact with Harold Pinter was when he produced and Pinter directed Simon Gray's *Rear Column* for the BBC. Dr. Marks has also produced Pinter's *One for the Road* and *Mountain Language* as well as Pinter's adaptation of Kafka's *The Trial* for film. In addition to working with Pinter, Dr. Marks has produced more than seventy productions for the BBC, some of which have been aired in the United States.

SUSAN HOLLIS MERRITT is the author of *Pinter in Play: Critical Strategies and the Plays of Harold Pinter* (Duke University Press) and the bibliographical editor of *The Pinter Review.* She is the recipient of a Fellowship for College Teachers from the National Endowment for the Humanities as well as a Fellowship from the NEH Summer Seminar Program. Most recently Visiting Scholar in English and Theatre Arts at Cornell University and Visiting Associate Professor of English at Keuka College, she has also published essays, interviews, and reviews pertaining to Pinter and literary criticism and theory. Her current research project is entitled "The Politics of Identity and Difference in Contemporary Drama."

CAREY PERLOFF was recently named Director of American Conservatory Theatre in San Francisco, one of America's most important regional theatres. Prior to her work for ACT, Ms. Perloff ran CSC Repertory, the Classic Stage Company, an off-Broadway theatre in New York devoted to innovative productions of classic plays. For CSC she directed the world premiere of Ezra Pound's *Elektra,* the American premiere of Tony Harrison's *Phaedra Brittanica,* the first major revival in 25 years of Pinter's *The Birthday*

Party, acclaimed versions of Strindberg's *Creditors,* Beckett's *Happy Days,* Tirso de Molina's *Don Juan of Seville,* and Dumas's *The Tower of Evil,* among others. Working closely with Pinter, she directed the American premiere of his *Mountain Language* at CSC. A graduate of Stanford University, Ms. Perloff was a Fulbright scholar at St. Anne's College, Oxford University, and received an Obie Award for Artistic Excellence in 1988.

PHYLLIS R. RANDALL is a professor of English at North Carolina Central University. She has published on David Storey, Sam Shepard, and Caryl Churchill, and has edited a critical collection, *Caryl Churchill: A Casebook* (1988). As Assistant Editor of *American Speech,* she has also published on language and on women's communication, including, with Elizabeth Jarrard, *Women Speaking: an Annotated Bibliography of Verbal and Nonverbal Communication 1970–80* (1982).

ALICE RAYNER teaches dramatic literature and theory at Stanford University and has published on dramatic theory in her book, *Comic Persuasion* (1987), and in *Theatre Journal, New Theatre Quarterly,* and *Journal of Dramatic Theory and Criticism.*

JUDITH ROOF is coeditor of *Feminism and Psychoanalysis* (Cornell University Press) and author of *A Lure of Knowledge* (Columbia University Press) as well as essays on Beckett, Pinter, Duras, film, feminist theory, and psychoanalysis. As Associate Professor of English, she teaches drama and film at the University of Delaware.

HERSH ZEIFMAN, Associate Professor of English and Drama at York University, Toronto, has published widely on contemporary British and American drama. He is coeditor of *Modern Drama,* president of the Samuel Beckett Society, a member of the executive board of *The Pinter Review,* editor of *David Hare: A Casebook* (forthcoming, Garland), and the coeditor of *Contemporary British Drama* (forthcoming, Macmillan).

Index

DATE DUE

JUL 14 PAID			
JUL 21 1998			
MAY 06 1999			